Portuguese
phrase book

D1350206

Berlitz Publishing / APA Publications GmbH & Co.
Verlag KG, Singapore Branch, Singapore

Contacting the Editors
Every effort has been made to provide accurate information in this publication, but changes are inevitable. The publisher cannot be responsible for any resulting loss, inconvenience or injury. We would appreciate it if readers would call our attention to any errors or outdated information by contacting Berlitz Publishing, 95 Progress Street, Union, NJ 07083, USA. Fax: 1-908-206-1103, e-mail: comments@berlitzbooks.com

Satisfaction guaranteed—If you are dissatisfied with this product for any reason, send the complete package, your dated sales receipt showing price and store name, and a brief note describing your dissatisfaction to: Berlitz Publishing, Langenscheidt Publishing Group, Dept. L, 46-35 54th Rd., Maspeth, NY 11378. You'll receive a full refund.

Contents

Stores & Services   129

Health   161

English–Portuguese dictionary & index   169
Portuguese–English dictionary   202

Reference   216

Pronunciation

This section is designed to make you familiar with the sounds of Portuguese by using our simplified phonetic transcription. You'll find the pronunciation of the Portuguese letters and sounds explained below, together with their "imitated" equivalents. To use this system, found throughout the phrase book, simply read the pronunciation as if it were English, noting any special rules below.

The Portuguese language

There are over 190 million speakers of Portuguese worldwide. These are the countries where you can expect to hear Portuguese spoken (figures are approximate):

Portugal Portugal

Portuguese is the national language and is spoken by practically all of the 11 million population.

Brasil Brazil

Portuguese is spoken by the great majority of the population of 170 million. Tupi and Arawak are the most important languages of the 200,000 native Indians.

África Africa

Portuguese is the official language in Angola (10 million), other languages are Mbundu (5 million), Kongo (1 million); Cape Verde (450,000), most of the population speak a version of Portuguese creole; Guinea-Bissau (1.2 million), other languages are Balante, Fulani and Malinke; Mozambique (18 million), other languages are Makua (4 million), Tsonga (1.5 million).

Espanha Spain

Galician, a dialect of Portuguese, is spoken by 3 million people in northwestern Spain.

Portuguese is also spoken in Macao (500,000), though Cantonese is the language of commerce. There are about 400,000 Portuguese speakers in the United States.

The Portuguese alphabet is the same as English, with the addition of several accented characters: **ã**, **ç**, **ê**, **ô** and **õ**. The acute accent (´) indicates stress, rather than a change in sound. Portuguese is closely related to Spanish. Many words are spelt the same in both languages; e.g. **norte** (north), **mesa** (table).

There are some differences in vocabulary, expressions, and pronunciation between the Portuguese spoken in Portugal and that in Brazil – although each is easily understood by the other. Brazilian terms are shown in brackets.

Consonants

Letter	Approximate pronunciation	Symbol	Example
f, l, p, t, v, b	similar to English, but somewhat less decisive		
c	1) before **e** and **i** like s in sit	s	**cedo** _say_doo
	2) otherwise, like k in kit	k	**casa** _ka_zer
ç	like s in sit	s	**começar** koomer_sar_
ch	like sh in shut	sh	**chamar** sher_mar_
d	as in English, but often less decisive;	d	**dia** _dee_er
	also sometimes as dg in judge (Braz. only)	dzh	**de** dzhi
g	1) before **a, o, u,** or **a,** like g in go, but often less decisive	g	**garfo** _gar_foo
	2) before **e** and **i**, like s in pleasure	zh	**gelo** _zhay_loo
h	always silent		**homem** _om_maym
j	like s in pleasure	zh	**já** zhah
lh	like lli in million	ly	**olho** _oal_yoo
m	1) when initial or between vowels, like m in met	m	**mais** mighsh
	2) between a vowel and a consonant, or if last letter of word, it indicates that the vowel is nasalized, but the m is generally silent	ym	**tempo** _taym_poo
n	1) when initial or between vowels, like n in no	n	**novo** _noa_voo
	2) in a consonant group and in plural endings it nasalizes the preceding vowel	wn ym	**branco** _brawn_koo **homens** _om_maymsh
nh	like ni in onion	ny	**vinho** _veen_yoo
q	like k in kit	k	**querer** ker_rair_
r	strongly trilled (like a Scottish r)	r	**rua** _r_wer

Consonants (continued)

s	1) like *s* in *sit*	s/ss	**saber** *serbair*	
	2) like *z* in *razor*	z	**casa** *kazer*	
	3) like *sh* in *shut*	sh	**país** *pereesh*	
t *(Braz.)*	before **e**, like *ch* in *church*	ch	**arte** *archi*	
x	1) generally like *sh* in *shut*	sh	**baixo** *bighshoo*	
	2) in **ex-** before a vowel, like *z* in *razor*	z	**exausto** *eezowshtoo*	
	3) sometimes like *x* in *exit*	ks	**táxi** *taksi*	
z	1) like *z* in *razor*	z	**zero** *zehroo*	
	2) like *sh* in *shut*	sh	**feliz** *ferleesh*	
	3) like *s* in *pleasure*	zh	**luz** *loozh*	

Vowels

a	1) like *u* in *cut*	u	**contas** *kontush*
	2) like *ar* in *party*	a/ah	**nado** *nadoo*
	3) like *er* in *other*	er	**porta** *porter*
e	1) like *e* in *get*	eh	**perto** *pehrtoo*
	2) like *a* in *late*	ay/ai	**cabelo** *kerbayloo*
	3) like *er* in *other*	er	**pesado** *perzadoo*
	4) occasionally, like *i* in *hit*	i	**antes** *ahntish*
é	like *e* in *get*	eh	**café** *kerfeh*
ê	like *a* in *late*	ay	**mês** *maysh*
i	1) like *ee* in *seed*	ee	**riso** *reezoo*
	2) like *i* in *sit*	i	**informação** *infoormersawm*
o	1) like *o* in *rod*	o	**fora** *forer*
	2) like *o* in *note*	oa	**voltar** *voaltahr*
	3) like *oo* in *foot*	oo	**caso** *kazoo*
ô, ou	something like *o* in *note*	oh/oa	**outro** *ohtroo*
u	1) like *oo* in *soon*	oo	**uma** *ooma*
	2) silent in **gu** and **qu** before **e** or **i**		**querer** *kerrair*
ai	like *igh* in *sigh*	igh	**mais** *mighsh*

Nasal vowels

These are similar to the French nasal vowels and also to the nasal twang heard in some areas of the United States and Britain.

ã, an	like *an* in French "*dans*"	ah	**amanhã** *amer-nyah*
am	like *ã* followed by *w*	aw	**falam** *falawm*
em, en	like *a* in *late* combined with *ng* in *sing*	aym(n)	**cento** *sayntoo*
im, in	a nasalized *ee* as in *feet*	eem(n)	**cinco** *seenkoo*
om, on	*on* as in French "*bon*"	awm(n)	**bom** *bawm*
um, un	a nasalized *oo* as in *foot*	oom(n)	**um** *oom*

8

Semi-nasalized diphthongs

In the following, the first element is nasalized and combined with a *y* as in *yet* or with a *w* in *was*.

ãe	*ã* followed by *y* in *yet*	*aym(n)*	**mãe**	*maym*
ão	*ã* followed by *w* in *was*	*awm(n)*	**mão**	*mawm*
õe	*orn* in *corncob*	*oym(n)*	**põe**	*poym*
	followed by *y* in *yet*			

Stress

Stress has been indicated in the phonetic transcription: <u>underlined</u> letters should be pronounced with more stress (i.e. louder) than the others.

Pronunciation of the Portuguese alphabet

A	*ah*		**N**	*enn*
B	*bay*		**O**	*oh*
C	*say*		**P**	*pay*
D	*day*		**Q**	*qay*
E	*eh*		**R**	*ehr*
F	*ef*		**S**	*ess*
G	*zhay*		**T**	*tay*
H	*er-<u>gah</u>*		**U**	*oo*
I	*ee*		**V**	*vay*
J	*<u>zho</u>tter*		**W**	*<u>doo</u>blervay*
L	*ehl*		**X**	*sheesh*
M	*emm*		**Z**	*zay*

Note: The letters **k**, **w**, and **y** occur only in foreign names and their derivatives, as well as in certain abbreviations.

Basic Expressions

ESSENTIAL

Yes.	**Sim.** *seem*
No.	**Não.** *nawm*
Okay.	**O.K.** *"okay"*
Please.	**Se faz favor [Por favor].**
	ser fash fer-voar [poor fer-voar]
Thank you very much.	**Muito obrigado(-a).**
	mweentoo obrigadoo(-er)

Greetings/Apologies Saudações/Desculpas

Hello./Hi!	**Olá!** *ollah*
Good morning.	**Bom dia.** *bawm deeer*
Good afternoon/evening.	**Boa tarde.** *boaer tard*
Good night.	**Boa noite.** *boaer noyt*
Good-bye.	**Adeus.** *er-deoosh*
Excuse me! *(getting attention)*	**Desculpe!** *dishkoolp*
Excuse me. *(May I get past?)*	**Com licença.** *kawm lysaynser*
Excuse me!/Sorry!	**Perdão!** *perdawm*
It was an accident.	**Foi sem querer.** *foy saym ker-rair*
Don't mention it.	**Não tem de quê.** *nawm taym der kay*
Never mind.	**Não tem importância.**
	nawm taym eenpoortawnsyer

Communication difficulties
Problemas de comunicação

Do you speak English? **Fala inglês?**
faler __eenglaysh__

Does anyone here speak English? **Há aqui alguém que fale inglês?**
ah er-__kee__ al__gaym__ ker __faler__ een__glaysh__

I don't speak (much) Portuguese. **Não falo (bem) português.**
nawm __faloo__ (baym) poortoo__gaysh__

Could you speak more slowly? **Pode falar mais devagar?**
pod fer-__lar__ mighsh der-ver-__gar__

Could you repeat that? **Pode repetir?** *pod rer-per-__teer__*

What was that? **Como disse?** *__koomoo__ __deeser__*

Could you spell it? **Pode soletrar?** *pod __sooler__-trar*

Please write it down. **Escreva, por favor.**
ish__krayver__ poor fer-__voar__

Can you translate this for me? **Pode traduzir-me isto?**
__pod__ trer-doozeermer __eeshtoo__

What does this/that mean? **O que significa isto/aquilo?**
oo ker signee__feeker__ __eeshtoo__/er-__keeloo__

How do you pronounce that? **Como se pronuncia isso?**
__koomoo__ seh proonoon__seeer__ __eesoo__

Please point to the phrase
in the book. **Mostre-me a frase no livro, por favor.**
__moshtrer__-mer er __frazer__ noo __leevroo__
poor fer-__voar__

I understand. **Compreendo [Entendo].**
kawmpree__ayn__doo [ayn__tayn__doa]

I don't understand. **Não compreendo [entendo].**
nawm kawmpree__ayn__doo [ayn__tayn__doa]

– São trinta euros.
(That's 30 euros.)
– *Perdão. Não compreendo.* (Sorry. I don't understand.)
– São trinta euros.
(That's 30 euros.)
– *Escreva, por favor.* (Please write it down.)
– Sim. (Yes.)
– … Ah, trinta euros. Aqui está.
(… Ah, 30 euros. Here you are.)

Questions Perguntas

GRAMMAR

Questions can be formed in Portuguese:
1. by a questioning intonation; often the personal pronoun is left out, both in affirmative sentences and in questions:

| **Falo inglês.** | I speak English. |
| **Fala inglês?** | Do you speak English? |

2. by using a question word (>12–17) + the inverted order (verb-noun):

| **Quando abre o museu?** | When does the museum open? |

In Portuguese there are two main verbs meaning "to be":

ser indicates a permanent state:

| **Sou inglês.** | I'm English. |
| **É portuguesa.** | She is Portuguese. |

estar indicates movement or a non-permanent state:

| **Está doente.** | He is ill. |
| **Estou a passear [passeando].** | I am walking. |

The verb **ficar** can also be used, meaning "to be situated."

Where? Onde?

Where is it?	**Onde é que fica/está?** *ond eh ker feeker/ishtah*
Where are you going?	**Onde vai?** *ond vigh*
to the meeting place [point]	**no ponto de encontro** *noo pontoo der aynkontroo*
away from me	**longe de mim** *lonzher der meem*
downstairs	**(lá) em baixo** *(lah) aym bighshoo*
from the U.S.	**dos Estados Unidos** *dooz ishtadoosh ooneedoosh*
here	**aqui** *er-kee*
in the car	**no carro** *noo karroo*
in Portugal	**em Portugal** *aym poortoogal*
opposite the market	**em frente ao mercado** *aym fraynt ow merkadoo*
on the left/right	**à esquerda/direita** *ah ishkairder/deerayter*
to the hotel	**para o hotel** *per-rer oo ottel*
toward Lisbon	**na direção de Lisboa** *ner deerehsawm der leeshboaer*

When ...? Quando ...?

When does the museum open?	**Quando abre o museu?** *kwandoo abrer oo mooseoo*
When does the train arrive?	**Quando chega o comboio [trem]?** *kwandoo shayger oo kawmboyoo [trayn]*
after lunch	**depois do almoço** *der-poysh doo almoasoo*
always	**sempre** *saymprer*
around midnight	**cerca da meia-noite** *serker der mayer noyt*
at 7 o'clock	**às 7 (horas)** *ash set (orush)*
before Friday	**antes de sexta-feira** *antish der sayshter fayrer*
by tomorrow	**(para) amanhã** *(per-rer) amer-nyah*
daily	**diariamente** *deeareeer-maynt*
during the summer	**durante o verão** *doorawnt oo ver-rawm*
every week	**todas as semanas** *toaderz ush ser-manush*
for 2 hours	**durante/por 2 horas** *doorawnt/poor dooush orush*
from 9 a.m. to 6 p.m.	**das 9 às 18 (horas)** *dush nov ash dzoytoo (orush)*
immediately	**imediatamente** *eemer-dyater-maynt*
in 20 minutes	**em 20 minutos** *aym veent minootoosh*
never	**nunca** *noonker*
not yet	**ainda não** *er-eender nawm*
now	**agora** *er-gorer*
often	**muitas vezes** *mweentush vayzush*
on March 8	**no 8 de Março** *noo oytoo der marsoo*
on weekdays	**durante a semana** *doorawnt er ser-maner*
once a week	**uma vez por semana** *oomer vaysh poor ser-maner*
since yesterday	**desde ontem** *deshd ontaym*
sometimes	**às vezes** *ash vayzush*
soon	**em breve/logo** *aym brev/logoo*
then	**então/depois** *ayntawm/der-poysh*
within 2 days	**dentro de 2 dias** *dayn-troo der doysh deeush*
10 minutes ago	**há dez minutos** *ah desh meenootoosh*

13

What kind of …? De que género …?

I'd like something …	**Queria algo …** ker-_reeer_ _algoo_
It's …	**É/Está …** eh/_ishtah_
beautiful/ugly	**bonito/feio** boo_nee_too/_fay_oo
better/worse	**melhor/pior** mer-_lyor_/_peeor_
big/small	**grande/pequeno** grawnd/per-_kay_noo
cheap/expensive	**barato/caro** ber-_ra_too/_ka_roo
clean/dirty	**limpo/sujo** _leem_poo/_soo_zhoo
dark/light	**escuro/claro** ish_koo_roo/_kla_roo
delicious/revolting	**delicioso/horrível** der-leesy_oa_zoo(-_ozz_er)/_orr_eevel
early/late	**cedo/tarde** _say_doo/tard
easy/difficult	**fácil/difícil** _fa_seel/di_fee_seel
empty/full	**vazio/cheio** ver-_zee_oo/_shay_oo
good/bad	**bom (boa)/mau (má)** bawm (_boa_er)/_ma_oo (mah)
heavy/light	**pesado/leve** per-_za_doo/lev
hot/warm/cold	**quente/morno/frio** kaynt/_moar_noo/_free_oo
modern/old-fashioned	**moderno/antigo** moo_dehr_noo/awm_tee_goo
narrow/wide	**estreito/largo** ish_tray_too/_lar_goo
next/last	**próximo/último** _pross_ymoo/_ool_tymoo
old/new	**velho/novo** _vel_yoo/_noa_voo (_nov_ver)
open/shut	**aberto/fechado** er-_behr_too/fer-_sha_doo
pleasant, nice/unpleasant	**agradável/desagradável** er-grer-_da_vell/der-zer-grer-_da_vell
quick/slow	**rápido/lento** _rap_ydoo/_layn_too
quiet/noisy	**sossegado/barulhento** sooser-_ga_doo/ber-rool_yayn_too
right/wrong	**certo/errado** _sehr_too/ee_rra_doo
tall/small	**alto/baixo** _al_too/_bigh_shoo
thick/thin	**grosso/fino** _groa_soo (_gross_er)/_fee_noo
vacant/occupied	**vago/ocupado** _va_goo/okkoo_pa_doo
young/old	**jovem/velho** _zhov_vaym/_vel_yoo

14

Nouns in Portuguese are either masculine or feminine and
the adjectival endings change accordingly. Many adjectives
end with **-a** in the feminine form, e.g. **bonito – bonita** ➤ 169.
Only more unusual feminine endings are given.

How much/many? Quanto/Quantos?

How much is that?	**Quanto é?** _kwan_too eh
How many are there?	**Quantos tem/há?** _kwan_toosh taym/ah
1/2	**um(a)/dois (duas)** oom(er)/doysh (_doo_ush)
3/4/5	**três/quatro/cinco** traysh/_kwa_troo/_seen_koo
none	**nenhum** ner-_nyoom_
about 20 euros [reais]	**cerca de vinte euros [reais]** _ser_ker der veent a_yoo_orosh [reh-ighsh]
a little	**um pouco** oom _poa_koo
a lot of traffic	**muito trânsito** _mween_too _tranz_ytoo
enough	**bastante/suficiente** bush_tawnt_/soofeesy_aynt_
few/a few of them	**poucos/alguns** _poh_koosh/al_goonsh_
many people	**muitas pessoas** _mween_tush per-_soa_ush
more than that	**mais do que isso** mighsh doo ker _ee_soo
less than that	**menos do que isso** _may_noosh doo ker _ee_soo
much more	**muito mais** _mween_too mighsh
nothing else	**mais nada** mighsh _nad_er
too much	**demasiado/demais** der-mer-zy_ad_oo/der-_mighsh_

Why? Porquê?

Why is that?	**Porquê?** poor_kay_
Why not?	**Porque não?** _poor_ker nawm
because of the weather	**por causa do tempo** poor _kow_zer doo _taymp_oo
because I'm in a hurry	**porque estou com pressa** _poor_ker ish_toh_ kawm _pres_er
I don't know why.	**Não sei porquê.** nawm say poor_kay_

NUMBERS ➤ 216

Who? / Which? Quem? / Qual?

Which one do you want?	**Qual deseja?** *kwal der-zayzher*
Who is it for?	**Para quem é?** *per-rer kaym eh*
him/her	**ele/ela** *ayl/eler*
me	**mim** *meem*
them	**eles/elas** *aylish/elush*
none	**nenhum** *ner-nyoom*
no one	**ninguém** *neengaym*
not that one	**esse não** *ayss nawm*
one like that	**um como esse** *oom koomoo ayss*
someone/something	**alguém/alguma coisa** *algaym/algoomer koyzer*
this one/that one	**este/esse** *aysht/ayss*

Whose? De quem?

Whose is that?	**De quem é isso?** *der kaym eh eesoo*
It's ...	**É ...** *eh*
mine	**meu/minha** *meoo/meenyer*
ours	**nosso/nossa** *nosoo/noser*
yours	**vosso/vossa** *vosoo/voser*
It's his.	**É o seu/a sua/dele.** *eh oo seoo/ah swer/dayl*
They are hers.	**São os seus/as suas/dela.** *sahwm oosh seoosh/ush sooush/deler*
It's ... turn.	**É a ... vez.** *eh er ... vaysh*
my/our/your	**minha/nossa/vossa** *meenyer/noser/voser*

GRAMMAR

Possessive adjectives and pronouns agree in gender and number with the object possessed, not the possessor.

	masculine	*feminine*
my	o meu	a minha
yours (fam./sing.)	o teu	a tua
his/hers/its	o seu	a sua
our	o nosso	a nossa
your	o vosso	a vossa
their	o seu	a sua

How? Como?

How would you like to pay?	**Como deseja pagar?** _koomoo der-zayzher per-gar_
by cash	**a dinheiro** _er deenyayroo_
by credit card	**com cartão de crédito** _kawm kertawm der kreditoo_
How are you getting here?	**Como vem para cá?** _koomoo vaym per-rer kah_
by car	**de carro** _der karroo_
on foot	**a pé** _er peh_
quickly	**rapidamente** _rapeeder-maynt_
slowly	**devagar** _der-ver-gar_
too fast	**demasiado depressa** _der-mer-zyadoo der-preser_
by chance	**por acaso** _poor er-kazoo_
entirely	**completamente** _kawmpletter-maynt_
equally	**igualmente** _eegwalmaynt_
totally	**totalmente** _tootalmaynt_
very	**muito** _mweentoo_
with a friend	**com um(a) amigo(-a)** _kawm oom(er) er-meegoo(-er)_
without a passport	**sem passaporte** _saym paser-port_

Is it …?/Are there …? Está …?/Há …?

Is it free of charge?	**Está livre?** _ishtah leevrer_
It isn't ready.	**Não está pronto.** _nawm ishtah prontoo_
There are showers in the rooms.	**Há chuveiros nos quartos.** _ah shoovayroos noosh kwartoosh_
Are there any buses into town?	**Há autocarros [ônibus] para a cidade?** _ah owtokarroosh [oanibooss] per-rer er sidad_
There isn't any hot water.	**Não há água quente.** _nawm ah agwer kaynt_
There aren't any towels.	**Não há toalhas.** _nawm ah tooalyush_
Here it is/they are.	**Aqui está/estão.** _er-kee ishtah/ishtawm_
There it is/they are.	**Ali está/estão.** _er-lee ishtah/ishtawm_

Can/May? Pode?

Can I have …?	**Pode dar-me …?**	*pod darmer*
May we have …?	**Pode dar-nos …?**	*pod darnoosh*
Can you show me …?	**Pode mostrar-me?**	*pod mooshtrarmer*
Can you tell me …?	**Pode dizer-me …?**	*pod deezairmer*
Can you help me?	**Pode ajudar-me?**	*pod er-zhoodarmer*
May I help you?	**Posso ajudar?**	*possoo er-zhoodar*
Can you direct me to …?	**Pode dizer-me onde fica …?**	*pod deezairmer ond feeker*
I can't.	**Não posso.**	*nawm possoo*

What do you want? O que deseja?

I'd like …	**Queria …**	*ker-reeer*
We'd like …	**Queríamos …**	*ker-reeer-moosh*
Give me …	**Dê-me …**	*daymer*
I'm looking for …	**Ando à procura de …**	*awndoo ah prokoorer der*
I need to …	**Preciso de …**	*prer-seezoo der*
go …	**ir …**	*eer*
find …	**encontrar …**	*aynkontrar*
see …	**ver …**	*vair*
speak to …	**falar com …**	*fer-lar kawm*

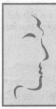 

– Desculpe! (Excuse me.)
    – Sim? (Yes?)
– Pode ajudar-me? (Can you help me?)
    – Com certeza. (Certainly.)
– Preciso de falar com o senhor Pinto.
(I would like to speak to Mr. Pinto.)
    – Um momento, por favor.
    (One moment, please.)

Other useful words
Outras palavras úteis

fortunately	**felizmente** *fer-leeshmaynt*
hopefully *(God willing)*	**se Deus quizer** *ser deoosh keezehr*
of course	**com certeza** *kawm sertayzer*
perhaps	**talvez** *talvaysh*
unfortunately	**infelizmente** *eenfer-leeshmaynt*
also/and	**também/e** *tawmbaym/ee*
but/or	**mas/ou** *mush/oh*

Exclamations Exclamações

At last!	**Finalmente/Até que enfim!** *feenalmaynt/er-teh ker aynfeem*
Go on.	**Continue.** *konteenooer*
Heck!/Damn!	**Bolas!** *bolush*
Good God!	**Meu Deus!** *meoo deoosh*
I don't mind.	**Não faz mal.** *nawm fash mal*
No way!	**De maneira nenhuma!** *der mer-nayrer ner-nyoomer*
Really?	**A sério?** *er sehryoo*
Rubbish!	**Disparate [Besteira]!** *deeshper-rat [behshtayrer]*
That's enough.	**Já chega!** *zhah shayger*
That's true.	**É verdade.** *eh verdad*
Well I never!	**Não posso crer!** *nawm possoo krair*
How are things?	**Tudo bem?** *toodoo baym*
terrific	**estupendo** *ishtoopayndoo*
great	**óptimo** *ottymoo*
not bad	**nada mau/mal** *nader mow/mal*
okay	**OK** *"okay"*
not good	**mal/mau** *mal/mow*
fairly bad	**bastante mau** *bushtawnt mow*
terrible	**terrível** *ter-rreevell*
awful	**horrível** *or-rreevell*

Accommodations

All types of acommodations can be found through the tourist information center (**Oficina de turismo**). Early reservations are essential in most major tourist centers, especially during high season or special events.

Turismo no Espaço Rural offers privately owned homes ranging from manor houses (**Turismo de Habitação**) to country houses in a rural setting **TR (Turismo Rural)** and farmhouses **AT (Agro-tourism)**. In the Algarve and other seaside resorts, you should have little trouble finding locals wanting to rent a room in their own house. The cheapest form of accommodations in Brazil is the **dormitório**, providing a shared room for a few reais per night.

Hotel *ottel*
In addition to the family-run hotel **rurais**, hotels in Portugal are graded from 2-star to 5-star deluxe; in Brazil, where most hotels are regulated by **Embratur**, there are five official categories.

Hotel-Apartamento *ottel er-purter-<u>mayn</u>too*
Apartment hotels ranging from 2- to 4-star.

Hotel fazenda *ottel fa<u>zayn</u>der*
Farmhouse lodges, generally equipped with a swimming pool, tennis court, and horseback-riding facilities; comparable to luxury hotels.

Pousada *poa<u>zah</u>der*
A state-owned inn converted from an old castle, monastery, convent, palace or in a location of interest to tourists. It's comfortable and serves good food.

Motel *mottel*
In Brazil, mostly intended for couples, with rooms charged by the hour.

Pensão *payng<u>sahwm</u>*
Corresponds to a boarding house. Usually divided into four categories.

Pousada de juventude *poa<u>zah</u>der der zhoovayn<u>tood</u>*
Youth hostel; there are nearly 20 in Portugal and over 90 in Brazil. In Brazil, hostels are open to anyone, though members obtain discounts.

Residencial *rer-zeedayn<u>seeahl</u>*
Bed and breakfast accommodations.

Reservations Reservas

In advance Previamente

Can you recommend
a hotel in …?

**Pode recomendar-me um
hotel em …?**
pod rer-koomayn<u>dar</u>mer oom <u>o</u>ttel aym

Is it near the center of town?

Fica perto do centro da cidade?
<u>fee</u>ker <u>pehr</u>too doo <u>sayn</u>troo der si<u>dad</u>

How much is it per night?

Quanto é por noite?
<u>kwan</u>too eh poor noyt

Is there anything cheaper?

Há mais barato?
ah mighsh ber-<u>ra</u>too

Could you reserve me a
room there, please?

Podia reservar-me lá um quarto?
poo<u>dee</u>er rer-zer<u>var</u>mer lah oom <u>kwar</u>too

How do I get there?

Como se vai para lá?
<u>koo</u>moo ser vigh <u>per</u>-rer lah

At the hotel No hotel

Do you have any rooms?

Tem quartos vagos?
taym <u>kwar</u>toosh <u>va</u>goosh

Is there another hotel nearby?

Há outro hotel perto daqui?
ah <u>oh</u>troo <u>o</u>ttel <u>pehr</u>too der-<u>kee</u>

I'd like a single/double room.

Queria um quarto individual/duplo.
ker-<u>ree</u>er oom <u>kwar</u>too eendivid<u>wal</u>/<u>doo</u>ploo

A room with …

Um quarto com … *oom <u>kwar</u>too kawm*

twin beds

duas camas *<u>doo</u>ush <u>ka</u>mush*

a double bed

cama de casal *<u>ka</u>mer der ker-<u>zal</u>*

a bath

banho *<u>ba</u>nyoo*

a shower

chuveiro *shoo<u>vay</u>roo*

– Tem quartos vagos? Queria um quarto duplo.
(Do you have any vacancies? I'd like a double room.)
– *Desculpe. Estamos cheios.* (Sorry, we're full.)
– Ó! Há outro hotel perto daqui?
(Oh! Is there another hotel nearby?)
– *Sim. O Hotel Ambassador é perto daqui.*
(Yes, the Ambassador Hotel is nearby.)

Reception Recepção

I have a reservation.	**Fiz uma reserva.** *feez oomer rer-zehrver*
My name is …	**O meu nome é …** *oo meoo noamer eh*
I confirmed my reservation by mail.	**Mandei uma carta para confirmar a reserva.** *mawnday oomer karter per-rer konfeermar er rer-zehrver*
I've reserved a room for two nights	**Tenho um quarto reservado para duas noites.** *taynyoo oom kwartoo rezervahdoo per-rer dooush noytish*
Could we have adjoining rooms?	**Os quartos podem ser juntos?** *oosh kwartoosh podaym sair zhoondoosh*

Amenities and facilities Comodidades e serviços

Is there (a) … in the room?	**O quarto tem …?** *oo kwartoo taym*
air conditioning	**ar condicionado** *ar kondeesyoonadoo*
TV/telephone	**TV/telefone** *tayvay/ter-ler-fon*
Does the hotel have a(n) …?	**O hotel tem …?** *oo ottel taym*
fax	**serviço de fax** *serveesoo der faks*
laundry service	**serviço de lavandaria** *serveesoo der ler-vawnder-reeer*
satellite TV	**parabólica** *per-rer-bollikker*
sauna	**sauna** *sowner*
swimming pool	**piscina** *peeshseener*
Could you put … in the room?	**Podia pôr … no quarto?** *poodeeer poar … noo kwartoo*
an extra bed	**outra cama** *ohtrer kamer*
a crib [child's cot]	**uma cama de bebé [nenê]** *oomer kamer de bebeh [naynay]*
Do you have facilities for …	**Há facilidades para …?** *ah fer-seeleedadish per-rer*
children/the disabled	**crianças/deficientes** *kryawnsush/deefeeseeyayntish*

How long ...? Quanto tempo ...?

We'll be staying ...	**Ficamos ...** *feekamoosh*
overnight only	**só esta noite** *so eshter noyt*
a few days	**alguns dias** *algoonsh deeush*
a week (at least)	**(pelo menos) uma semana** *(payloo maynoosh) oomer ser-manner*
I'd like to stay an extra night.	**Queria ficar mais uma noite.** *ker-reeer feekar mighsh oomer noyt*

– Boa tarde. O meu nome é John Newton.
(Good afternoon. My name is John Newton.)
– Boa tarde, senhor Newton. (Good afternoon, Mr. Newton.)
– Queria ficar duas noites.
(I'd like to stay for two nights.)
– Ah sim. Preencha esta ficha, por favor.
(Oh yes. Please fill out this form.)

Posso ver seu passaporte?	May I see your passport, please?
Preencha esta ficha, por favor.	Please fill out this form.
Assine aqui, por favor.	Please sign here.
Qual é a matrícula [placa] do seu carro?	What is your license plate [registration] number?

SÓ QUARTO ...	room only ...
EUROS [REAIS]	euros [reais]
PEQUENO ALMOÇO [CAFÉ DA MANHÃ] INCLUÍDO	breakfast included
SERVEM-SE REFEIÇÕES	meals available
APELIDO [SOBRENOME]	last name
NOME PRÓPRIO	first name
MORADA [ENDEREÇO]/RUA/N.º	home address/street/ number
NACIONALIDADE/PROFISSÃO	nationality/profession
DATA/LUGAR DE NASCIMENTO	date/place of birth
ORIGEM/DESTINO	coming from/going to
NÚMERO DO PASSAPORTE	passport number
MATRÍCULA [PLACA] DO AUTOMÓVEL	license plate [registration] number
LUGAR/DATA	place/date (of signature)
ASSINATURA	signature

Price Preço

How much is it …?	**Quanto é …?** _kwantoo eh_
per night/week	**por noite/semana** _poor noyt/ser-manner_
for bed and breakfast	**por cama e pequeno almoço [por noite e café da manhã]** _poor kamer ee per-kaynoo almoasoo [poor noyt ee kerfeh dah manyah]_
excluding meals	**sem refeições** _saym rer-faysoynsh_
for full board (American Plan [A.P.])	**com pensão completa (P.C.)** _kawm paynsawm kawmpletter_
for half board (Modified American Plan [M.A.P.])	**com meia-pensão (M.P.)** _kawm mayer paynsawm_
Does the price include …?	**O preço inclui …?** _oo praysoo eenklooy_
breakfast	**pequeno almoço [café da manhã]** _per-kaynoo almoasoo [kerfeh dah manyah]_
service	**serviço** _serveesoo_
sales tax [VAT]	**IVA** _eever/ee vay ah_
Do I have to pay a deposit?	**Tenho que dar um sinal?** _taynyoo ker dar oom seenal_
Is there a reduction for children?	**Há desconto para crianças?** _ah dishkontoo per-rer kryawnsush_

Decisions Decisões

May I see the room?	**Posso ver o quarto?** _possoo vair oo kwartoo_
That's fine. I'll take it.	**Está bem. Fico com ele.** _ishtah baym. feekoo kawm ayl_
It's too …	**É demasiado …** _eh der-mer-zyadoo_
cold/hot	**frio/quente** _freeoo/kaynt_
dark/small	**escuro/pequeno** _ishkooroo/per-kaynoo_
noisy	**barulhento** _ber-roolyayntoo_
Do you have anything …?	**Tem alguma coisa …?** _taym algoomer koyzer_
bigger/cheaper	**maior/mais barata** _mighor/mighsh ber-rater_
quieter/warmer	**mais sossegada/mais quente** _mighsh sooser-gader/mighsh kaynt_
No, I won't take it.	**Não fico com ele.** _nawm feekoo kawm ayl_

24

Problems Problemas

The … doesn't work.	**… não funciona.** *… nawm foonsyonner*
air conditioning	**O ar condicionado** *oo ar kondeesyoonadoo*
fan	**A ventoinha [o ventilador]** *er vayntweenyer [oo venteeladoar]*
heat [heating]/light	**O aquecimento/A luz** *oo er-keseemayntoo/er loosh*
television	**A televisão** *er ter-ler-veezawm*
I can't turn the heat [heating] on/off.	**Não consigo ligar/desligar o aquecimento.** *nawm konseegoo leegar/dishleegar oo er-keseemayntoo*
There is no hot water / toilet paper.	**Não há água quente/papel higiénico.** *nawm ah agwer kaynt/papel eezhyenykoo*
The faucet [tap] is dripping.	**A torneira está a pingar [pingando].** *er toornayrer ishtah er peengar [peengandoo]*
The sink is blocked.	**O lavatório [A pia] está entupido/a.** *oo ler-ver-toryoo [ah peeer] ishtah ayntoopeedoo/er*
The window / door is jammed.	**A janela/porta está empenada.** *er zher-neler/porter ishtah aymper-nader*
My room has not been made up.	**O meu quarto não foi arrumado.** *oo meoo kwartoo nawm foy er-rroomadoo*
The … is broken.	**… está partido(-a) [quebrado](-a)].** *ishtah purteedoo(-er) [kaybradoo]*
blind	**o estore** *oo ishtor*
lamp	**o candeeiro [abajur]** *oo kawndyayroo [abazhoor]*
lock	**a fechadura** *er fer-sher-doorer*
There are insects in our room.	**Há insectos no quarto.** *ah eensettoosh noo kwartoo*

Action Acção

Could you have that taken care of?	**Podia mandar arranjar [arrumar] isso?** *poodeeer mawndar er-rrawnzhar [arroomar] eesoo*
I'd like to move to another room.	**Queria mudar de quarto.** *ker-reeer moodar der kwartoo*
I'd like to speak to the manager.	**Queria falar com o/a gerente.** *ker-reeer fer-lar kawm oo/er zher-raynt*

Requirements Perguntas gerais

The 220-volt, 50-cycle AC is the norm throughout Portugal. If you bring your own electrical appliances, buy an adapter plug (round pins, not square) before leaving home. The electrical current in Brazil is not completely standardized. Most of Brazil, including Rio de Janeiro and São Paulo, are 110 or 120V, 60 Hz AC.

About the hotel Sobre o hotel

Where's the …?	**Onde é …?** *ondy eh*
bar	**o bar** *oo bar*
dining room	**a sala de jantar** *er saler der zhawntar*
elevator [lift]	**o elevador** *oo eelver-doar*
parking lot [car park]	**o parque de estacionamento** *oo park der ishter-syooner-mayntoo*
shower room	**o chuveiro** *oo shoovayroo*
swimming pool	**a piscina** *er peeshseener*
TV room	**a sala de televisão** *er saler der ter-ler-veezawm*
restroom	**a casa de banho [o banheiro]** *er kazer der banyoo [oo bahnyayro]*
tour operator's bulletin board	**o quadro de avisos das agências turísticas** *oo kwadroo der-veezoosh der-zer-zhaynsyush tooreeshtikush*
What time is the door locked?	**A que horas fecham a porta?** *er kee orush fayshawm er porter*
What time is breakfast served?	**A que horas servem o pequeno almoço [café da manhã]?** *er kee orush sehrvaym oo per-kaynoo almoasoo [kerfeh dah manyah]*
Is there room service?	**Há serviço de quartos?** *ah serveesoo der kwartoosh*

MARQUE … PARA OBTER UMA LINHA EXTERNA	dial … for an outside line
NÃO INCOMODAR	do not disturb
SAÍDA DE EMERGÊNCIA	emergency exit
SAÍDA DE INCÊNDIO	fire door
SÓ MÁQUINAS DE BARBEAR	razors [shavers] only

Personal needs Necessidades pessoais

The key to room ..., please.	**A chave do quarto ...,** **por favor.** *er shav doo* <u>kwar</u>*too ... poor fer-*<u>voar</u>
I've lost my key.	**Perdi a minha chave.** *per*<u>dee</u> *er* <u>mee</u>*nyer shav*
I've locked myself out of my room.	**Fechei-me fora do quarto.** *fer-*<u>shay</u>*mer* <u>fo</u>*rer doo* <u>kwar</u>*too*
Could you wake me at ...?	**Podia acordar-me às ...?** *poo*<u>dee</u>*er er-koor*<u>dar</u>*mer ash*
I'd like breakfast in my room.	**Queria o pequeno almoço [café da manhã] no quarto.** *ker-*<u>ree</u>*er oo per-*<u>kay</u>*noo al*<u>moa</u>*soo [ker*<u>feh</u> *dah man*<u>yah</u>] *noo* <u>kwar</u>*too*
Can I leave this in the safe?	**Posso deixar isto no cofre?** <u>pos</u>*soo day*<u>shar</u> <u>eesh</u>*too noo* <u>kof</u>*fer*
Could I have my things from the safe?	**Queria tirar as minhas coisas do cofre.** *ker-*<u>ree</u>*er tee*<u>rar</u> *ush* <u>mee</u>*nyush* <u>koy</u>*zush doo* <u>kof</u>*fer*
Could you contact our tour representative?	**Podia contactar com o nosso guia turístico?** *poo*<u>dee</u>*er konter-k*<u>tar</u> *kawm oo* <u>no</u>*soo* <u>gee</u>*er too*<u>reesh</u>*tykoo*
Where can I find a ...?	**Onde posso encontrar ...?** *ond* <u>pos</u>*soo* <u>ayn</u>*kontrar*
maid	**a criada** *er kree*<u>a</u>*der*
bellman [porter]	**o porteiro** *oo poor*<u>tay</u>*roo*
May I have a/some ...?	**Pode dar-me ...?** *pod* <u>dar</u>*mer*
bath towel	**uma toalha de banho** <u>oo</u>*mer too*<u>a</u>*lyer der* <u>ban</u>*yoo*
blanket	**um cobertor** *oom koober*<u>toar</u>
hangers	**cabides** *ker-*<u>bee</u>*dish*
pillow	**uma almofada [um travesseiro]** <u>oo</u>*mer almoo*<u>fa</u>*der [oom traves*<u>say</u>*roo]*
soap	**um sabonete** *oom ser-boo*<u>nayt</u>
Is there any mail for me?	**Há correio [correspondência] para mim?** *ah koo*<u>rray</u>*oo [coorespon*<u>dayn</u>*syer]* <u>per</u>*-rer meem*
Are there any messages for me?	**Há alguma mensagem para mim?** *ah al*<u>goo</u>*mer mayn*<u>sa</u>*zhaym* <u>per</u>*-rer meem*

BREAKFAST ➤ 43; CHANGING MONEY ➤ 138

Renting Aluguer

We've reserved an apartment in the name of …
Reservamos um apartamento em nome de … *rer-zervamooz oom er-purter-mayntoo aym noamer der*

Where do we pick up the keys?
Onde vamos buscar as chaves? *ond vamoosh booshkar ush shavish*

Where is the…?
Onde está …? *ond ishtah*

electric meter / fuse box
o contador de electricidade/o quadro da electricidade *oo konter-doar der eelettreesidad/ oo kwadroo dah eelettreesidad*

water heater
o esquentador [aquecedor] *oo ishkaynter-doar [erkehse-doar]*

Are there any spare …?
Há mais …? *ah mighsh*

fuses / gas bottles
fusíveis/botijas [botijões] de gás *foozee- vaysh/booteezhush [booteezhoynsh] der gash*

sheets
lençóis *laynsoysh*

Which day does the maid come?
Em que dia vem a empregada da limpeza? *aym ker deeer vaym er aymprer-gader dah leempayzer*

Where / When do I put out the trash?
Onde/Quando ponho o lixo lá fora? *ond/kwandoo poanyoo oo leeshoo lah forer*

Is the cost of electricity included?
A electricidade está incluída? *er eelettreesidad ishtah eenklweeder*

Problems Problemas

Where can I contact you?
Onde posso contactá-lo? *ond possoo konter-ktar-loo*

How does the stove [cooker]/ water heater work?
Como funciona o fogão/esquentador [aquecedor]? *koomoo foonsyonner oo foogawm/ishkaynter-doar [erkehse-doar]*

The … is dirty.
… está sujo(-a). *… ishtah soozhoo(-er)*

The … has broken down.
… está avariado(-a) [quebrado(-a)]. *… ishtah er-ver-ryadoo(-er) [kaybradoo]*

We accidentally broke/lost …
Partimos [Quebramos]/Perdemos sem querer … *perteemoosh [kaybramoosh]/ perdaymoosh saym ker-rair*

That was already damaged when we arrived.
Isso já estava avariado quando chegamos. *eesoo zhah ishtaver er-ver-ryadoo kwandoo sher-gamoosh*

Useful terms Vocabulário útil

boiler	**o cilindro** oo see*leen*droo
dishes [crockery]	**a louça** er *loh*ser
freezer	**a arca frigorífica [o congelador]** er *arker* freegoo*ree*fikker [oo kownzehler*doar*]
frying pan	**a frigideira** aa freezhee*day*rer
kettle	**a chaleira** er sha*lay*rer
refrigerator	**o frigorífico [a geladeira]** oo freegoo*ree*fykoo [er zhehler*day*rer]
saucepan	**o tacho [a caçarola]** oo *ta*shoo [er kase*roa*ler]
stove [cooker]	**o fogão** oo foo*gawm*
toaster	**a torradeira** er toorrer-*day*rer
utensils [cutlery]	**os talheres** oosh ter-*lyeh*rish
washing machine	**a máquina de lavar (roupa)** er *ma*kinner der ler-*var* (*roh*per)

Rooms Quartos

balcony	**a varanda** er ver-*rawn*der
bathroom	**a casa de banho [o banheiro]** er *ka*zer der *ba*nyoo [oo bah*nyay*roo]
bedroom	**o quarto de dormir** oo *kwar*too der door*meer*
dining room	**a sala de jantar** er *sa*ler der zhawn*tar*
kitchen	**a cozinha** er koo*zee*nyer
living room	**a sala de estar** er *sa*ler dish*tar*

Youth hostel Pousada da juventude

Do you have any places left for tonight?	**Ainda há vagas para hoje à noite?** er-*een*der ah *va*gush *per*-rer oazh *ah* noyt
Do you rent out bedding?	**Alugam roupa de cama?** er-*loo*gawm *roh*per der *ka*mer
What time are the doors locked?	**A que horas fecham as portas?** er kee *o*rush *fay*shawm ush *por*tush
I have an International Student Card.	**Tenho um Cartão Internacional de Estudante.** *tay*nyoo oom ker*tawm* eenterner-syo*nal* dishtoo*dawnt*

REQUIREMENTS ➤ 26; CAMPING ➤ 30

Camping Campismo

Most Portuguese campsites are within easy reach of the beach. They range from basic grounds to vast recreational centers with all amenities. You must register with your passport. Certain sites require membership of a national or international camping association. The **Guia Quatro Rodas** camping guide provides details of facilities throughout Brazil.

Registration Registro

Is there a campsite near here?	**Há um parque de campismo [camping] aqui perto?** *ah oom park der kawmpeeshmoo [kamping] er-kee pehrtoo*
Do you have space for a tent?	**Há lugar para uma tenda [barraca]?** *ah loogar per-rer oomer taynder [berahker]*
Do you have space for a trailer [caravan]?	**Há lugar para uma rulote [trailer]?** *ah loogar per-rer oomer roolot ["trailer"]*
What is the charge …?	**Qual é a tarifa …?** *kwaleh er ter-reefer*
per day/week	**por dia/semana** *poor deeer/ser-manner*
for a tent/car	**por tenda [barraca]/carro** *poor taynder [berahker]/karroo*
for a trailer [caravan]	**por rulote [trailer]** *poor roolot ["trailer"]*

Facilities Serviços

Are there cooking facilities on site?	**Há uma área para se cozinhar?** *ah oomer aryer per-rer ser koozeenyar*
Are there any electrical outlets [power points]?	**Há electricidade?** *ah eelettreesidad*
Where is/are the …?	**Onde é/são …?** *ond eh/sawm*
drinking water	**água potável** *agwer pootavell*
trash cans [dustbins]	**as lixeiras** *ush leeshayrush*
laundry facilities	**uma lavandaria** *oomer ler-vawnder-reeer*
showers	**o chuveiro** *oo shoovayroo*
Where can I get some butane gas?	**Onde posso obter gás butano?** *ond possoo obtayr gash bootanoo*

É PROIBIDO ACAMPAR	no camping
ÁGUA POTÁVEL	drinking water
É PROIBIDO ACENDER FOGOS	no fires/barbecues

Complaints Reclamações

It's too sunny.	**Aqui há sol demais.** *er-kee ah sol der-mighsh*
It's too shady/crowded here.	**Aqui há sombra/gente demais.** *er-kee ah sonbrer/zhaynt der-mighsh*
The ground's too hard/uneven.	**O solo é demasiado duro/acidentado.** *oo solloo eh der-mer-zyadoo dooroo/aceedayntadoo*
Do you have a more level spot?	**Tem um lugar mais nivelado?** *taym oom loogar mighsh neevladoo*
You can't camp here.	**Não pode acampar aqui.** *nawm pod er-kawmpar er-kee*

Camping equipment Material de campismo

butane gas	**o gás butano** *oo gash bootanoo*
campbed	**o colchão de campismo/a cama portátil** *oo kolshawm der kawmpeeshmoo/er kamer poortatil*
charcoal	**o carvão** *oo kervawm*
compass	**o compasso** *oo kawmpasoo*
firelighters	**os acendedores** *oozer-saynder-doarish*
flashlight [torch]	**a lanterna** *er lawntehrner*
guy rope	**a corda de firmar (de tenda [da barraca])** *er korder der feermar (der taynder [dah berahker])*
hammer	**o martelo** *oo murteloo*
knapsack	**a mochila** *er moosheeler*
matches	**os fósforos** *oosh foshfooroosh*
(air) mattress	**o colchão (pneumático)** *oo koolshawm (pneoomatykoo)*
sleeping bag	**o saco de dormir** *oo sakoo der doormeer*
tarpaulin	**o plástico de estender no chão** *oo plashtykoo der ishtayndair noo shawm*
tent	**a tenda [barraca]** *er taynder [berahker]*
tent pegs	**as cavilhas** *ush ker-veelyush*
tent pole	**a estaca** *er ishtaker*

Checking out Partida

What time do we have to check out?	**A que horas temos de deixar o quarto?** *er kee orush taymoosh der dayshar oo kwartoo*
Could we leave our baggage here until …?	**Podemos deixar a bagagem aqui até às …?** *poodaymoosh dayshar er ber-gazhaym er-kee er-teh ash*
I'm leaving now.	**Parto agora mesmo.** *partoo er-gorer mayshmoo*
Could you call me a taxi, please?	**Chame-me um táxi, por favor.** *shamer-mer oom taxi poor fer-voar*
It's been a very enjoyable stay.	**Foi uma estadia muito agradável.** *foy oomer ishter-deeer mweentoo er-grer-davell*

Paying Pagamento

May I have my bill, please?	**Queria a conta, por favor.** *ker-reeah er konter poor fer-voar*
I think there's a mistake on this bill.	**Creio que se enganou na conta.** *krayoo ker ser aynger-noh ner konter*
I've made … telephone calls.	**Fiz … telefonemas.** *feesh … ter-ler-foonaymush*
I've taken … from the minibar.	**Tirei … do mini-bar [frigobar].** *tiray … doo mini-bar [freegoabar]*
Can I have an itemized bill?	**Pode dar-me uma conta detalhada?** *pod darmer oomer konter der-ter-lyader*
Could I have a receipt?	**Queria uma factura [um recibo].** *ker-reeer oomer fatoorer [oom rehseeboo]*

Tipping: a service charge is generally included in hotel and restaurant bills. However, if the service has been particularly good, you may want to leave an extra tip. The following chart is a guide:

	Portugal	Brazil
Bellman, per bag	€0.50	R$ 0.35–0.50
Hotel maid, per week	€3	R$ 5
Restroom attendant	€0.20	R$ 0.50–1
Waiter	10%	10%

Eating Out

Restaurants   Restaurantes

In Portugal, most distinctive are the **pousadas** and **casas de fados** or **adegas típicas**, the little restaurants where you eat or drink to the sound of the **fado**, the national folk song. In Brazil, don't miss the **churrascarias**, restaurants specializing in excellent barbecues.

Adega típica *er-deger teepyker*
Typical small Portuguese restaurant; you may be treated to **fado** singing.

Café *ker-feh*
Coffee shop and bar, where hot and cold drinks are served; you should be able to get a snack there.

Cantina *kawnteener*
Restaurant, specializing in Italian cuisine (*Braz.*).

Casa de fados *kazer der fadoosh*
A typical Portuguese restaurant, where you can hear **fado** sung.

Cervejaria *server-zher-reeer*
A beerhouse where you can drink beer and eat seafood snacks.

Churrascaria *shoorrushkayree-er*
Restaurant, specializes in barbecues and grills (*Braz.*).

Comida a quilo/Buffet *koomeeder er keeloo/boofeh*
Kind of restaurant open only at lunchtime, serving a varied buffet of salads, meat, vegetables, and fruits; you pay by the weight of your plate.

Confeitaria *konfayter-reeer*
A pastry shop, also serving coffee, tea, and other drinks.
Estalagem *ishter-lazhaym*
Privately owned inn, serving regional specialties.
Marisqueira *mer-reeshkayrer*
Restaurant specializing in seafood.
Pousada *pohzader*
State-owned inn, specializing in local dishes; located near places of interest to tourists.
Restaurante *rishtowrawnt*
According to the cuisine and standard of service: **de luxo** (luxury), **de primeira**, **de segunda** or **de terceira classe** (first, second or third class).
Rodízio *roodeezyoo*
A **churrascaria** where you pay a fixed price and eat as much as you want (*Braz.*).

Meal times Horas de comer

o pequeno almoço *oo perkaynoo ahlmoassoo*
Breakfast (known as **café da manhã** – *kahfeh dah mahnyah* in Brazil) is usually served from 7 to 10 a.m. In Portugal it consists of coffee, rolls, butter, and jam. In Brazil, the addition of fresh fruit juice, fruit, toast, and pastry make a heartier meal.
o almoço *oo ahlmoassoo*
Lunch is the main meal of the day, served from 12:30 to 2:30 p.m. In Brazilian resorts, it is often served uninterruptedly from 12:30 till evening. It generally consists of soup, fish or meat, and a dessert; salad might replace soup in Brazil.
o jantar *oo zhahntahr*
Dinner is served from about 7:30 to 9:30 p.m., except in a Portuguese **casa de fado**, where the show is likely to start around 10 p.m. In Brazil dinner is from 8 to 11 p.m.

Portuguese / Brazilian cuisine
Cozinha portuguesa/brasileira

Portuguese cuisine may not be the most sophisticated, although there is no shortage of freshly picked vegetables and fruit, and fish and seafood straight from the sea. **Bacalhau**, dried cod, served with boiled potatoes, remains the favorite national dish, followed by custards and all kinds of pastries. Pork comes in many guises, as do chicken and veal.
Brazilian cuisine has adopted many elements from Portugal, refined with the use of spices and exotic fruit, and a greater variety of barbecued meat. Most Portuguese and Brazilian restaurants display a menu (**ementa** or **cardápio**). A **prato do dia** (dish of the day) usually offers a good meal at a fair price.

A table for …	**Uma mesa para …**
	oomer mayzer per-rer
1/2/3/4	**um(a)/dois/três/quatro**
	oom(er)/doysh/traysh/kwatroo
Thank you.	**Obrigado(-a).** *obrigadoo(-er)*
I'd like to pay.	**Queria pagar.** *ker-reeer per-gar*

Finding a place to eat Onde comer?

Can you recommend a restaurant?	**Pode recomendar-me um restaurante?** *pod rer-koomayndarmer oom rishtowrawnt*
Is there a(n) … near here?	**Há … perto daqui?** *ah … pehrtoo der-kee*
traditional local restaurant	**um restaurante com especialidades regionais** *oom rishtowrawnt kawm ishper-syalidadish rer-zhyoonighsh*
Chinese restaurant	**um restaurante chinês** *oom rishtowrawnt sheenaysh*
fish restaurant	**uma marisqueira [um restaurante de frutos do mar]** *oomer mer-reeshkayrer [oom rishtowrawnt der frootoosh doo mar]*
inexpensive restaurant	**um restaurante barato** *oom rishtowrawnt ber-ratoo*
Italian restaurant	**um restaurante italiano** *oom rishtowrawnt eeter-lyanoo*
vegetarian restaurant	**um restaurante vegetariano** *oom rishtowrawnt ver-zher-ter-ryanoo*
Where can I find a(n) …?	**Onde posso encontrar …?** *ond possoo aynkontrar*
burger stand	**uma casa de hambúrgueres** *oomer kazer der awmboorgehrish*
café (with a terrace)	**um café (com esplanada [terraço])** *oom ker-feh kawm ishpler-nader [tehrrassoo]*
fast-food restaurant	**um restaurante de comidas rápidas [uma cadeia de fast food]** *oom rishtowrawnt der koomeedush rapidush [oomer ker-dayer de "fast food"]*
ice cream parlor	**uma gelataria/casa de gelados [sorveteria]** *oomer zher-ler-ter-reeer/ kazer der ger-ladoosh [sawveht-ter-ree-er]*
pizzeria	**uma pizzaria** *oomer peezzer-reeer*

DIRECTIONS ➤ 94

Reserving a table Reservas

I'd like to reserve a table …	**Queria reservar uma mesa** *ker-reeer rer-zervar oomer mayzer*
for today at …	**para hoje às …** *per-rer oazh ash*
for two	**para dois** *per-rer doysh*
We'll come at 8:00.	**Vamos às oito.** *vamooz ash oytoo*
A table for two.	**Uma mesa para dois.** *oomer mayzer per-rer doysh*
We have a reservation.	**Fizemos uma reserva.** *feezemoosh oomer rer-zehrver*

Em que nome?	What's the name, please?
Desculpe, mas estamos cheios.	I'm sorry. We're very busy / full.
Temos uma mesa livre daqui a … minutos.	We'll have a free table in … minutes.
Volte(m) daqui a … minutos.	Please come back in … minutes.

Where to sit Onde sentar-se?

Could we sit …?	**Podemos sentar-nos …?** *podaymoosh sayntarnoosh*
over there / outside	**ali/lá fora** *er-lee/lah forer*
in the non-smoking area	**na área para não-fumadores [não-fumantes]** *ner aryer per-rer nawm foomer-doarish* *[nawm foomantish]*
by the window	**(junto) à janela** *(zhoontoo) ah zher-neler*

– Queria reservar uma mesa para hoje.
(I'd like to reserve a table for today.)
– *Para quantas pessoas? (For how many people?)*
– Quatro. (Four.)
– *Para que horas? (For what time?)*
– Para as oito. (We'll come at 8.)
– *E em que nome? (And what's the name?)*
– Evans. (Evans.)
– *Então, até logo. (OK. See you later.)*

Ordering Encomendas

Waiter!/Waitress!	**Se faz favor!** ser fash fer-_voar_
May I see the wine list, please?	**A carta dos vinhos, se faz favor.** er _karter_ doosh _veenyoosh_ ser fash fer-_voar_
Do you have a set menu?	**Tem ementa [cardápio] a preço fixo?** taym ee_maynter_ [_kardapyoo_] er _praysoo_ _feeksoo_
Can you recommend some typical local dishes?	**Pode recomendar-me alguns pratos regionais?** pod rer-koomayn_darmer_ al_goonsh_ _pratoosh_ rer-zhyoo_nighsh_
Could you tell me what … is?	**Pode dizer-me o que é …?** pod dee_zairmer_ oo kee eh
What's in it?	**Tem/Leva o quê?** taym/_lever_ oo kay
What kind of … do you have?	**Que variedade de … tem?** ker ver-rye_dad_ der … taym
I'd like …	**Queria …** ker-_reeer_
a bottle/glass/carafe of …	**uma garrafa/um copo/jarro de …** _oomer_ ger-_rrafer_/oom _koppoo_/ _jarroo_ der

Deseja(m) encomendar?	Are you ready to order?
O que deseja(m)?	What would you like?
Gostaria(m) de uma bebida primeiro?	Would you like to order drinks first?
Recomendo …/Não temos …	I recommend …/We don't have …
Isso leva/demora … minutos.	That will take … minutes.
Bom apetite!	Enjoy your meal.

– Deseja encomendar? (Are you ready to order?)
– *Pode recomendar-me alguns pratos regionais?*
(Can you recommend some typical local dishes?)
– Com certeza. Recomendo o bife na frigideira.
(Yes, I recommend the "bife na frigideira.")
– *O.K. Quero isso. (Good, I'll have that.)*
– Com certeza. E para beber?
(Certainly. And what would you like to drink?)
– *Uma garrafa de tinto da casa. (A carafe of house red wine.)*
– Com certeza. (Certainly.)

DRINKS ➤ 49; MENU READER ➤ 52

Accompaniments Acompanhamentos

Could I have ... without the ...?	**Podia me trazer ... sem ...?** *po<u>dee</u>er-mer trer-<u>zair</u> ... saym*
With a side order of ...	**Com ... à parte?** *kawm ... ah part*
May I have salad instead of vegetables, please?	**Pode ser com salada em vez de legumes?** *pod sair kawm ser-lader aym vaysh doosh ler-goomish*
Does the meal come with vegetables/potatoes?	**Vem com legumes/batatas?** *vaym kawm ler-goomish/ber-tatush*
Do you have any sauces?	**Que molhos tem?** *ker mollyoosh taym*
I'd like ... with that.	**Queria ... a acompanhar.** *ker-<u>ree</u>er ... ah akawmpah<u>nyar</u>*

vegetables/salad	**legumes/salada** *ler-<u>goo</u>mish/ser-<u>la</u>der*
potatoes/fries	**batatas/batatas fritas** *ber-<u>ta</u>tush/ber-<u>ta</u>tush <u>free</u>tush*
sauce	**molho** *<u>moa</u>lyoo*
ice	**gelo** *<u>zhay</u>loo*
May I have some ...?	**Pode trazer-me ...?** *pod trer-<u>zair</u>mer*
bread	**pão** *pawm*
butter	**manteiga** *mawn<u>tay</u>ger*
lemon	**limão** *lee<u>mawm</u>*
mustard	**mostarda** *moosh<u>tar</u>der*
olive oil	**azeite** *er-<u>zay</u>ter*
pepper	**pimenta** *pee<u>mayn</u>ter*
salt	**sal** *sal*
seasoning	**tempero** *taym<u>pay</u>roo*
sugar	**açúcar** *er-<u>soo</u>kar*
(artificial) sweetener	**adoçante (artificial)** *er-doo<u>sawnt</u> (urteefee<u>syal</u>)*
vinegar	**vinagre** *vee<u>na</u>grer*

38

MENU READER ➤ 52

General requests Pedidos gerais

Could I have a (clean) ..., please?	**Pode trazer-me ... (limpo/-a)?** *pod trer-zairmer ... (leempoo/-er)*
ashtray	**um cinzeiro** *oom seenzayroo*
cup / glass	**uma chávena [xícara]/um copo** *oomer shav-ner [sheekarah]/oom koppoo*
fork / knife	**um garfo/uma faca** *oom garfoo/oomer faker*
spoon / plate	**uma colher/um prato** *oomer koolyehr/oom pratoo*
napkin	**um guardanapo** *oom gwerder-napoo*
I'd like some more ..., please.	**Queria mais ..., se faz favor.** *ker-reeer mighsh ... ser fash fer-voar*
Nothing more, thanks.	**Mais nada, obrigado(-a).** *mighsh nader obrigadoo(-er)*
Where are the restrooms [toilets]?	**Onde são as casas de banho [os banheiros]?** *ond sawm ush kazush der banyoo [oosh bahnyayroass]*

Special requirements Pedidos especiais

I can't eat food containing ...	**Não posso comer alimentos que contenham ...** *nawm possoo koomair er-leemayntoosh ker kontaynyawm*
salt / sugar	**sal/açúcar** *sal/er-sookar*
Do you have meals/drinks for diabetics?	**Tem pratos/bebidas para diabéticos?** *taym pratoosh/ber-beedush per-rer dyer-bettikoosh*
Do you have vegetarian meals?	**Tem pratos vegetarianos?** *taym pratoosh ver-zher-ter-ryanoosh*

For the children Para as crianças

Do you have children's portions?	**Tem doses [porções] para crianças?** *taym dozish [pawsoyns] per-rer kryawnsush*
Could we have a child's seat, please?	**Pode trazer uma cadeirinha de criança?** *pod trer-zair oomer ker-dayreenyer der kryawnser*
Where can I feed / change the baby?	**Onde posso alimentar/mudar o bebé [nenê]?** *ond possoo er-leemayntar/moodar oo bebeh [naynay]*

Fast food/Café
Refeições rápidas/Café

Something to drink Para beber

I'd like …	**Queria …** ker-_reeer_
beer	**uma cerveja** _oo_mer ser_vay_zher
coffee/tea/chocolate	**um café/um chá/um chocolate** _oom ker-_feh_/oom shah/oom shookoo_lat
black/with milk	**uma bica [um cafezinho]/um garoto** **[café-com-leite]** _oo_mer _beeker_ [oom ker-_fehzinyoo_]/oom ger-_roa_too [ker_feh_ kawm layt]
cola/lemonade	**uma cola [um refrigerante]/uma limonada** _oo_mer _koler_ [oom rerfrizher_ranti_]/ _oo_mer leemoo_nader_
fruit juice	**um sumo [suco] de frutas** oom _soo_moo [_soo_koo] der _froo_tush
mineral water	**uma água mineral** _oo_mer _ag_wer meene_ral_
(a glass of) red/white wine	**(um copo de) vinho tinto/branco** (oom _kop_poo der) _vee_nyoo _teen_too/_brawn_koo

And to eat E para comer

A piece of …	**Uma fatia de …** _oo_mer fer-_tee_er der
I'd like two of those.	**Queria dois desses.** ker-_reeer_ doysh _day_sish
burger/fries	**um hambúrguer/batatas fritas** oom awm_boor_gehrish/ber-_ta_tush _free_tush
sandwich/cake	**uma sandes [um sanduíche]/um bolo** _oo_meer _sawn_dish [oom sand_wee_chi]/ oom _boa_loo
A … ice cream, please.	**Um gelado [sorvete] de …** oom zher-_la_doo [saw_veh_ti] der
chocolate/strawberry/vanilla	**chocolate/morango/baunilha** shookoo_lat_/moo_rawn_goo/bow_nee_lyer
A … portion	**Uma dose [porção] …** _oo_mer doz [paw_sawm_]
small/regular [medium]/large	**pequena/média/grande** per-_kay_ner/_me_dyer/grawnd
It's to take out.	**É para levar.** eh _per_-rer ler-_var_
That's all, thanks.	**É tudo, obrigado(-a).** eh _too_doo obri_ga_doo(er)

– Que desejam? (What would you like?)
– *Dois cafés, por favor.* (Two coffees, please.)
– Com ou sem leite? (With or without milk?)
– *Com leite, por favor.* (With milk, please.)
– Mais alguma coisa? (Anything else?)
– *É tudo, obrigado.* (That's all, thanks.)

Complaints Reclamações

I have no knife/fork/spoon.	**Não tenho faca/garfo/colher.** *nawm taynyoo faker/garfoo/koolyehr*
There must be some mistake.	**Deve haver engano.** *dev er-vair aynganoo*
That's not what I ordered.	**Não encomendei isso.** *nawm aynkoomaynday eesoo*
I asked for ...	**Pedi ...** *per-dee*
I can't eat this.	**Não posso comer isto.** *nawm possoo koomair eeshtoo*
The meat is ...	**A carne ...** *er karn*
overdone	**está cozida demais** *ishtah koozeeder der-mighsh*
rare	**está mal cozida** *ishtah mal koozeeder*
too tough	**é muito dura** *eh mweentoo doorer*
This is too bitter/sour.	**Isto está azedo demais.** *eeshtoo ishtah er-zaydoo der-mighsh*
The food is cold.	**A comida está fria.** *er koomeeder ishtah freeer*
This isn't fresh.	**Isto não é fresco.** *eeshtoo nawm eh frayshkoo*
How much longer will our food be?	**Ainda demora muito?** *er-eender der-morer mweentoo*
We can't wait any longer. We're leaving.	**Não podemos esperar mais. Vamo-nos embora.** *nawm poodaymoosh ishper-rar mighsh. vamoonoosh aymborer*
This isn't clean.	**Isto não está limpo.** *eeshtoo nawm ishtah leempoo*
I'd like to speak to the manager.	**Queria falar com o/a gerente.** *ker-reeer fer-lar kawm oo/er zher-raynt*

Paying Ao pagar

I'd like to pay.	**Queria pagar.** *ker-<u>ree</u>er per-<u>gar</u>*
We'd like to pay separately.	**Queriamos contas separadas.** *ker-<u>ree</u>ermoosh <u>kon</u>tush ser-per-<u>ra</u>dush*
It's all together.	**É tudo junto.** *eh <u>too</u>doo <u>zhoon</u>too*
I think there's a mistake in this bill.	**Creio que há um engano na conta.** *<u>kray</u>oo ker ah oom <u>ayn</u>ganoo ner <u>kon</u>ter*
What is this amount for?	**Isto é de quê?** *<u>eesh</u>too eh der kay*
I didn't have that. I had …	**Não escolhi isso. Eu escolhi …** *nawm ishkol<u>yee</u> <u>ee</u>soo. eoo ishkol<u>yee</u>*
Is service included?	**O serviço está incluído?** *oo ser<u>vee</u>soo ish<u>tah</u> eenklw<u>ee</u>doo*
Can I pay with this credit card?	**Posso pagar com este cartão de crédito?** *<u>pos</u>soo per-<u>gar</u> kawm aysht ker<u>tawm</u> der <u>kre</u>ditoo*
I forgot my wallet.	**Esqueci-me da carteira.** *ishke<u>see</u>mer der ker<u>tay</u>rer*
I don't have enough money.	**Não tenho dinheiro que chegue.** *nawm <u>tay</u>nyoo deen<u>yay</u>roo ker shayg*
Could I have a receipt?	**Queria uma factura [um recibo].** *ker-<u>ree</u>er <u>oo</u>mer fa<u>too</u>rer [oom rer<u>see</u>boo]*
Can I have an itemized receipt, please?	**Queria uma factura [um recibo] detalhada, se faz favor.** *ker-<u>ree</u>er <u>oo</u>mer fa<u>too</u>rer [oom rer<u>see</u>boo] der-terl<u>ya</u>der sef fash fer-<u>voar</u>*
That was a very good meal.	**Foi uma refeição excelente.** *foy <u>oo</u>mer rer-fay<u>sawm</u> <u>ay</u>shser-laynt*

> – A conta, se faz favor. (The bill, please.)
> – Com certeza. Aqui está. (Certainly. Here you are.)
> – O serviço está incluído? (Is service included?)
> – Está, sim. (Yes, it is.)
> – Posso pagar com este cartão de crédito? (Can I pay with this credit card?)
> – Com certeza. (Certainly.)
> – Obrigada. Foi uma refeição excelente. (Thank you. That was a very good meal.)

Course by course Pratos

Breakfast Pequeno almoço [Café da manhã]

I'd like …	**Queria …** ker-<u>reeer</u>
bread	**pão** pawm
butter	**manteiga** mawn<u>tayg</u>er
eggs	**ovos** <u>o</u>voosh
fried eggs	**ovos estrelados [fritos]** ovooz ishtrer-<u>la</u>doosh [<u>free</u>toosh]
scrambled eggs	**ovos mexidos** <u>o</u>voosh mer-<u>shee</u>doosh
fruit juice	**sumo [suco] de fruta** <u>soo</u>moo [<u>soo</u>koo] der <u>froo</u>ter
jam	**doce de fruta [geleia]** doass der <u>froo</u>ter [zher-<u>lay</u>er]
(cold/hot) milk	**leite (frio/quente)** layt (<u>free</u>oo/kaynt)
rolls	**papo-secos [pãozinhos]** <u>pa</u>poo <u>say</u>koosh [paym<u>zy</u>nyoosh]
toast	**torradas** too<u>rra</u>dush

Appetizers/Starters Acepipes [Entradas]

If you feel like something to whet your appetite, choose carefully, for Portuguese appetizers can be filling. Appetizers/starters may also be listed on the menu under **Petiscos**.

assorted cold cuts (meat)	**carnes frias [frios]** <u>kar</u>nersh <u>free</u>ersh [<u>free</u>ush]
squid Milanese	**lula à milanesa** <u>loo</u>ler ah meeler<u>neh</u>sa
smoked pork fillet (Port.)	**paio** <u>pigh</u>oo
spicy chicken stew	**pipis** pip<u>pee</u>sh

Chouriço shoh<u>ree</u>soo
Smoked pork sausage flavored with paprika and garlic.

pimentos assados pee<u>mayn</u>toosh er-<u>sa</u>doosh
Sweet peppers, roasted and served cold with olive oil and vinegar.

santola recheada sawn<u>to</u>ller rer-<u>shy</u>ader
Spider-crab stuffed with its own meat.

Soups Sopas

Portuguese meals often start with a soup, a fairly substantial dish based on potatoes.

sopa ...	*soaper*	soup
açorda à Alentejana	*erssoarder ah erlaynterzherner*	bread soup with garlic and herbs
à pescador	*ah pishker-doar*	fish soup
canja	*kanzher*	chicken soup with rice
de agriões	*der gryoynsh*	potato and watercress soup
de cozido	*der koozeedoo*	meat broth with vegetables and macaroni
de feijão	*der fayzhawm*	red kidney bean and cabbage soup
de feijão verde	*der fayzhawm vaird*	potato and green bean soup
de grelos	*der grayloosh*	turnip sprout soup
transmontana	*trawnshmontarner*	vegetable soup with bacon and bread

Caldo verde *kaldoo vaird*
Thick potato and kale soup with smoked sausage.

Gaspacho *gushpashoo*
Chilled soup with diced tomatoes, sweet peppers, onions, cucumber, and croutons.

Migas de bacalhau *meegush der ber-ker-lyow*
Dried cod soup flavored with garlic and thickened with bread.

Sopa seca *soaper sayker*
Thick soup with beef, chicken, ham, smoked sausage, cabbage, and bread.

Salads Saladas

salada	*ser-lader*	salad
de alface	*dalfass*	green salad
de atum	*der ertoong*	tuna and potato
de palmito	*der palmeeto*	palm heart (*Braz.*)
mista	*meeshter*	tomato and lettuce
russa	*rooser*	boiled potatoes and carrots with mayonnaise

Salada completa *ser-lader komplehter*
Salad of green leaves, tomato, palm hearts, boiled eggs, onions, and carrots.

Fish/Seafood
Peixes/Mariscos [Frutos do mar]

While touring in coastal areas, don't miss the opportunity to
sample some of the wide variety of fresh fish and seafood.
The Portuguese are fond of boiled fish dishes served with
cabbage and boiled potatoes – doused with oil and vinegar.

atum	*ertoong*	tuna
camarões grandes	*kermerrawms grawndis*	shrimp [king prawns]
espadarte	*ishper-darter*	swordfish
lagosta	*lergoashter*	lobster
linguado	*leengwadoo*	sole
lulas	*loolersh*	squid
pargo	*pargoo*	bream
polvo	*poalvoo*	octopus

Amêijoas à Bulhão Pato *er-mayzhoosh ah boolyawm patoo*
Clams with coriander, garlic, and onion.

Amêijoas à Portuguesa *er-mayzhoosh ah poortoogayzer*
Clams cooked with garlic, parsley, and olive oil.

Arroz de atum *er-rroash der-toom*
Tuna with rice, egg, tomato, and mayonnaise.

Cabeça de pescada cozida *ker-bayser der pishkader koozeeder*
Fish stew, made from fish heads, especially hake.

Bacalhau à Brás *ber-ker-lyow ah brash*
Strips of dried cod fried with onions and potatoes, cooked in beaten egg.

Bacalhau à Gomes de Sá *ber-ker-lyow ah goamish der sah*
Dried cod with olives, garlic, onions, parsley, and hard-boiled eggs.

Bacalhau podre *ber-ker-lyow poadrer*
Baked layers of cod and fried potatoes.

Caldeirada *kaldayrader*
Several kinds of fish with onions, tomatoes, potatoes, and olive oil.

Lulas recheadas *loolush rer-shyadush*
Squid cooked with a stuffing of egg yolk, minced ham, onion,
and tomato.

Moqueca de peixe *mookeker der paysh*
Stew made of fish, shellfish or shrimp with coconut milk (*Braz.*).

Vatapá *vatapah*
Fish and shrimp in a paste made of rice flour or breadcrumbs (*Braz.*).

Meat and poultry Carnes e aves

In Portugal, **bife** is the word for steak, even if it is veal, pork, or fish rather than beef. In Brazil, don't miss the barbecue specialties.

carne de vaca	*karn der vakker*	beef
galinha/frango	*ger-leenyer/frawngoo*	chicken
costeleta	*kooshter-layter*	chop/cutlet
presunto	*prer-soontoo*	cured ham
borrego [carneiro]	*boorraygoo [karnayroo]*	lamb
carne de porco	*karn der poarkoo*	pork
coelho	*kwaylyoo*	rabbit
bife [filete]	*beef [feeleti]*	steak
medalhão	*mer-der-lyawm*	tenderloin steak
vitela	*veeteler*	veal

Arroz de frango *er-rroash der frawngoo*
Fried chicken with white wine, ham, and rice in a casserole.

Bife na frigideira *beef ner freezheedayrer*
Beef steak fried in butter, white wine, and garlic; served with ham and fried bread.

Carne de sol com feijão verde *karn der sol kawm fayzhawm vaird*
Meat dried in the sun (jerky) with green beans *(Braz.)*.

Coelho assado *kwaylyoo er-sadoo*
Roast rabbit with onions, cooked with white wine.

Cozido à Portuguesa *koozeedoo ah poortoogayzer*
Boiled beef, bacon, smoked sausage, and vegetables; served with rice.

Ensopado de cabrito *aynsoopadoo der ker-breetoo*
Stew of kid (goat) and vegetables, served on slices of bread.

Feijoada *fayzhooader*
Brazil's national dish: black beans cooked with bacon, dried and salted pork, jerky, and sausage, served with rice, slices of orange and **farofa**, manioc (cassava) flour roasted in butter or oil.

Frango na púcara *frawngoo ner pookerer*
Chicken stewed in port and cognac, then fried with almonds.

Rojões à moda do Minho *roozhoynsh ah modder doo meenyoo*
Chopped pork, marinated in white wine, onions, and herbs, and then fried.

Tripas à moda do Porto *treepush ah modder doo poartoo*
Tripe cooked with pork products, beans, and chicken, served with rice.

Xinxim de galinha *sheensheem dzhee galleenyer*
Chicken cooked in a sauce of dried shrimp, peanuts, and parsley *(Braz.)*.

Vegetables Legumes

You'll recognize **brócolos, espargos, lentilhas, tomates**. In
Portugal, many dishes are served with both rice and potatoes.

alface	*alfass*	lettuce
cebolas	*serboalush*	onions
cogumelos	*koogoomeloosh*	mushrooms
ervilhas	*eerveelyush*	peas
favas	*favush*	broad beans
feijão	*fayzhawm*	kidney beans
feijão verde	*fayzhawm vaird*	green (runner) beans
pimentos	*peemayntoosh*	sweet peppers

Arroz *erroash*
Rice, which may be served **~ de alhos** (with garlic), **~ de cozido** (cooked in
meat stock), **~ de feijão** (with red or white beans), **~ de frango** (with fried
chicken in a casserole).

Batatas *bertatush*
Potatoes, these may be **~ cozidas** (boiled), **~ cozidas com pele** (boiled in their
skins), **~ fritas** (fries [chips]), **~ palha** (matchsticks), **puré de ~** (mashed).

Acarajé *akarazheh*
Grated beans fried in **dendê** (palm oil), served with pepper sauce, onions.
and shrimp (*Braz.*).

Tutu à mineira *tootoo ah meenayrer*
Dish made of beans, manioc (cassava) flour, pork, cabbage, fried eggs, and
streaky bacon (*Braz.*).

Fruit Frutas

You'll recognize **banana, coco, lima, limão, melão, pêra, tangerina**.
In northern Brazil, there is a tremendous variety of exotic fruits – but be
careful if you have a sensitive digestion and try only a few at a time.

abacate	*er-ber-kat*	avocado
abacaxi	*er-bakashee*	pineapple (*Braz.*)
ameixas	*er-mayshush*	plums
cerejas	*ser-rayzhush*	cherries
laranja	*ler-rawnzher*	orange
maçã	*mer-sah*	apple
morangos	*moorawngoosh*	strawberries
pêssego	*paiser-goo*	peach

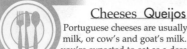

Cheeses Queijos

Portuguese cheeses are usually a mixture of sheep's and goat's milk, or cow's and goat's milk. Brazil produces cheese that you're expected to eat as a dessert. accompanied by preserves or sweets – **goiabada**, a paste of guava, for example.

creamy	**Queijo da Serra**, **Azeitão**, **Évora**, **Castelo Branco** (blue), **Serpa**; **Requeijão** (Brazilian cheese produced in Minas Gerais)
goat's milk cheese	**Cabreiro** (must be eaten fresh), **Cardiga**
cow's milk cheese	**São João**, **São Jorge**, **Bola** (hard cheese), **Ilha** (from the Azores Islands); **Queijo do Sertão** (Brazilian), **Queijo de Minas** (Brazilian, delicious with **goiabada**)

Desserts/Pastries Sobremesas/Pastelaria

Cakes, custards and sweets – usually made of egg yolks *(Portugal)* or grated coconut *(Brazil)* – are part of every meal. You may find them a bit too sweet.

arrufada de Coimbra	*er-rroofader der kooeembrer*	cinnamon dough cake
bolo podre	*boaloo poadrer*	honey and cinnamon cake
broas castelares	*broaersh kershterlahrish*	sweet-potato biscuits
goiabada	*goyabader*	thick paste made of guavas *(Braz.)*
leite-creme	*layt krem*	custard, often with caramel topping
marmelada	*murmer-lader*	thick quince paste
mousse de maracujá	*mooss der marakoozhah*	passion fruit mousse *(Braz.)*
ovos moles de Aveiro	*ovoosh mollish davayroo*	beaten egg yolks cooked in syrup
pudim flan	*poodeem flan*	caramel custard
quindim	*keendeen*	coconut and egg yolk pudding *(Braz.)*

Babá-de-moça *babah dzhee moaser*
Dessert made of egg yolk, coconut milk, and syrup *(Braz.)*.

Canjica *kawnzheeker*
Dessert made with dried white sweet corn and milk *(Braz.)*.

Pastel de Tentúgal *pushtell der tayntoogal*
Very thin flaky pastry filled with beaten egg yolks cooked in syrup.

Pudim Molotov *poodeem mollotof*
Fluffy egg-white mousse immersed in caramel sauce.

Drinks Bebidas

Aperitifs Aperitivos

The Portuguese like to sip an aperitif before dinner; some
drink vermouth while others prefer a dry port or madeira, or a
Moscatel de Setúbal served chilled. Brazilians like to drink a
batida, a blend of **cachaça** (white sugar-cane rum), ice, sugar, and fruit
juice.

Please bring me a vermouth.   **Por favor, traga-me um vermute.**
                                por fervoar trager mer oom vehrmooter

Beer Cerveja

Beer is a popular drink in Portugal and Brazil, always served very cold. Try
local brews, such as **Sagres** in Portugal, **Antártica** in Brazil. In Portugal, beer is
often served with **tremoços** (salted lupin seeds) or **amendoins** (peanuts).

I'd like …	**Queria…** *ker-reeer*
a dark beer	**uma cerveja preta** *oomer servayzher prayter*
a draft [draught] beer	**uma imperial [um chope]** *oomer eenperryal [oom shoppi]*
a lager	**uma cerveja (branca)** *oomer servayzher (branker)*
a bottle/glass/mug	**uma garrafa/um copo/uma caneca** *oomer ger-rafer/oom koppoo/oomer ker-nehker*

Wines Vinhos

Portugal may be best known abroad for its blush [rosé] and fortified wines,
but you'll find a variety of excellent red and white wines as well. The
Portuguese themselves seem to prefer the drier, lighter types as aperitifs or
dessert wine.

Brazilian wines are produced in the southern part of the country, which
turns out some good reds and whites. Labels to look for include **Almadén**
and **Forestier**.

I'd like a (half) bottle of … wine.	**Queria uma (meia-)garrafa de vinho …** *ker-reeer oomer (mayer) ger-rafer der veenyoo*
red/white/blush [rosé]	**tinto/branco/rosé** *teentoo/brawnkoo/rozeh*
a carafe/half liter/glass	**um jarro/meio-litro/copo** *oom zharoo/mayoo leetroo/koppoo*

Types of wine Tipos de vinho

dry, light white	**vinhos verdes, Porca de Murça** and **Pérola** (Douro region); **Bucelas, Óbidos** and **Alcobaça** (Estremadura)
dry white	**Sercial** (Madeira), medium-dry **Verdelho**
sweet white	**Moscatel** (Setúbal); **Carcavelos** and **Favaios** regions; bottles labeled **Grandjó** (Douro)
blush [rosé]	**Pinhel** region; **Mateus rosé** (Trás-os-Montes)
light-bodied red	**Clarete** (Douro), **Lafões** region; red **vinhos verdes**
full-bodied red	**Colares, Dão, Lagoa,** and **Bairrada** regions
sweet red	**Malmsey,** and drier **Bual** (Madeira); port wine (Douro)
sparkling	**Bairrada,** especially **vinhos espumantes naturais** from **Caves da Raposeira**

um (vinho da) Madeira *oom (veenyoo der) merdayrer*

Excellent red and white aperitif and dessert wines from the island of Madeira:
Sercial is the driest, and **Verdelho** (medium-dry) can be drunk as an aperitif;
Boal (or **Bual**) is smoky and less sweet than the rich dark-amber **Malmsey** (or
Malvásia), which is best served as a dessert wine at room temperature.

um (vinho do) Porto *oom (veenyoo doo) poartoo*

Port, famous fortified wine from the upper Douro valley, east of Oporto,
classified by vintage and blend. The vintage ports, only made in
exceptional years, are bottled at least two years after harvesting and then
stored for 10 to 20 years, while the blended ports are kept in barrels for a
minimum of five years. There are two types: the younger ruby variety
(**tinto aloirado**) is full-colored and full-bodied, while the tawny (**aloirado**) is
less sweet, amber-colored and delicate.

um vinho verde *oom veenyoo vaird*

"Green wine," produced in the Minho area in northwest Portugal, made
from unripened grapes. **Vinho verde** is faintly sparkling and extremely acid
in taste, very refreshing and with low alcohol content.

Reading the label

adega vineyard/winery	**espumante** sparkling	**tinto** red
branco white	**extra-seco** very dry	**vinho** wine
casta grape	**IPR** quality wines	**vinho de mesa**
colheita vintage	**ligeiro** light	table wine
DOC highest quality wines	**palacio** vineyard	**vinho regional**
doce sweet	**quinta** vineyard	regional wine
encorpado full-bodied	**rosé** blush [rosé]	**VQPRD** quality wines
engarrafado na Origem	**seco** dry	from smaller defined
wine bottled at estate	**solar** vineyard	regions

Spirits/Liqueurs Espíritos/Licores

You'll recognize **gim tónico** [tônica], **rum**, **porto** (port wine), **vermute**, **vodka**, **whisky com soda**. You may also like to try a Portuguese brandy, like **Antiqua**, **Borges** or **Constantino**. In Brazil, why not try a **cachaça** (white rum) – but watch out for the effects!

aguardente ...	*agwahdent*	... spirit
de figo	*der feegoo*	fig spirit
de medronho	*der mer-droanyoo*	arbutus berry* spirit
velha	*vehlya*	brandy
batida ...	*batsheeder*	cachaça cane spirit with fruit juice, sugar, ice (*Braz.*)
de caju	*dzhee kazhoo*	batida, as above with cashew nut
de coco	*der koakoo*	batida with coconut
de maracujá	*der mer-rer-koozhah*	batida with passion fruit
caipirinha	*kighpeereenyah*	cachaça, crushed lime, sugar and ice (*Braz.*)
caipirinha de vodka	*kighpeereenyah dzhee vodka*	caipirinha made with vodka (*Braz.*)
Cuba livre	*koober leebrer*	rum and Coke®
ginjinha	*zhenzheenyer*	spirit distilled from morello cherries

* small strawberry-like fruit

Non-alcoholic drinks Bebidas não alcoólicas

Look for the bars advertising **sucos** (juices) with lots of fresh fruit on display.

I'd like some ...	**Queria ...** *ker-reeer*
fruit juice	**um sumo [suco]** *oom soomoo [sookoo]*
orange juice	**um sumo [suco] de laranja natural** *oom soomoo [sookoo] der ler-rawnzher ner-tooral*
mineral water	**uma água mineral** *oomer agwer meener-ral*
carbonated/non-carbonated	**com gás/sem gás** *kawm gash/saym gash*
tea/coffee	**um chá/um café** *oom shah/oom ker-feh*
with milk/lemon	**com leite/limão** *kawm layt/lymawm*
coconut juice	**água de coco** *agwer dzhi koakoo* (*Braz.*)
sugar-cane juice (*Braz.*)	**caldo de cana** *kaldoo dzhi kanner*
coconut milk (*Braz.*)	**leite de coco** *laytshee dzhi koakoo*

alourado(-a) [dourado(-a)] no forno	er-lohradoo(-er) [dohradoo(-er)] noo foarnoo	oven-browned
aos cubos	owsh kooboosh	diced
assado(-a)	er-sadoo(-er)	roasted
com natas	kawm natush	creamed
cozido(-a)	koozeedoo(-er)	boiled
cozido(-a) a vapor	koozeedoo(-er) er ver-poar	steamed
escalfado(-a)	ishkalfadoo(-er)	poached
estufado(-a)	ishtoofadoo(-er)	braised
frito(-a)	freetoo(-er)	fried
[de]fumado(-a)	[day]foomadoo(-er)	smoked
grelhado(-a)	gre-lyadoo(-er)	grilled
guisado(-a) [ensopado(-a)]	geezadoo(-er)	stewed
marinado(-a)	mer-reenadoo(-er)	marinated
no forno	noo foarnoo(-er)	baked
panado(-a) [empanado(-a)]	per-nadoo(-er) [emper-nadoo(-er)]	breaded
mal passado(-a)	mal per-sadoo(-er)	rare/underdone
meio passado(-a)	mayoo per-sadoo(-er)	medium
bem passado(-a)	baym per-sadoo(-er)	well-done
picante	peekawnt	spicy
recheado(-a)	rer-shyadoo(-er)	stuffed
salteado(-a)	saltyadoo(-er)	sautéed

A à .../à moda de ... ... style
   à escolha of your choice
à la carte/lista a la carte
abacate avocado
abacaxi pineapple (*Braz.*)
abóbora pumpkin
açafrão saffron
acarajé fried beans ➤47

acepipes (variados) (assorted) appetizers
açorda thick soup with bread;
  ~ alentejana with poached eggs;
  ~ à moda de Sesimbra with fish
açorda à Alentejana bread soup with garlic and herbs
açúcar sugar
adocicado slightly sweet
agrião, agriões watercress
água water

água de coco coconut juice

água mineral mineral water; **~ com gás** carbonated [fizzy]; **sem gás** non-carbonated [still]

água-pé weak wine

aguardente spirit; **~ bagaceira** distilled from grape husks; **~ de figo** fig spirit; **~ de medronho** arbutus berry spirit; **~ velha** well-aged brandy

aipo celery

alcachofra artichoke

alcaparras capers

alecrim rosemary (*Braz.*)

aletria sweet noodle pudding

alface lettuce

Algarvia almond layer cake

alheira garlic sausage of breadcrumbs and minced meat; **~ à transmontana** served with fried eggs, fried potatoes and cabbage

alho garlic

alho porro leek

almoço lunch

almôndegas fish- or meatballs

alourado no forno oven-browned

alperces apricots

amargo bitter

amêijoas baby clams; **~ à Bulhão Pato** fried in olive oil with garlic and coriander; **~ à espanhola** baked with onions, tomatoes and peppers; **~ ao natural** steamed with herbs; **~ na cataplana** steamed with smoked ham

ameixas plums; **~ secas** prunes

amêndoa amarga almond liqueur

amêndoas almonds

amendoins peanuts

amoras blackberries

ananás pineapple

anchovas anchovies

anis anise liqueur

Antiqua aged Portuguese grape brandy

ao ... in the style of ...

aos cubos diced

aperitivos aperitifs

arenque herring

arroz rice ➤47;
~ à grega with diced vegetables;
~ de alhos with garlic; **~ de Cabidela** with chicken blood; **~ de cenoura** with carrots; **~ de coco** with coconut milk; **~ de cozido** cooked in a meat stock; **~ de feijão** with red or white beans; **~ de frango** with fried chicken casserole ➤46; **~ de grelos** with turnip sprouts; **~ de manteiga** with butter; **~ de pato no forno** baked with duck, cooked with bacon and *chouriço* ➤43; **~ de tomate** with tomato; **~ tropeiro** cooked with meat (*Braz.*)

arroz doce rice pudding

arrufada de Coimbra raised dough cake flavored with cinnamon

assado roast

atum tuna; **bife de ~** tuna steak marinated and fried

aveia oats

avelãs hazelnuts

aves poultry

azeda sorrel

azedo sour

azeite olive oil

azeitonas (pretas/de Elvas/ recheadas) olives (black/green/stuffed)

B **babá-de-moça** egg yolk dessert (*Braz.*) ➤48

bacalhau cod ➤45; **~ à Brás** fried with onions and potatoes ➤45; **~ à Gomes de Sá** dried cod with olives and eggs ➤45

~ à provinciana poached, with potatoes and broccoli; **~ à transmontana** braised with cured pork or *chouriço*; **~ com leite de coco** stewed in coconut milk (*Braz.*); **~ cozido com todos** poached, with boiled cabbage, onions, and potatoes; **~ de caldeirada** braised, with onions and tomatoes; **~ e ovos** salted, with potatoes and black olives

bagaço spirit made from grape husks

banana banana

barriga-de-freira dessert made of egg yolk, bread and syrup

batatas potatoes ➤47

batatas cozidas (com pele) boiled potatoes (in their skins)

batatas doces sweet potatoes

batatas fritas fries [chips]

batatas palha potato matchsticks

batida mixed drink of *cachaça*, fruit juice, sugar, ice (*Braz.*); **~ de caju** with cashew nut; **~ de coco** with coconut; **~ de maracujá** with passion fruit

batido milk shake

baunilha vanilla

bebida drink; **~ sem álcool/não alcoólica** soft drink; **~ espirituosa** spirits

bebidas incluídas drinks included

bem passado well-done

berbigão type of cockle

beringela eggplant

besugo bream (fish)

beterraba beet [beetroot]

bica espresso

bife steak/escalope

bife acebolado steak with onions (*Braz.*)

bife na frigideira fried beef steak ➤46

bife à milanesa breaded escalope of veal

bifinhos de vitela slices of veal fillet served with Madeira wine sauce

bobó dish of dried shrimp, onions, cassava root, fish stock, palm-oil, coconut milk (*Braz.*)

bola de Berlim doughnut

bolachas cookies

bolachas de água e sal crackers

bolinhos de amêndoa almond biscuits

bolinhos de bacalhau fried dried cod balls

bolinhos de canela cinnamon biscuits

bolo cake, pastry; **~ de arroz** rice cake; **~ de chila do Algarve** pumpkin jam cake (*Algarve*); **~ de fubá** corn flour cake (*Braz.*); **~ inglês** cake with candied fruit; **~ podre** cake flavored with honey and cinnamon; **~ rei** Christmas cake

Borges aged Portuguese grape brandy

borracho squab

borrego lamb

(na) brasa charcoal-grilled

broas castelares sweet-potato cookies

broas de mel corn flour and honey cookies

brócolos broccoli

bunuelos dough fritters (*Braz.*)

 C/ with
cabrito kid

caça game

cacau cocoa

cachaça spirit distilled from sugar cane (*Braz.*)

cachorro quente hot dog

cafezinho strong black coffee

café coffee; **~ sem cafeína** caffeine-free; **~ duplo** large cup; **~ frio** iced; **~ com leite** with milk; **~ instantâneo** instant

caipirinha *cachaça* (sugar cane spirit), crushed lime, sugar and ice (*Braz.*); **~ de vodka** caipirinha made with vodka, rather than *cachaça*

caju cashew nut (*Braz.*)

(em) calda (in) syrup

caldeirada fish simmered with tomatoes and potatoes ►45; **~ à fragateira** fish, shellfish, and mussels simmered in a fish stock with tomatoes and herbs, served on toast; **~ à moda da Póvoa** hake, skate, sea-bass, and eel simmered with tomatoes in olive oil

caldo consommé

caldo de cana sugar-cane juice

caldo verde potato and kale soup ►44

camarões shrimp; **~ à baiana** served in spicy tomato sauce with boiled rice; **~ fritos** fried; **~ grandes** large shrimp [king prawns] (*Braz.*); **~ no espeto** shrimps on a stick (*Braz.*)

cambuquira squash [pumpkin] shoots stewed with meat (*Braz.*)

canapé small open sandwich

caneca pint-size beer mug

canela cinnamon

canja chicken soup with rice

canjica sweet corn and milk dessert (*Braz.*) ►48

capão capon

caqui persimmon (*Braz.*)

caracol snail; spiral bun with currants

caracóis à Algarvia snails flavored with oregano (*Algarve*)

caranguejo crab

carapau mackerel; **~ de escabeche** fried and dipped in vinegar and olive-oil sauce

cardápio menu

caril curry powder

carioca small weak coffee

carne de porco pork; **~ à alentejana** chopped pork cooked with clams, tomatoes and onions (*Alentejo*)

carne de sol sun-dried meat, jerky

carne de vaca beef

carne picada chopped (minced) meat

carneiro mutton; **~ guisado [ensopado]** stewed with tomatoes, garlic, bay leaves, and parsley

carnes meat ►46; **~ frias** assorted cold cuts

caruru dish of minced herbs stewed in oil and spices (*Braz.*)

caseiro homemade

casquinha de siri crab in its shell (*Braz.*)

castanhas chestnuts; **~ de caju** cashew nuts

(água de) Castelo carbonated mineral water

(na) cataplana steamed in a copper pan

cavacas glazed cookies

cavala mackerel

cebolas onions

cenouras carrots

cerejas cherries

cerveja beer ►49; **~ branca** lager; **~ em garrafa** bottled; **~ imperial** draft [draught]; **~ preta** stout

cherne black grouper

chicória chicory

55

chispalhada pig's feet [trotters] stewed with white beans, cabbage, bacon, and blood sausage [black pudding]

chispe pig's foot [trotter]

chocolate quente hot chocolate

chocos cuttlefish; ~ **com tinta** cooked in their own ink

chope draft [draught] beer (*Braz.*)

chouriço smoked pork sausage ➤43

chuchu type of rutabaga (*Braz.*)

churrasco charcoal-grilled meat served with *farofa* (cassava-root meal) and hot-pepper sauce (*Braz.*); ~ **misto** mixed barbecue (beef, sausage, and pork)

chá tea; ~ **com leite** with milk; ~ **com limão** with lemon; ~ **de limão** made from lemon peel infusion; ~ **maté** infusion from maté-tree leaf, usually served chilled with slice of lemon

cobrança de suplemento para grupos de ... ou mais service charge for parties of ... or more

cocadas coconut macaroons (*Braz.*)

coco coconut

codorna quail (*Braz.*)

codorniz quail

coelho rabbit; ~ **assado** roast ➤46

coentro coriander

cogumelos (button) mushrooms

colorau paprika

com leite with milk

com natas creamed

comida caseira homemade

cominhos cumin

compota compote, stewed fruit

condimentos seasoning

congro conger eel

conhaque cognac

Constantino aged Portuguese brandy

conta bill

copo glass

coração heart

cordeiro lamb

corvina croaker (*fish*)

costeleta chop/cutlet

couve cabbage

couve lombarda savoy cabbage

couve portuguesa kale

couve roxa red cabbage

couve à Mineira sautéed collards [kale] in bacon fat and garlic (*Braz.*)

couve-de-Bruxelas brussels sprouts

couve-flor cauliflower

couvert cover charge; starter, appetizer (*Braz.*)

coxinha de galinha pastry filled with chicken

cozido stewed; boiled; cooked; ~ **em lume brando** simmered; ~ **à portuguesa** beef and pork boiled with *chouriço* (*northern Port.*) ➤46

cozido a vapor steamed

cozinha cooking/cuisine

cravinhos cloves

creme de abacate avocado sieved with lime juice and sugar (*Braz.*)

creme cream; ~ **leite** custard

crepe pancake

criação poultry

cru raw

crustáceos shellfish

Cuba livre rum and cola

curau mashed sweet corn cooked in coconut milk with sugar and cinnamon

D **da época** in season

da estação subject to availability

damascos apricots (*Braz.*)

dendê palm oil

doce sweet; **meio-~** medium-sweet; **~ de fruta** jam; **~ de laranja** marmalade

doce de abóbora pumpkin dessert

doces desserts; **~ de ovos e amêndoa** marzipan

dose portion

E **eiró** eel

ementa menu/set menu; **~ turística** tourist menu

empada de galinha chicken pie

empadinha roasted pastry; **~ de carne** filled with meat; **~ de palmito** filled with palm hearts (*Braz.*)

empadão large type of pie; **~ de batata** shepherd's pie (minced meat and mashed potato topping)

enchidos assorted pork products made into sausages

enguia eel

ensopado de cabrito kid stew ➤46

entrada starter/appetizer

entrecosto sparerib

erva-doce aniseed

ervilhas peas

escalfado poached

espadarte swordfish

espargos asparagus

espaguete spaghetti

esparregado purée of assorted greens in cream

especialidades specialties; **~ da casa** of the house; **~ regionais/da região** local specialties

espetada cooked on a skewer/kebab

(no) espeto spit-roasted

espinafres spinach

espumante sparkling (*wine*)

estufado braised

esturjão sturgeon

F **faisão** pheasant

farinha flour

farofa manioc (cassava) meal browned in oil or butter (*Braz.*)

farofel manioc (cassava) flour

farófias beaten egg white poached in milk, topped with cinnamon and egg custard

fatias slices; **~ da China** cold, baked egg yolks topped with syrup flavored with lemon and cinnamon; **~ douradas** slices of bread dipped into milk and egg yolk, fried and sprinkled with sugar (French toast)

favas broad beans

febras de porco à alentejana pieces of pork fillet grilled with onions, *chouriço*, and bacon

feijoada black beans, bacon, pork, jerky, and sausage; eaten with rice, orange and *farofa* (*Braz.*) ➤46

feijão bean; **~ branco** navy; **~ catarino** pink; **~ encarnado** red; **~ frade** black-eyed; **~ guisado [ensopado]** stewed with bacon in a tomato sauce; **~ preto** black; **~ tropeiro** black beans fried with chopped *carne de sol* (jerky) and served with *farofa* (*Braz.*); **~ verde** green (runner) beans

feito a pedido made to order

fiambre boiled ham

fígado liver; **~ de aves** chicken

figos figs

filete fillet of fish

filhó fritter; **~ de abóbora** of pumpkin purée

filé steak (*Braz.*)

fios de ovos fine golden strands of egg yolk cooked in syrup

folhado sweet puff-pastry delicacy

(no) forno baked
framboesas raspberries
frango chicken;
~ **assado** roast chicken;
~ **na púcara** chicken stewed in Port wine (*northern Port.*) ➤46
fresco fresh, chilled
(na) frigideira sautéed
frio cold
fritada de peixe deep-fried fish
frito fried; fritter
fruta fruit ➤47; ~ **em calda** in syrup; ~ **do conde** custard apple
frutos do mar seafood
fubá corn flour/maize flour (*Braz.*)
fumado [defumado] smoked

G **galantina** pressed meat in gelatine
geleia de fruta jam
geleia de laranja marmalade
galeto com polenta fried chicken with polenta (*Braz.*)
galinha stewing chicken
galinhola woodcock
galão weak milky coffee served in a glass
gambas shrimp [king prawns]
ganso goose
garoto (white) coffee served in a small cup
garoupa large grouper (*fish*)
garrafa bottle; **meia-~** half bottle
gasosa lemonade
gaspacho chilled soup ➤44
gelado ice cream; chilled/iced
gelatina jelly
geleia jelly; jam (*Braz.*)
gelo ice, ice cubes; **com ~** with ice; **sem ~** without ice
genebra Dutch gin
gengibre ginger

gim gin
ginjinha spirit distilled from morello cherries
girafa draft [draught] beer served in fluted glass
goiaba guava (*Braz.*)
goiabada thick paste made of guava (*Braz.*)
gombo okra (*Braz.*)
gratinado oven-browned
grelos turnip sprouts
groselha red currant
grão chickpeas; ~ **com bacalhau** stew of chickpeas, potatoes, and dried cod fillets
grelhado grilled
guaraná a tropical fruit drink
guisado stew; stewed

H **hortaliça** fresh vegetables
hortelã mint

I **incluído no preço** included in price
imperial draft [draught] beer
inhame yam
iogurte yogurt
isca de peixe fried small fish (*Braz.*)
iscas sliced liver; ~ **à portuguesa** marinated in white wine with garlic and herbs, then fried
iva incluído sales tax [VAT] included

J **jabuticaba** type of cherry (*Braz.*)
jambu variety of cress (*Braz.*)
jantar dinner
jardineira mixed vegetables
jarro carafe
javali wild boar

K **kibe** meat and bulgur (cracked wheat) croquette (*Braz.*)

L **lagosta** lobster; **~ americana** fried with onions and garlic, flambéed in brandy, served in Madeira wine sauce; **~ suada** with onions, garlic, and tomatoes

lagostim crayfish; **~-do-rio** fresh-water crayfish

lampreia lamprey; **~ à moda do Minho** marinated, then poached and served with rice

lanche snack

laranja orange

laranjada orangeade

lavagante lobster

lebre hare

legumes vegetables ➤47

leite milk; **~ com chocolate** chocolate drink

leite de coco coconut milk

leite-creme custard, often with caramel topping

leitão suckling pig; **~ à Bairrada** coated with spicy lard and spit-roasted; **~ recheado** stuffed with spicy minced bacon, *chouriço*, and giblets, then roasted

lentilhas lentils

licor liqueur

lima lime

limonada type of lemon drink

limão lemon

limão verde lime (*Braz.*)

língua tongue

linguado sole; **~ à meunière** sautéed in butter, served with parsley and lemon juice; **~ com recheio de camarão** filled with shrimps in a white sauce

linguíça very thin *chouriço* ➤43

lista dos vinhos wine list

lombo loin

louro bay leaf

lulas squid; **~ à milanesa** fried squid (*Braz.*); **~ à provençal** squid stew (*Braz.*); **~ de caldeirada** simmered with white wine, onions, and parsley; **~ recheadas** braised and stuffed ➤45

M **maçã** apple

maçapão marzipan

macarrão macaroni

macaxeira cassava root (*Braz.*)

Madeira Madeira wine ➤50

maduro mature

maionese mayonnaise

mal passado rare/underdone

malagueta hot pepper

malsadas raised, fried dough (*Braz.*)

mamão papaya

mandioca manioc (cassava) root (*Braz.*)

manga mango

manjar de coco coconut pudding (blancmange) topped with plum syrup (*Braz.*)

manjericão basil

manteiga butter

mãozinhas de vitela guisadas calves' trotters braised with onions, parsley, and vinegar

maracujá passion fruit (*Braz.*)

marinado marinated

(à) marinheira with white wine, onions, and parsley

mariscos seafood ➤45

marmelada thick quince paste

massa pasta; dough, pastry

massapão marzipan

massapães almond macaroons

mate ice-cold Paraguay tea *(Braz.)*

mazagrã chilled black coffee served on the rocks with sugar and lemon slice

medalhão tenderloin steak

medronho arbutus berry *(small strawberry-like fruit)*

meia desfeita poached pieces of dried cod fried with chickpeas, onions, and vinegar, topped with hard-boiled eggs and chopped garlic

meia dose half portion

meio-frango assado half a roast chicken

mel honey

melancia watermelon

melão melon; **~ com presunto** with ham

mero red grouper *(fish)*

mexerica tangerine *(Braz.)*

mexilhões mussels

migas de bacalhau dried cod soup ➤44

mil-folhas millefeuille/puff pastry with jam and cream

milho sweet corn

mioleira brains

miolos brains; **~ mexidos com ovos** lamb brains fried and served with scrambled eggs

misto quente ham-and-cheese toasted sandwich *(Braz.)*

moelas spicy stew of chicken stomach

moqueca de peixe fish, shellfish or shrimp stew ➤45 *(Braz.)*

morangos strawberries; **~ silvestre** wild

morcela blood sausage [black pudding]

mortadela mortadella *(Bologna sausage)*

mostarda mustard

mousse de chocolate chocolate pudding

mousse de maracujá passion fruit mousse

muito mal passado rare *(meat, etc.)*

 nabiças turnip greens
nabos turnips

nata(s) fresh cream; **~ batida(s)** whipped

(ao) natural plain, without dressing, sauce, etc.

nêsperas loquat *(fruit)*

no forno baked

noz nut; **~ moscada** nutmeg

 óleo oil; **~ de amendoim** peanut oil

omelete omelet; **~ de camarão** shrimp; **~ de chouriço** smoked sausage; **~ de espargos** asparagus

orégão [orégano] oregano

osso bone

ostras oysters; **~ do Algarve** oysters baked in butter and dry wine *(Algarve)*; **~ recheadas** oyster shells stuffed with oysters, onions, garlic, breadcrumbs, egg yolk, lemon juice, then oven-browned

ou servido com ... the same served with ...

ovos eggs; **~ Portuguesa** baked in a tomato shell with spices and breadcrumbs; **~ cozidos** boiled; **~ escalfados** poached; **~ estrelados/fritos** fried; **~ mexidos** scrambled; **~ moles de Aveiro** beaten yolks cooked in syrup *(Aveiro)*; **~ quentes** soft-boiled eggs; **~ verdes** eggs stuffed with boiled yolks, onions and parsley, and fried

P **paçoca** roast *carne de sol* (jerky) ground with manioc (cassava) root and served with sliced bananas; dessert made with roast peanuts crushed with sweetened manioc (cassava) meal (*Braz.*)

paio smoked, rolled pork fillet; **~ com ervilhas** simmered with peas and chopped onions

palmito palm hearts (*Braz.*)

pamonha made with grated sweetcorn and milk (*Braz.*)

panado [empanado] breaded

panqueca pancake

pão (escuro/integral) bread (brown/wholewheat); **~ de centeio** rye bread

pão de queijo pastry made with cheese and manioc flour

pão-de-ló coffee cake

pãozinho bread roll

papo-seco roll

papos-de-anjo egg yolk macaroons

para dois for two

pargo bream (*fish*)

passado cooked; (*meat, etc.*) **mal ~** rare/underdone; **meio ~** medium; **bem ~** well-done

passas (de uvas) raisins

pastel small pie

pastel de coco coconut pastry

pastel de feijão bean pastry

pastel de massa tenra soft crust pastry pie filled with minced meat

pastel de nata/de Belém small cream tart

pastel de Santa Clara tartlet with almond-paste filling

pastel de Tentúgal flaky pastry filled with beaten egg yolks

pastelão de palmito e camarão shrimp and palm-heart pie (*Braz.*)

pato duck; **~ estufado** braised in white wine with onions, parsley, and bay leaf

pato ao tucupi roast duck with tucupi (manioc juice) (*Braz.*)

pé de moleque peanut brittle (*Braz.*)

peito de galinha chicken breast

peixe fish ➤45; **~-agulha** garfish; **~-espada** cutlass fish; **~-galo** John Dory

pepino cucumber

pepinos de conserva pickles

pequeno almoço breakfast

pêra pear

perca perch

perdiz partridge; **~ à caçador(a)** simmered with carrots, onions, white wine, and herbs; **~ com molho de vilão** poached and served with cold sauce of olive oil, vinegar, and onions

perna de galinha chicken leg

pernil ham

pêro variety of eating apple

peru turkey

pés de porco pig's feet [trotters]

pescada whiting; **~ cozida com todos** poached and served with boiled potatoes and green beans

pescadinhas de rabo na boca fried whole whiting

pêssego peach

petiscos appetizers/starters

pevide pip (seed); salted pumpkin seed

picanha desfiada charcoal-grilled meat in pieces (*Braz.*)

picante hot, spicy

pikles pickled vegetables

pimenta pepper

pimentos sweet peppers; **~ assados** roasted ➤43

pinga wine; crude white rum (*Braz.*)

pinhoada pine nut brittle

pinhão pine nut

pipis spicy giblet stew

pirarucu fish from the Amazon (*Braz.*)

piri-piri seasoning of hot chili pepper and olive oil

polvo octopus

pombo pigeon; **~ estufado** braised with bacon, onions and white wine, served with fried bread

porco pork

porções variados assorted appetizers (*Braz.*)

(vinho do) Porto port ➤50

posta slice of fish or meat

prato do dia dish of the day

prato feito set meal

prato principal main course

pratos combinados set dishes

pratos frios cold dishes

pré-pagamento payment in advance

preço suplementar extra charge/supplement

prego small steak, often served in a roll

presunto cured ham; **~ cru** dried ham

preço price

primeiro prato first course

pudim de bacalhau dried-cod loaf, served with tomato sauce

pudim flan caramel custard

pudim Molotov mousse in caramel sauce

pudim à portuguesa custard flavored with brandy and raisins

puré de batatas mashed potatoes with milk and butter

puro straight/neat

Q **queijada** small cottage-cheese tart; **~ de Sintra** flavored with cinnamon

queijinhos do céu marzipan balls rolled in sugar

queijo cheese ➤48

quente hot; **~ e frio** hot fudge sundae

quiabo okra

quindim pudding made with coconut and egg yolks (*Braz.*)

R **rabanada** slice of bread dipped into egg batter and sprinkled with sugar (French toast)

rabanetes radishes

raia skate (*fish*)

rainha-cláudia greengage plum

recheado stuffed

recheio stuffing, forcemeat

refeição meal; **~ completa** set menu; **~ ligeira** snack

refogado onions fried in olive oil

refrescos soft drinks

repolho cabbage

requeijão curd cheese (*Braz.*)

rins kidneys

rissóis [risoles] de camarão deep-fried pastry envelopes filled with shrimp

robalo sea bass

rodela round slice

rodízio selection of chargrilled meats (*Braz.*)

rojões à alentejana pork cubes fried with baby clams, diced potatoes, and onions

rojões à moda do Minho fried chopped pork ➤46

rolo de carne picada meatloaf

rolos de couve lombarda savoy cabbage leaves stuffed with mince or sausage meat

romã pomegranate

rosca ring-shaped white bread

rosmaninho rosemary

ruivo red gurnard *(fish)*

S **sal** salt
salada salad ➤44;
~ **completa** with tomato, palm hearts, boiled eggs; ~ **de alface/escarola** green salad; ~ **de agrião** watercress; ~ **de atum** tuna and potato; ~ **de feijão frade** black-eyed bean; ~ **de pimentos assados** made with grilled sweet peppers; ~ **de tomate** tomato; ~ **mista** tomato and lettuce; ~ **russa** diced boiled potatoes and carrots with mayonnaise

salambôs oval puffs with cream and caramel glaze *(Braz.)*

salgado salty / salted

salmonete red mullet; ~ **grelhado com molho de manteiga** grilled and served with melted butter, chopped parsley, and lemon; ~ **setúbalense** grilled red mullet

salmão (fumado) [defumado] (smoked) salmon

salsa parsley

salsicha sausage

salteado sautéed

salva sage

sandes/sanduíche sandwich

santola spider-crab; ~ **recheada** stuffed with its own meat ➤43

sarapatel pork or mutton stew, thickened with blood

sarda mackerel

sardinhas sardines

sável shad *(herring-like fish)*

seco dry; **meio-** ~ medium-dry

sêmola semolina

sericá alentejano cinnamon soufflé

serviço incluído service included

sidra cider

siri crab *(Braz.)*

só por encomenda made to order

sobremesas dessert ➤48

solha plaice *(fish)*

sonho type of doughnut

sopa soup ➤44; ~ **à pescador** fish soup

sopa de ~ type of soup; ~ **abóbora** pumpkin; ~ **agriões** potato and watercress; ~ **camarão** shrimp; ~ **cenoura** carrot; ~ **coentros** with coriander, bread, and poached eggs; ~ **cozido** meat broth with vegetables and macaroni; ~ **ervilhas** green pea; ~ **favas** broad bean; ~ **feijão frade** black-eyed bean; ~ **grelos** turnip sprout; ~ **grão** chickpea; ~ **hortaliça** vegetable; ~ **rabo de boi** oxtail; ~ **tomate** tomato with poached eggs and bread

sopa do dia soup of the day

sopa juliana soup with shredded vegetables

sopa seca thick beef and chicken soup ➤44

sopa transmontana vegetable soup with bacon and bread

sorvete ice cream *(Braz.)*; ~ **com água** sherbet / water-ice

suco fruit juice *(Braz.)*; ~ **de abacaxi** pineapple; ~ **de laranja** orange; ~ **de mamão** papaya; ~ **de manga** mango; ~ **de tamarindo** tamarind; ~ **de toranja** grapefruit

sugestão do chefe the chef recommends

sumo [suco] fruit juice

sururu type of cockle (*Braz.*)

suspiro meringue

 taça long-stemmed glass, cup

taínha gray mullet (*fish*)

tâmaras dates

tangerinas tangerines

tarte de amêndoa almond tart

tempero seasoning

tenro tender

tigelada dessert of eggs beaten with milk and cinnamon

tinto red (*wine*)

todos os pratos servidos com ... all meals served with ...

tomates tomatoes

tomilho thyme

toranja grapefruit

tornedó round cut of prime beef

torrada toast

torrão de ovos marzipan candy

torta swiss roll; **~ de laranja** with orange juice; **~ de Viana** filled with lemon curd

tosta toasted sandwich; **~ mista** with ham-and-cheese

toucinho [bacon] bacon; **~ do céu** kind of marzipan pudding

tremoço salted lupin seed

tripas à moda do Porto tripe cooked with pork, served with rice ➤46

trouxa de vitela veal olive

trouxas de ovos egg yolks poached in sweetened water and topped with syrup

trufa truffle

truta trout

túberas truffles

tucupi manioc (cassava) juice (*Braz.*)

tutano marrow

tutu à mineira dish of beans, pork, and cabbage ➤47 (*Braz.*)

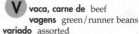 **umbu** a tropical fruit (*Braz.*)

uvas grapes

uísque whisky

 vaca, carne de beef

vagens green/runner beans

variado assorted

vatapá fish and shrimp (dried and fresh) in a paste ➤45 (*Braz.*)

veado venison

vegetais variados choice of vegetables

vieira scallop

vinagre vinegar

vinho wine ➤49–50; **~ da casa** house wine; **~ da Madeira** Madeira wine ➤50; **~ do Porto** port ➤50; **~ da região** local wine; **~ generoso** well-aged and fortified; **~ licoroso** naturally sweet; **~ verde** "green wine" ➤50

vitamina cold drink of several fruits blended with milk or water (*Braz.*)

vitela veal

xinxim de galinha chicken in shrimp sauce (*Braz.*) ➤46

Travel

Portugal has a fairly well-developed transport system, so you should
enjoy trouble-free traveling. Distances in Brazil mean that air travel is
often the best option; alternatively buses are comfortable and economical.
Petty crime and robbery are a problem in tourist spots, buses, and city
beaches in Brazil. Portugal is a relatively safe country and violent crimes
against tourists are rare.

ESSENTIAL

A ticket to …	**Um bilhete para …**
	oom billyayt per-rer
one-way [single]	**de ida** *der eeder*
round-trip [return]	**de ida e volta** *der eeder ee volter*
How much …?	**Quanto …?** *kwantoo*
When will … arrive/leave?	**Quando chega/parte …?**
	kwando shayger/part

Safety Questões de segurança

Would you accompany me to the bus stop?	**Podia ir comigo até à paragem do autocarro [parada de ônibus]?** *podeeer eer koomeegoo er-teh ah per-rahzhaym doo owtokarroo [paradah der oanibooss]*
I don't feel safe (here).	**Não me sinto em segurança (aqui).** *nawm mer seentoo aym ser-goorawnser (er-kee)*

Arrival Chegada

Citizens of EU countries require a valid passport for entry to Portugal and Brazil. Citizens of the US, Canada, Australia, and New Zealand require a valid passport and visa for entry to Brazil but only a valid passport for entry to Portugal. Visas, valid for 90 days in Brazil, can be extended at federal police stations.

Duty free into:	Cigarettes	Cigars	Tobacco	Spirits	Wine
Portugal	200 or	50 or	250 g.	1 l. or	2 l.
Canada	200 and	50 and	200 g.	1 l. or	1 l.
U.K.	200 or	50 or	250 g.	1 l. and	2 l.
U.S.	200 and	100 and	discretionary	1 l. or	1 l.

Import restrictions between EU countries have been relaxed on items for personal use or consumption that are bought duty-paid within the EU. Suggested maximum: 90 l. wine or 60 l. sparkling wine; 20 l. fortified wine; 10 l. spirits and 110 l. beer.

Passport control Controle de passaportes

We have a joint passport.	**Temos um passaporte em conjunto.** _taymoosh oom paser-port aym konzhoontoo_
The children are on this passport.	**As crianças estão neste passaporte.** _ush kryawnsush ishtawm naysht paser-port_
I'm here on vacation [holiday].	**Estou de férias.** _ishtoh der fehryush_
I'm here on business.	**Estou em negócios.** _ishtoh aym ner-gossyoosh_
I'm just passing through.	**Estou só de passagem.** _ishtoh so der per-sahzhaym_
I'm going to …	**Vou para …** _voh per-rer_
I won't be working here.	**Não vou trabalhar aqui.** _nawm voh trer-ber-lyar er-kee_
I'm …	**Estou …** _ishtoh_
on my own	**sozinho(-a)** _sozzeenyoo(-er)_
with my family	**com a minha família** _kawm er meenyer fer-meelyer_
with a group	**com um grupo** _kawm oom groopoo_

WHO ARE YOU WITH? ➤ 120

Customs Alfândega

I have only the normal allowances.	**Trago apenas o que é permitido.** *tragoo er-paynush oo ker eh permeeteedoo*
It's a gift.	**É um presente.** *eh oom prer-zaynter*
It's for my personal use.	**É para meu uso pessoal.** *eh per-er meoo oozoa per-ssoaerl*

Tem alguma coisa a declarar?	Do you have anything to declare?
Tem de pagar direitos (alfandegários).	You must pay duty on this.
Onde comprou isto?	Where did you buy this?
Abra este saco, por favor.	Please open this bag.
Tem mais bagagem?	Do you have any more luggage?

I would like to declare …	**Queria declarar …** *ker-reeer der-kler-rar*
I don't understand.	**Não compreendo.** *nawm kawmpreeayndoo*
Does anyone here speak English?	**Há aqui alguém que fale inglês?** *ah er-kee algaym ker faler eenglaysh*

CONTROLE DE PASSAPORTES	passport control
FRONTEIRA	border crossing
ALFÂNDEGA	customs
NADA A DECLARAR	nothing to declare
ARTIGOS A DECLARAR	goods to declare
POLÍCIA	police

Duty-free shopping Duty-free

What currency is this price in?	**Em que moeda está este preço?** *aym ker mooehder ishtah aysht praysoo*
Can I pay in …	**Posso pagar em …** *possoo per-gar aym*
dollars/pounds	**dólares/libras** *doller-rish/leebrush*
euros/reais *(Port./Braz.)*	**euros/reais** *ayoorosh/reh-ighsh*

Plane De avião

In Portugal, there are airports at Lisbon, Oporto, Faro, Funchal (Madeira), Ponta Delgada (Azores), and Lajes (Azores). The national airline is TAP Air Portugal. The main Brazilian airlines are Varig, Vasp, and Transbrasil.

Individual flight tickets in Brazil can be expensive, so it may be worth buying an air-pass (only available outside the country). It is advisable to reserve in advance in the summer, when Brazilians themselves travel most frequently.

Tickets and reservations Bilhetes e reservas

When is the … flight to …?	**Quando é o … voo [vôo] para …?** _kwandoo eh oo … voohoo per-rer_
first/next/last	**primeiro/próximo/último** _primayroo/prossymoo/ooltymoo_
I'd like 2 … tickets to …	**Queria dois bilhetes … para …** _ker-reeer doysh billyaytish … per-rer_
one-way [single]	**só de ida** _so der eeder_
round-trip [return]	**de ida e volta** _der eeder ee volter_
first class	**em primeira classe** _aym primayrer klass_
business class	**em business/navigator** _aym business/navigator_
economy class	**em classe económica** _aym klass eekonnoomeeker_
How much is a flight to …?	**Quanto é o bilhete para …?** _kwantoo eh oo billyayt per-rer_
I'd like to … my reservation for flight number …	**Queria … a minha reserva no voo …** _ker-reeer … er meenyer rer-zehrver noo voohoo_
cancel/change/confirm	**cancelar/mudar/confirmar** _kawnser-lar/moodar/konfeermar_

Inquiries about the flight Perguntas sobre o voo

How long is the flight?	**Quanto tempo demora o voo [vôo]?** _kwantoo taympoo der-moarer oo voohoo_
What time does the plane leave?	**A que horas parte o avião?** _er kee orush part oo er-vyawm_
What time will we arrive?	**A que horas chegamos?** _er kee orush shegamoosh_
What time do I have to check in?	**A que horas tenho de registar [fazer o check in]?** _er kee orush taynyoo de rezheeshtrahr [fer-zair oo "check in"]_

Checking in Registro

Where is the check-in
counter for flight ...?

**Onde é o registro
[check in] para o voo ...?**
*ond eh oo rezheeshtroo
['check in'] per-rer oo vohoo*

I have ...

Tenho ... *taynyoo*

3 suitcases

três malas *traysh malush*

2 carry-ons [pieces of
hand luggage]

duas peças de bagagem de mão
dooush pesush der ber-gazhaym der mawm

O seu bilhete/passaporte, se faz favor.	Your ticket/passport, please.
Prefere à janela ou na coxia [no corredor]?	Would you like a window or an aisle seat?
Fumadores [fumates] ou não-fumadores [não-fumantes]?	Smoking or non-smoking?
Quantas peças de bagagem tem?	How many pieces of baggage do you have?
Pode levar trinta quilos de bagagem.	You are allowed 30 kilos of baggage.
Tem excesso de peso na sua bagagem.	You have excess baggage.
Isso é demasiado pesado/ volumoso para bagagem de mão.	That's too heavy/large for carry-on [hand baggage].
Tem de pagar um suplemento de ... por quilo em excesso.	You'll have to pay a supplement of ... per kilo of excess baggage.
Foi o senhor/a senhora quem fez as malas?	Did you pack these bags yourself?
Contêm qualquer artigo cortante ou eléctrico?	Do they contain any sharp or electronic items?

CHEGADAS	arrivals
PARTIDAS	departures
CONTROLE DE SEGURANÇA	security check
NÃO ABANDONAR A BAGAGEM	do not leave bags unattended

BAGGAGE ➤ 71

Information Informações

Is flight … delayed?	**Há atraso no voo …?** *ah er-trazoo noo vohoo*
How late will it be?	**Qual é o atraso?** *kwal eh oo er-trazoo*
Has the flight from … landed?	**O avião de … já aterrou [aterrizou]?** *oo er-vyawm der … zhah er-terroh [er-terrizoh]*
Which gate does the flight to … leave from?	**Qual é a porta do voo [vôo] para …?** *kwal eh er porter doo vohoo per-rer*
Could I have a drink, please?	**Queria uma bebida, se faz favor.** *ker-reeer oomer ber-beeder ser fash fer-voar*
Please wake me for the meal.	**Acorde-me para a refeição, se faz favor.** *er-korder-mer per-rer er rer-faysawm ser fash fer-voar*
What time will we arrive?	**A que horas vamos chegar?** *er kee orush vamoosh sher-gar*
I feel airsick.	**Sinto-me enjoado(-a).** *seentoomer aynzhwadoo(-er)*
An airsickness bag, please.	**Um saco de enjoo, se faz favor.** *oom sakoo daynzhohoo ser fash fer-voar*

Arrival Chegada

Where is/are …?	**Onde é/são …?** *ond eh/sawm*
buses	**os autocarros [ônibus]** *oosh owtokarroosh [oanibooss]*
car rental	**o aluguer de carros** *oo er-loogehr der karroosh*
exit	**a saída** *er ser-eeder*
taxis	**os táxis** *oosh taksish*
telephone	**o telefone** *oo ter-ler-fon*
Is there a bus into town?	**Há um autocarro [ônibus] para o centro?** *ah oom owtokarroo [oanibooss] per-rer oo sayntroo*
How do I get to the … Hotel?	**Como é que vou para o Hotel …?** *koomoo eh ker voh per-rer oo ottel*

Baggage Bagagem

There are storage lockers (**cacifos**) at the main bus and train stations. Carts are only available at airports.

Porter! Excuse me!	**Carregador! Se faz favor!** *ker-rrer-ger-doar ser fash fer-voar*
Could you take my luggage to …?	**Pode levar a minha bagagem ao …?** *pod ler-var er meenyer ber-gazhaym ow*
a taxi/bus	**táxi/autocarro [ônibus]** *taksi/owtokarroo [oanibooss]*
Where is/are (the) …?	**Onde é/estão …?** *ond eh/ishtawm*
luggage carts [trolleys]	**os carrinhos** *oosh kerreenyos*
luggage lockers	**os cacifos de bagagem** *oosh ker-seefoosh der ber-gazhaym*
baggage check [left-luggage office]	**o depósito de bagagem** *oo der-pozzytoo der ber-gazhaym*
Where is the luggage from flight …?	**Onde está a bagagem do voo [vôo] …?** *ond ishtah er ber-gazhaym doo vohoo*

Loss, damage, and theft Perdas, danos e roubos

I've lost the key/ticket.	**Perdi a chave/o talão.** *perdee er shav/oo ter-lawm*
My luggage has been lost/stolen.	**Perdi/Roubaram a minha bagagem.** *perdee/rohbarawm er meenyer ber-gazhaym*
My suitcase was damaged.	**A minha mala foi danificada.** *er meenyer maler foy der-neefikader*
Our luggage has not arrived.	**A nossa bagagem não chegou.** *er noser ber-gazhaym nawm sher-goh*

Como é a sua bagagem?	What does your baggage look like?
Tem o talão da reclamação?	Do you have the claim check [reclaim tag]?
A sua bagagem …	Your luggage …
pode ter sido enviada para …	may have been sent to …
talvez chegue mais logo.	may arrive later today
Por favor venha amanhã.	Please come back tomorrow.
Ligue para este número, para saber se a sua bagagem já chegou.	Call this number to check if your baggage has arrived.

POLICE ➤ 152; COLOR ➤ 143

Train De comboio [trem]

Expresso *ishprehssoo*

Express train running from Lisbon through Coimbra to Oporto (**Alfa** trains); regional trains (**Intercidades** and **Inter-regionais**) connect different areas of Portugal, offering fast and comfortable traveling.

Lisboa-Expresso, TEF *lizhboaer ishprehssoo, tehf*

Express train linking Lisbon with Madrid, reservation compulsory, surcharge payable; also **Lusitânia-Expresso** (Lisbon–Madrid) and **Sud-Express** (Lisbon-Paris), for which early booking is advisable.

Internacional *eengterrnerssyoonahl*

Direct train for a trip abroad; you'll have to book a seat in advance, as only one car [carriage] crosses the border.

Rápido *rahpiddoo*

Direct train, stops only at main stations, early booking advisable.

Regional *rizhyoonal*

Local train providing an opportunity to those with time to observe people and their habits.

Automotora *owtoamootoarer*

Small diesel train used on short runs.

Correio *koorrayoo*

Long-distance postal train, stops at all stations; also takes passengers.

The Portuguese railway, **Caminhos de Ferro Portugueses** (**C.P.**), handles almost all train services. Tickets can be purchased and reservations made in travel agencies and at train stations.

Check out the various reductions and travel cards available (for 7, 14, and 21 days). Rates are cheaper on "Blue Days" (**dias azuis**). A "Gold Card" is available for people over 65.

Lisbon has four main train stations, so don't go to the wrong one: Santa Apolónia (international, northern Portugal), Cais do Sodré (Estoril, Cascais, western suburbs), Rossio (Sintra and west), and Sul e Sueste (Algarve).

In Brazil, the rail network is small and not very efficient.

Brazilian railways, **Estrada de Ferro Central do Brasil** (**E.F.C.B.**), offer few passenger services. The São Paulo–Rio de Janeiro night journey is comfortable but long and expensive.

To the station Caminho da estação

How do I get to the train station?	**Como vou para a estação de caminho de ferro [estação ferroviária]?** _koomoo voh per-rer er ishter-sawm der ker-meenyoo der fehrroo [ishter-sawm fehrooveeahree-er]_
Do trains to … leave from … station?	**Os comboios [trens] para … partem da estação …?** _oosh kawmboyoosh [traynsh] per-rer … partaym der ishter-sawm_
Can I leave my car there?	**Posso deixar lá o meu carro?** _possoo dayshar lah oo meoo karroo_

At the station Na estação

Where's the …?	**Onde é …?** _ond eh_
baggage check [left-luggage office]	**o depósito da bagagem** _oo der-pozzytoo der ber-gazhaym_
currency exchange	**o bureau de câmbio** _oo "bureau de change"/kawmbyoo_
snack bar	**o snack bar [a lanchonete]** _oo "snack bar" [er lanshoanehti]_
ticket office	**a bilheteira [bilheteria]** _er billyer-tayrer [billyer-tayreeer]_
waiting room	**a sala de espera** _er saler di shpehrer_
Where is/are the …?	**Onde é/são …?** _ond eh/sawm_
information desk	**as informações** _ush infoormer-soynsh_
lost-and-found [lost property office]	**os perdidos e achados** _oosh perdeedoosh ee er-shadoosh_
luggage lockers	**os cacifos de bagagem** (Portugal only) _oosh ker-seefoosh der ber-gazhaym_
platforms	**as linhas [plataformas]** _ush leenyush [plataformush]_

ENTRADA	entrance
SAÍDA	exit
PARA AS LINHAS	to the platforms
INFORMAÇÕES	information
RESERVAS	reservations
CHEGADAS	arrivals
PARTIDAS	departures

DIRECTIONS ➤ 94

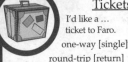

Tickets Bilhetes

I'd like a … ticket to Faro.	**Queria um bilhete … para Faro.** *ker-reeer oom billyayt … per-rer fahroo*
one-way [single]	**de ida** *der eeder*
round-trip [return]	**de ida e volta** *der eeder ee volter*
first/second class	**de primeira/segunda classe** *der primayrer/ser-goonder klass*
I'd like a discounted ticket.	**Queria um meio-bilhete.** *ker-reeer oom mayoo billyayt*
I'd like to reserve a(n) …	**Queria marcar …** *ker-reeer murkar*
seat	**um lugar** *oom loogar*
aisle seat	**um lugar de coxia [de corredor]** *oom loogar der koosheeer [der koorehdor]*
window seat	**um lugar à janela** *oom loogar ah zher-ner-ler*
berth	**um beliche** *oom ber-leesh*
Is there a sleeping car [sleeper]?	**Há couchettes/carruagem-cama [vagão-leito]?** *ah kooshettish/ker-rwazhaym kamer [vagawn laytoo]*
I'd like a(n) … berth.	**Queria um beliche …** *ker-reeer oom ber-leesh*
upper/lower	**superior/inferior** *sooper-ryoar/infer-ryoar*
Can I buy a ticket on board?	**Posso comprar o bilhete no comboio [trem]?** *possoo kawmprar oo billyayt noo kawmboyoo [trayn]*

Prices Preços

How much is that?	**Quanto custa?** *kwantoo kooshter*
Is there a discount for …?	**Há desconto para …?** *ah dishkontoo per-rer*
children/families	**crianças/famílias** *kryawnsush/fer-meelyush*
senior citizens	**os reformados [idosos]** *oosh rer-foormadoosh [eedoasoosh]*
students	**estudantes** *ishtoodawntish*
Do you offer a cheap same-day round-trip ticket?	**Há desconto para uma ida e volta no mesmo dia?** *ah dishkontoo per-rer oomer eeder ee volter noo mayshmoo deeer*

NUMBERS ➤ 216; DAYS OF THE WEEK ➤ 218

Queries Perguntas

Do I have to change trains?	**Tenho de mudar de comboio [trem]?** _taynyoo der moodar der kawmboyoo [trayn]_
It's a direct train.	**É directo [direto].** _eh deerettoo_
You have to change at …	**Tem de mudar em …** _taym der moodar aym_
How long is this ticket valid?	**Este bilhete é válido por quanto tempo?** _aysht billyayt eh validoo poor kwantoo taympoo_
Can I take my bicycle on the train?	**Posso levar a minha bicicleta no comboio [trem]?** _possoo ler-var er meenyer beeseekletter noo kawmboyoo [trayn]_
Can I return on the same ticket?	**Este bilhete é válido para a volta?** _aysht billyayt eh validoo per-rer er volter_
In which car [coach] is my seat?	**Em que compartimento fica o meu lugar?** _aym ker kawmpertimayntoo feeker oo meoo loogar_
Is there a dining car on the train?	**Há serviço de restaurante no comboio [trem]?** _ah serveesoo der rishtowrawnt noo kawmboyoo [trayn]_

> – Queria um bilhete para Lisboa, se faz favor.
>   (I'd like a ticket to Lisbon, please.)
> – *De ida ou de ida e volta?* (One-way or round-trip?)
> – De ida e volta. (Round-trip, please.)
> – *São vinte e cinco euros.* (That's 25 euros.)
> – Tenho de mudar? (Do I have to change trains?)
> – *Sim. Tem de mudar em Beja.*
>   *(Yes. You have to change in Beja.)*
> – Obrigada. Adeus. (Thank you. Good-bye.)

Train times Horários de comboios [trens]

Could I have a timetable, please?	**Queria um horário, se faz favor.** _ker-reeer oom oraryoo ser fash fer-voar_
When is the … train to Oporto?	**Quando é o … comboio [trem] para o Porto?** _kwandoo eh oo … kawmboyoo [trayn] per-rer poartoo_
first/next/last	**primeiro/próximo/último** _primayroo/prossymoo/ooltymoo_

How frequent are the trains to …?	**Qual é a frequência dos comboios [trens] para …?** *kwal eh er frer-kwaynsyer doosh kawmboyoosh [traynsh] per-rer*
once/twice a day	**um/dois por dia** *oom/doysh poor deeer*
5 times a day	**cinco por dia** *seenkoo poor deeer*
every hour	**de hora em hora** *dorer aym orer*
What time do they leave?	**A que horas partem?** *er kee orush partaym*
on the hour	**na hora** *ner orer*
20 minutes past the hour	**vinte minutos depois da hora** *veent minootoosh der-poysh der orer*
What time does the train arrive in …?	**A que horas chega o comboio [trem] a …** *er kee orush shayger oo kawmboyoo [trayn] er*
How long is the trip [journey]?	**Quanto tempo demora a viagem?** *kwantoo taympoo der-morer er vyazhaym*
Is the train on time?	**O comboio [trem] vem à tabela [está no horário]?** *oo kawmboyoo [trayn] vaym ah ter-beler [ishtah noo orahreeoo]*

Departures Partidas

Which platform does the train to … leave from?	**De que linha [plataforma] parte o comboio [trem] para …?** *der ker leenyer [plataformah] part oo kawmboyoo [trayn] per-rer*
Where is platform 4?	**Onde é a linha [plataforma] n.º 4?** *ond eh er leenyer [plataformer] noomeroo kwatroo*
over there	**ali** *er-lee*
on the left/right	**à esquerda/direita** *ah ishkairder/deerayter*
under the underpass	**por baixo da passagem inferior** *poor bighshoo der per-sazhaym eenfer-ryoar*
Where do I change for …?	**Onde é que mudo para …?** *ond eh ker moodoo per-rer*
How long will I have to wait for a connection?	**Quanto tempo tenho de esperar pela ligação [conexão]?** *kwantoo taympoo taynyoo der eeshper-rar payler leeger-sawm [konnehksawn]*

Boarding À partida

Is this the right platform for the train to …?	**É daqui que parte o comboio [trem] para …?** *eh der-kee ker partoo kawmboyoo [trayn] per-rer*
Is this the train to …?	**É este o comboio [trem] para …** *eh aysht oo kawmboyoo [trayn] per-rer*
Is this seat taken?	**Este lugar está ocupado?** *aysht loogar ishtah okkoopadoo*
I think that's my seat.	**Acho que esse é o meu lugar.** *ashoo ker ayss eh oo meoo loogar*
Are there any seats/berths available?	**Há lugares/beliches vagos?** *ah loogarish/ber-leeshish vagoosh*
Do you mind …?	**Importa-se …?** *eemporter-ser*
if I sit here	**que eu me sente aqui** *ker eoo mer saynt er-kee*
if I open the window	**que eu abra a janela** *ker eoo abrer er zher-neler*

During the trip Na viagem

How long are we stopping here?	**Quanto tempo paramos aqui?** *kwantoo taympoo per-ramoosh er-kee*
When do we get to …?	**Quando chegamos a …?** *kwandoo shegamoosh er*
Have we passed …?	**Já passamos por …?** *zhah per-samoosh poor*
Where is the dining/ sleeping car?	**Onde é a carruagem- [vagão-] restaurante/ cama?** *ond eh er ker-rrwazhaym [vagawn] rishtowrawnt/kamer*
Where is my berth?	**Onde é o meu beliche?** *ond eh oo meoo ber-leesh*
I've lost my ticket.	**Perdi o meu bilhete.** *perdee oo meoo billyayt*

⊕	**TRAVÃO [FREIO] DE EMERGÊENCIA**	emergency brake	⊗
	ALARME	alarm	
⊘	**PORTAS AUTOMÁTICAS**	automatic doors	⊖

TIME ➤ 220

Long-distance bus [Coach]
Camioneta [Ônibus]

Intercity bus services are frequent and cover most of Portugal. Some buses are run by the Portuguese Transport Company, **Rodoviária Nacional (R.N.)**, others are private.

In Brazil, intercity buses are fairly cheap and comfortable, usually with air conditioning. If you are traveling overnight, look for **leitos**, buses with reclining seats, clean sheets, and pillows provided. Tickets (**passagens**) are available from bus stations (**rodoviárias**).

Where is the bus station?	**Onde é a estação de camionetas [ônibus]?** *ond eh er ishter-sawm der kamyoonettush [oanibooss]*
When's the next bus [coach] to …?	**A que horas é a próxima camioneta [o próximo ônibus] para …?** *er kee orush eh a prossymer kamyoonetter [oo prossymoo oanibooss] per-rer*
Which stop does it leave from?	**Onde é a paragem [parada]?** *ond eh er per-razhaym [parader]*
Does the bus stop at …?	**A camioneta [O ônibus] para em …?** *er kamyoonetter [oo oanibooss] parer aym*
How long does the trip take?	**Quanto tempo demora a viagem?** *kwantoo taympoo der-morer er vyazhaym*

Bus/Streetcar Autocarros [Ônibus]/Eléctricos

In most buses you pay a flat fare to the driver as you enter, or buy a booklet of tickets from bus company kiosks.

Where is the bus station?	**Onde é a paragem de autocarros [o terminal de ônibus]?** *ond eh er per-razhaym der owtokarroosh [oo terminal der oanibooss]*
Where can I get a tram to …?	**Onde posso apanhar [pegar] um eléctrico [bonde] para …?** *ond possoo er-per-nyar [paygar] oom eelettrikoo [bawmdzhi] per-rer*
What time is the bus to …?	**A que horas é o autocarro [ônibus] para …?** *er kee orush eh oo owtokarroo [oanibooss] per-rer*

PARAGEM DE AUTOCARROS [PARADA DE ÔNIBUS]	bus stop
NÃO-FUMADORES [-FUMANTES]	no smoking
SAÍDA (DE EMERGÊNCIA)	(emergency) exit

78

DIRECTIONS ➤ 94; TIME ➤ 220

Buying tickets Para comprar bilhetes

Where can I buy tickets?
Onde posso comprar bilhetes? *ond possoo kawmprar billyaytish*

A ... ticket/train pass to ...
Um bilhete/passe ... para ... *oom billyayt/pass ... per-rer*

one-way [single]
só de ida *so der eeder*

round-trip [return]
de ida e volta *der eeder ee volter*

day/weekly/monthly
para o dia/semanal/mensal *per-rer oo deeer/semer-nal/maynsal*

a booklet of tickets
um livro de bilhetes *oom leevroo der bilyaytish*

How much is the fare to ...?
Quanto é o bilhete para ...? *kwantoo eh oo billyayt per-rer*

Traveling Para viajar

Is this the right bus to ...?
É este o autocarro [ônibus] para ...? *eh aysht oo owtokarroo [oanibooss] per-rer*

Could you tell me when to get off?
Pode dizer-me onde devo sair? *pod deezairmer ond dayvoo ser-eer*

Do I have to change trams/buses?
Tenho de mudar de eléctrico [bonde]/de autocarro [ônibus] *taynyoo der moodar der eeletrikoo [bawmdzhi]/der owtokarroo [oanibooss]*

How many stops are there to ...?
Há quantas paragens [paradas] até ...? *ah kwantush per-razhaynsh [paradush] er-teh*

Next stop!
A próxima paragem [parada]! *er prossymer per-razhaym [paradah]*

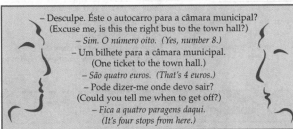

– Desculpe. Éste o autocarro para a câmara municipal?
(Excuse me, is this the right bus to the town hall?)
– Sim. O número oito. (Yes, number 8.)
– Um bilhete para a câmara municipal.
(One ticket to the town hall.)
– São quatro euros. (That's 4 euros.)
– Pode dizer-me onde devo sair?
(Could you tell me when to get off?)
– Fica a quatro paragens daqui.
(It's four stops from here.)

NUMBERS ➤ 216; *DIRECTIONS* ➤ 94

Subway [Metro] Metro

The subway system in Lisbon has two main lines. Buy a single flat-rate ticket (**senha**) or a booklet of ten tickets at ticket offices or automatic machines, found in every station.

São Paulo, Rio de Janeiro, Belo Horizonte, Porto Alegre, and Recife have modern subway systems, though not covering the whole city. Tickets available are: **unitário** (one-way), **múltiplo 2** (round-trip), **múltiplo 10** (10 trips), and **integração** (1 metro + 1 bus).

General inquiries Perguntas gerais

Where's the nearest subway [metro] station?	**Onde é a estação de metro mais próxima?** ondeh er ishter-_sawm_ der _me_ttroo mighsh _pro_ssymer
Where can I buy tickets?	**Onde se compram bilhetes?** ond ser _kawm_prawm bi_lly_aytish
Could I have a map of the subway [metro]?	**Pode dar-me um mapa do metro.** pod _dah_mer oom _ma_pper doo _me_ttroo

Traveling Para viajar

Which line should I take for …?	**Qual é a linha para …?** kwal eh er _lee_nyer _per_-rer
Is this the train for …?	**Este comboio [trem] vai para …?** aysht kawm_boy_oo [trayn] vigh _per_-rer
Which stop is it for …?	**Qual é a estação para …?** kwal eh er ishter-_sawm_ _per_-rer
How many stops is it to …?	**Quantas estações até à/ao …?** _kwan_tush ishter-_soynsh_ er-_teh_ ah/ow
Is the next stop …?	**A próxima estação é o/a …?** er _pro_ssymer ishter-_sawm_ eh oo/er
Where are we?	**Onde estamos?** ond isht_a_moosh
Where do I change for …?	**Onde devo mudar para …?** ond _day_voo moo_dar_ _per_-rer
What time is the last train to …?	**A que horas é o último comboio [trem] para o/a …?** er kee _o_rush eh o _ool_tymoo kawm_boy_oo [trayn] _per_-rer oo/er

PARA OUTRAS LINHAS/ CORRESPONDÊNCIA [CONEXÃO]	to other lines/ transfer

NUMBERS ➤ 216; BUYING TICKETS ➤ 79, 74

Ferry Ferry-boat [Balsa]

Popular cruises in Portugal run down the Douro and Tagus rivers and all along the Algarve coast in Portugal. In Brazil there are specially organized cruises in all coastal towns for visits to main beaches and nearby islands.

Transport between Belém, Manaus and Santarém can also be done by boat across the Amazon river, departing from **hidroviárias** (ferry terminals); for the long night journey, a hammock on deck is preferable to a hot cabin. Cruises on the Amazon are run by the state-owned **Empresa de Navegação da Amazônia (E.N.A.S.A.)** and a number of private companies.

When is the … boat/car ferry to …?	**Quando é o … barco/ferry-boat [a … balsa] para …?** _kwandoo eh oo … barkoo/ferry-boat [er … balser] per-rer_
first/next/last	**primeiro/próximo/último** _primayroo/prossymoo/ooltymoo_
hovercraft/ship	**hovercraft/navio** _overkraft/ner-veeoo_
A round-trip [return] ticket for …	**Um bilhete de ida e volta para …?** _oom billyayt der eeder ee volter per-rer_
one car and one trailer	**um carro e um reboque [trailer]** _oom karroo ee oom rer-bok ['trailer']_
two adults and three children	**dois adultos e três crianças** _doysh er-dooltoosh ee traysh kryawnsush_
I'd like to reserve a … cabin.	**Queria marcar um camarote …** _ker-reeer murkar oom ker-mer-rot_
single/double	**individual/duplo** _eendividwal/dooploo_

BARCO SALVA-VIDAS	lifeboat	
CINTO DE SALVAÇÃO [DE SEGURANÇA]	life preserver [lifebelt]	
POSTO DE INSPECÇÃO	muster station	
PROIBIDO O ACESSO	no access	

Boat trips Excursões de barco

Is/Are there …?	**Há … ?** _ah_
river cruise/boat trips	**um cruzeiro no rio/excursões de barco** _oom kroozayroo noo reeoo/ ayshkoorsoynsh der barkoo_
What time does it leave/return?	**A que horas parte/regressa?** _er kee orush part/rer-greser_

TIME ➤ 220; BUYING TICKETS ➤ 74, 79

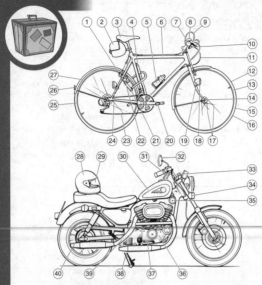

1 brake pad **calço** m **do travão [freio]**
2 bicycle bag **saco** m **[bolsa** f**] de bicicleta**
3 seat [saddle] **selim** m
4 pump **bomba** f
5 water bottle **garrafa** f **de água**
6 frame **quadro** m
7 handlebars **guiador [guidão]** m
8 bell **campainha [buzina]** f
9 brake cable **cabo** m **do travão [freio]**
10 gear shift [lever] **alavanca** f **das velocidades [marchas]**
11 gear control cable **cabo** m **de direcção**
12 inner tube **câmara-de-ar** f
13 front/back wheel **roda** f **dianteira/ traseira**
14 axle **eixo** m
15 tire [tyre] **pneu** m
16 wheel **roda** f
17 spokes **raios** mpl
18 bulb **lâmpada** f
19 headlamp **farol** m **dianteiro**
20 pedal **pedal** m
21 lock **cadeado** m

22 generator [dynamo] **dínamo** m
23 chain **corrente** f
24 rear light **farol** m **traseiro**
25 rim **aro** m
26 reflectors **reflectores** mpl
27 fender [mudguard] **guarda-lamas [pára-lamas]** m
28 helmet **capacete** m
29 visor **viseira** f
30 fuel tank **depósito [tanque]** m **de gasolina**
31 clutch **alavanca** f **de embraiagem [embreagem]**
32 mirror **espelho** m
33 ignition switch **chave** f **de ignição**
34 turn signal [indicator] **pisca-pisca** m
35 horn **buzina** f
36 engine **motor** m
37 gear shift [lever] **alavanca** f **das velocidades [marchas]**
38 kick stand **assento** m
39 exhaust pipe **tubo** m **de escape**
40 chain guard **protector de corrente**

REPAIRS ➤ 89

Bicycle / Motorbike
Bicicleta / Motocicleta

I'd like to rent a ...	**Queria alugar uma ...** *ker-reeer er-loogar oomer*
3-/10-speed bicycle	**bicicleta de 3/10 velocidades [marchas]** *beeseekletter der traysh/desh ver-loosidadish [merchersh]*
moped	**lambreta/acelera** *lawmbrayter/er-ser-lerer*
mountain bike	**bicicleta de montanha** *beeseekletter der montanyer*
motorbike	**motocicleta** *mottoseekletter*
How much does it cost per day/week?	**Quanto custa por dia/semana?** *kwantoo kooshter poor deeer/ser-maner*
Do you require a deposit?	**Quer que eu deixe um sinal?** *kehr kee eoo daysher oom seenal*
The brakes don't work.	**Os travões [freios] não funcionam.** *oosh trer-voynsh [frayoosh] nawm foonsyonnawm*
There isn't a pump.	**Não tem bomba.** *nawm taym bawmber*
There aren't any lights.	**Não tem luzes.** *nawm taym loozish*
The front/rear tire [tyre] has a flat [puncture].	**O pneu dianteiro/traseiro tem um furo.** *oo pneeoo dyawntayroo/trer-zayroo taym oom fooroo*

Hitchhiking   À boleia [carona]

Always take care before hitchhiking anywhere.

Where are you heading?	**Para onde vai?** *per-rer ond vigh*
I'm heading for ...	**Vou para ...** *voh per-rer*
Can you give me/us a lift?	**Pode dar-me/-nos boleia [carona]?** *pod darmer/darnoosh boolayer [karoanah]*
Is that on the way to ...?	**Isso fica a caminho de ...?** *eesoo feeker er ker-meenyoo der*
Could you drop me off ...?	**Pode deixar-me... ?** *pod daysharmer*
here/at the ... exit	**aqui/na ... saída** *er-kee/ner ... ser-eeder*
downtown	**no centro** *noo sayntroo*
Thanks for the lift.	**Obrigado(-a) pela boleia [carona].** *obrigadoo(-er) payler boolayer [karoanah]*

DIRECTIONS ➤ 94; DAYS OF THE WEEK ➤ 21

Taxi/Cab Táxi

Taxis in Portugal are cream colored or black with a green roof. Rural taxis, including those at airports, are marked "A" (**aluguer**) and are usually unmetered, but follow a standard-fare table. All Brazilian taxis have meters, except in small towns, where the fare should be agreed in advance.

Tipping suggestions: 10% in Portugal and R$ 0.20–0.90 in Brazil.

Where can I get a taxi?	**Onde posso apanhar [pegar] um táxi?** ond _posso_ er-per-_nyar_ [_paygar_] oom _taksi_
Do you have the number for a taxi?	**Tem o número de telefone dos táxis?** taym oo _noo_meroo der ter-ler-_fon_ doosh _taksish_
I'd like a taxi …	**Queria um táxi …** ker-_reeer_ oom _taksi_
now/in an hour	**agora/daqui a uma hora** er-_gorer_/der-_kee_ er _oomer orer_
for tomorrow at 9:00	**amanhã às 9 horas** amer-_nyah_ ash nov _orush_
The address is …	**A morada [O endereço] é …** er moo_rader_ [oo endeh_reh_soo] eh …
I'm going to …	**E vai para …** ee vigh _per_-rer
Please take me to …	**Leve-me …** _lever_-mer
airport	**ao aeroporto** ow er-_ehro_poartoo
rail station	**à estação dos comboios [trens]** ah ishter-_sawm_ doosh kawm_boy_oosh [traynsh]
… Hotel	**ao Hotel …** ow _ottel_
this address	**a esta morada [neste endereço]** er _eshter_ moo_rader_ [naysht endeh_reh_soo]
How much will it cost?	**Quanto vai custar?** _kwan_too vigh koosh_tar_
Please stop here.	**Pare aqui, se faz favor.** _parer_ er-_kee_ ser fash fer-_voar_
How much is that?	**Quanto é?** _kwan_too eh
You said … euros.	**Disse … euros.** _deeser_ … _ayoorosh_
Keep the change.	**Guarde o troco.** _gwarder_ oo _troakoo_

> – Leve-me à estação de comboios.
> (Take me to the train station.)
> – Com certeza. (Certainly.)
> – Quanto vai custar? (How much will it cost?)
> – Quatro euros. … Já chegamos.
> (4 euros. … Here we are.)
> – Obrigada. Guarde o troco. (Thank you. Keep the change.)

Car/Automobile Automóvel

In Portugal, the minimum driving age is 18, and 21 for rental cars. While driving in Portugal the following documents must be carried at all times: valid driver's license, vehicle registration document, and insurance documentation. If you don't hold an EC format license, an international driving permit is also required.

A special certificate (**autorização**) is required if the vehicle you are driving is not registered in your name. Insurance for minimum third party risks is compulsory in Europe. It is recommended that you take out international motor insurance (Green Card) through your insurer.

Essential equipment: warning triangle, nationality plate, a set of spare headlight and taillight bulbs. Seat belts (**o cinto de segurança**) are compulsory. Children under 12 must travel in the rear.

Traffic from the right has priority in Portugal, unless otherwise indicated.

Traffic police can give on-the-spot fines (ask for a receipt).

The use of horns is prohibited in built-up areas except for emergencies.

Alcohol limit in blood: max. 50mg/100ml in Portugal.

Conversion chart

km	1	10	20	30	40	50	60	70	80	90	100	110	120	130
miles	0.62	6	12	19	25	31	37	44	50	56	62	68	74	81

Road network

Portugal	**AE** – highway [motorway]; **EP** – principal road; **EN** – national road; **EM** – municipal road, **CM** – secondary municipal road

Speed limits	Built-up area	Outside built-up area	Highway [motorway]
Portugal	50 (31) max.	90 (56)	120 (74)

Some highways [motorways] and bridges are subject to tolls (**a portagem [a pedágio]**).

Speed limits in Brazil vary and are indicated by road-side signs. Although these are enforced by traffic police, the Brazilian tendency to speed demands foreign drivers that have strong nerves.

Fuel

Gas [Petrol]	Leaded	Unleaded	Diesel
Portugal	**Regular (85)/ Super (98)**	**Super (95/98)**	**gasóleo/diesel**

Brazilians also use **álcool** (a mixture of petroleum and alcohol) as a fuel, so you have to specify whether you want that or **gasolina** (gas [petrol]).

Car rental Aluguer de automóveis

In Portugal, third-party insurance is included in the basic rental charge. Most firms require a minimum age of 21; holders of major credit cards are normally exempt from deposit payments. In Brazil, insurance may only cover 80% of the full cost of theft.

Where can I rent a car?	**Onde posso alugar um carro?** *ond possoo er-loogar oom karroo*
I'd like to rent a(n) …	**Queria alugar …** *ker-reeer er-loogar*
2-/4-door car	**um carro de 2/4 portas** *oom karroo der dooush/kwatroo portush*
automatic	**um carro automático** *oom karroo owtoomatikoo*
car with 4-wheel drive	**um carro com tracção às 4 rodas** *oom karroo kawm trasawm ash kwatroo rodush*
car with air conditioning	**um carro com ar condicionado** *oom karroo kawm ar kondeesyoonadoo*
I'd like it for a day/week.	**Queria-o por um dia/uma semana.** *ker-reeer oo por oom deeer/oomer ser-maner*
How much does it cost per day/week?	**Quanto é por dia/semana?** *kwantoo eh poor deeer/ser-maner*
Is mileage included?	**A quilometragem está incluída?** *er keelomer-trazhaym ishtah eenklweeder*
Is insurance included?	**O seguro está incluído?** *oo ser-gooroo ishtah eenklweedoo*
Are there special weekend rates?	**Há tarifas especiais para os fins-de-semana?** *ah ter-reefush ishper-syighsh per-rer oosh feensh der ser-maner*
Can I return the car at your office in …?	**Posso deixar o carro na vossa agência em …?** *possoo dayshar oo karroo ner voaser er-zhaynsyer aym*
What kind of fuel does it take?	**Que combustível gasta?** *ker kawmbooshteevell gashter*
Could I have full insurance?	**Pode dar-me um seguro contra todos os riscos [seguro total]?** *pod darmer oom ser-gooroo kontrer toadooz oosh reeshkoosh [ser-gooroo toatal]*

Gas [petrol] station
Nas bombas de gasolina [No posto]

Where's the next gas [petrol] station, please?	**Onde é a bomba de gasolina [o posto] mais próxima[-o]?** *ond eh er bawmber der gerzooleener [oo poostoa] mighsh prossymer[-oo]*
Is it self-service?	**É auto-serviço?** *eh owtosserveesoo*
Fill it up, please.	**Encha o depósito [tanque], se faz favor.** *aynsher oo der-pozzytoo [tankay] ser fash fer-voar*
… liters, please.	**… litros, se faz favor.** *leetroosh ser fash fer-voar*
premium [super]/regular	**super/normal** *soopehr/normal*
lead-free/diesel	**sem chumbo/gasóleo [diesel]** *saym shoomboo/gazollyoo ["diesel']*
I'm at pump number …	**Sou à bomba número …** *soh er bawmber noomeroo*
Where is the air pump/ water?	**Onde é a máquina pneumática [bomba de ar]/água?** *ond eh er makinner pneoomaticker [bomber dzhi ahr]/agwer*

⊖	**PREÇO POR LITRO**	price per liter/litre ⊙

Parking Estacionamento

In Portugal, metered parking is common in most towns. Certain cities have blue zones; parking tokens/discs are available from the police or the Portuguese motoring organization (**ACP**).

In Brazil, permits may be sold by traffic wardens or at street stalls. The use of parking lots is advisable in Brazilan cities to avoid parking fines, car theft, and offers to "look after" your car.

Is there a parking lot [car park] nearby?	**Há um parque de estacionamento perto daqui?** *ah oom park der ishter-syooner-mayntoo pehrtoo der-kee*
What's the charge per hour/day?	**Qual é a tarifa por hora/dia?** *kwal eh er ter-reefer poor orer/deeer*
Where do I pay?	**Onde pago?** *ond pagoo*
Do you have some change for the parking meter?	**Tem dinheiro trocado [troco] para o parquímetro?** *taym deenyayroo trookadoo [trookoo] per-rer oo perkeemer-troo*

NUMBERS ➤ 216; DIRECTIONS ➤ 94

Breakdown Avaria

In Portugal, for help in the event of a breakdown: refer to your breakdown assistance documents; or if you are far from a service station: ☎ 115 (Portugal); or contact the **Automóvel Club de Portugal**.

Where is the nearest garage?	**Onde fica a garagem mais próxima?** *ond feeker er ger-razhaym mighsh prossymer*
My car broke down.	**Tive uma avaria. [Meu carro quebrou.]** *teev oomer er-ver-reeer. [meoo karroa ker-broh]*
Can you send a mechanic/ tow [breakdown] truck?	**Pode mandar-me um mecânico/ pronto-socorro?** *pod mawndarmer oom mer-kanykoo/prontoo sookoarroo*
I belong to … auto club.	**Pertenço ao Automóvel Clube de …** *pertaynsoo ow owtoomovell kloob der*
My license plate [registration] number is …	**A minha matrícula [placa] é o …** *er meenyer mertrikooler [plaker] eh oo*
The car is …	**O carro está …** *oo karroo ishtah*
on the highway [motorway]	**na auto-estrada** *ner owtoshtrader*
2 km from …	**a dois km de …** *er doysh keelomer-troosh der*
How long will you be?	**Quanto tempo vai demorar?** *kwantoo taympo vigh der-moorar*

What's wrong? Qual é o problema?

I don't know what's wrong.	**Não sei qual é o problema.** *nawm say kawleh oo prooblaymer*
My car won't start.	**O motor não pega.** *oo mootoar nawm peger*
The battery is dead.	**A bateria está descarregada.** *er ber-tereeer ishtah dishker-rregader*
I've run out of gas [petrol].	**Acabou a gasolina.** *er-ker-boh er ger-zooleener*
I have a flat [puncture].	**Tenho um furo.** *taynyoo oom fooroo*
There is something wrong with …	**Há um problema qualquer no(-a) …** *ah oom prooblaymer kwalkehr noo(-er)*
I've locked the keys in the car.	**Deixei as chaves dentro do carro.** *dayshay ush shavish dayntroo doo karroo*

Repairs Reparações

Do you do repairs? **Faz reparações?**
fash rer-per-rer-soynsh

Can you repair it (temporarily)? **Pode arranjá-lo [consertá-lo] (temporariamente)?** *pod
er-rranzhaloo [konserta loo] (taympooraryer-maynt)*

Please make only essential repairs. **Faça apenas os consertos essenciais.**
fasser er-paynush oosh konsairtoosh eesaynsyighsh

Can I wait for it? **Vale a pena esperar?**
vall er payner ishper-rar

Can you repair it today? **Pode consertá-lo hoje?**
pod konsertaloo oazher

When will it be ready? **Quando estará pronto?**
kwandoo ishter-rah prontoo

How much will it cost? **Quanto custará?**
kwantoo kooshter-rah

That's outrageous! **Isso é ridículo!**
eesoo eh rrideekooloo

Can I have a receipt for the insurance? **Pode dar-me uma factura [um recibo] para
o seguro?** *pod darmer oomer fatoorer [oom reseebo] per-rer oo ser-gooroo*

O/A ... não funciona.	The ... isn't working.
Não tenho as peças necessárias.	I don't have the necessary parts.
Tenho de encomendar as peças.	I will have to order the parts.
Só posso consertá-lo temporariamente.	I can only repair it temporarily.
O seu carro só serve para a sucata.	Your car is beyond repair.
Não tem conserto.	It can't be repaired.
Vai estar pronto ...	It will be ready ...
hoje à tarde	this afternoon
amanhã	tomorrow
em ... dias	in ... days

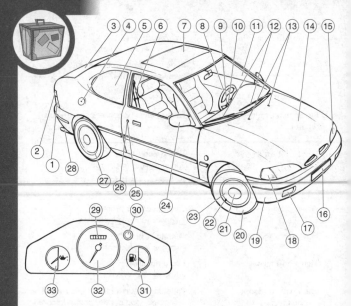

1 tail lights [back lights] **faróis** mpl **traseiros**
2 brake lights **farolins** mpl **de travagem** [luzes fpl **de freio**]
3 trunk [boot] **porta-bagagens** [porta-malas] m
4 gas tank door [petrol cap] **tampa** f **do depósito [tanque] de gasolina**
5 window **janela** f
6 seat belt **cinto** m **de segurança**
7 sunroof **tecto** m **de abrir [teto solar]**
8 steering wheel **volante** m
9 ignition **ignição** f
10 ignition key **chave** f **de ignição**
11 windshield [windscreen] **pára-brisas** m
12 windshield [windscreen] wipers **limpa [limpador de]** m **pára-brisas**
13 windshield [windscreen] washer **líquido** m **do pára-brisas**
14 hood [bonnet] **capota** f
15 headlights **faróis** mpl

16 license [number] plate **matrícula [placa]** f
17 fog lamp **farol** m **de nevoeiro [luz** f **de neblina]**
18 turn signals [indicators] **pisca-pisca** mpl
19 bumper **pára-choques** m
20 tires [tyres] **pneus** mpl
21 wheel cover [hubcap] **tampão** m **de roda [acalota]**
22 valve **válvula** f
23 wheels **rodas** fpl
24 outside [wing] mirror **retrovisor/ espelho** m **lateral**
25 automatic locks [central locking] **fecho** m **[fechadura** f**] central**
26 lock **fecho** m **[fechadura** f**]**
27 wheel rim **aro** m **da roda**
28 exhaust pipe **tubo [cano]** m **de escape**
29 odometer [milometer] **conta-quilómetros [hodômetro]** m

90

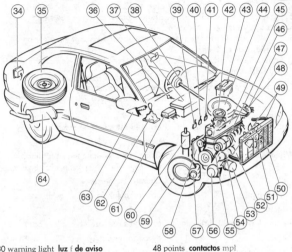

30 warning light **luz** f **de aviso [emergência]**
31 fuel gauge **manómetro** m **do nível de gasolina**
32 speedometer **velocímetro** m
33 oil gauge **filtro** m **do óleo**
34 backup [reversing] lights **farolins** mpl **[luzes** fpl**] de marcha-atrás [ré]**
35 spare tire [wheel] **roda** f **sobresselente [oestepe]**
36 choke **ar** m
37 heater **chauffage [calefação]** f
38 steering column **eixo** m **de direcção**
39 accelerator **acelerador** m
40 pedal **pedal** f
41 clutch **embraiagem [embreagem]** f
42 carburetor **carburador** m
43 battery **bateria** f
44 alternator **alternador** m
45 camshaft **eixom do motor**
47 distributor **distribuidor** m

48 points **contactos** mpl
49 radiator hose (top/bottom) **mangueira** f **do radiador**
50 radiator **radiador** m
51 fan **ventoinha** f
52 engine **motor** m
53 oil filter **filtro** m **do óleo**
54 starter motor **motor** m **de arranque**
55 fan belt **correia** f **da ventoinha**
56 horn **buzina** f
57 brake pads **calços** mpl**/pastilhas** fpl **dos travões [freios]**
58 transmission [gearbox] **caixa** f **das velocidades [de câmbio]**
59 brakes **travões [freios]** mpl
60 shock absorbers **amortecedores** mpl
61 fuses **fusíveis** mpl
62 gear shift [lever] **alavanca** f **das velocidades [marchas]**
63 handbrake **travão [freio]** m **de mão**
64 muffler [silencer] **silenciador** m

Accidents Acidentes

In the event of an accident:
1. put your red warning triangle 100 meters behind your car;
2. report the accident to the police (in Brazil, the road police – **polícia rodoviária**); don't leave before they arrive;
3. show your driver's license and green card;
4. give your name, address, insurance company to the other party;
5. contact your insurance company;
6. don't make any written statement without advice of a lawyer or automobile club official;
7. note all relevant details of the other party, any independent witnesses, and the accident.

There has been an accident.	**Houve um acidente.** *ohv oom aseedent*
It's …	**Foi …** *foy*
on the highway [motorway]	**na auto-estrada** *ner owtoshtrader*
near …	**perto de …** *pehrtoo der*
Where's the nearest telephone?	**Onde fica o telefone mais próximo?** *ond feeker oo ter-ler-fon mighsh prossymoo*
Call …	**Chame …** *shamer*
an ambulance	**uma ambulância** *oomer awmboolansyer*
a doctor	**um médico** *oom medikoo*
the fire department [brigade]	**os bombeiros** *oosh bawmbayroosh*
the police	**a polícia** *er pooleesyer*
Can you help me?	**Pode ajudar-me?** *pod er-zhoodarmer*

Injuries Ferimentos

There are people injured.	**Há pessoas feridas.** *ah per-sohush fer-reedush*
No one is hurt.	**Não há feridos.** *nawm ah fer-reedoosh*
He is bleeding heavily.	**Ele está gravemente a sangrar [sangrando].** *ayl ishtah graver-maynt er sawngrar [sawngrandoo]*
She's unconscious.	**Ela perdeu os sentidos.** *eler perdeoo oosh saynteedoosh*
He can't breathe/move.	**Ele não respira/se mexe.** *ayl nawm rishpeerer/ser mesh*
Don't move him.	**Não o mexam.** *nawm oo mayshawm*

Legal matters Assuntos legais

What's your insurance company?	**Qual é a sua companhia de seguros?** *kwal eh ah swer kawmper-nyer der ser-gooroosh*
What's your name and address?	**Qual é o seu nome e morada [endereço]?** *kwal eh oo seoo noamer ee moorader [endehresoo]*
He ran into me.	**Ele chocou contra mim.** *ayl shookoh kontrer meem*
She was driving too fast/too close.	**Ela ia a guiar [guiando] demasiado depressa/perto.** *eler eeer er gyar [gyandoo] der-mer-zyadoo der-preser/pehrtoo*
I had the right of way.	**Eu tinha prioridade.** *eoo teenyer preeooridad*
I was only driving ... kmph.	**Eu ia apenas a ... km à hora.** *eoo eeer er-paynush er ... keelomer-troosh ah orer*
I'd like an interpreter.	**Preciso de um tradutor.** *prer-seezoo der oom trer-dootoar*
I didn't see the sign.	**Não vi o sinal.** *nawm vee oo seenal*
He/She saw it happen.	**Ele/Ela viu o que aconteceu.** *ayl/eler vyoo oo ker er-konter-seoo*
The license plate [registration] number was ...	**A matrícula [placa] foi ...** *er mer-treekooler [plaker] foy*

Mostre-me ..., se faz favor.	Can I see ..., please?
a sua carta de condução [carteira de motorista]	your driver's license
a sua apólice de seguro	your insurance card
os documentos do carro	your vehicle registration
A que horas aconteceu?	What time did it happen?
Onde é que aconteceu?	Where did it happen?
Esteve mais alguém envolvido?	Was anyone else involved?
Há testemunhas?	Are there any witnesses?
Ia com excesso de velocidade.	You were speeding.
As suas luzes não estão a funcionar [funcionando].	Your lights aren't working.
Tem de pagar uma multa.	You'll have to pay a fine (on the spot).
Precisamos que vá fazer um depoimento à esquadra [delegacia].	You have to make a statement at the station.

TIME ➤ 220

Asking directions
Para perguntar o caminho

Excuse me.	**Desculpe.** *dishkoolp*
How do I get to …?	**Como se vai para …?** *koomoo ser vigh per-rer*
Where is …?	**Onde fica …?** *ond feeker*
Can you show me on the map where I am?	**Pode indicar-me onde estou no mapa?** *pod eendykarmer ond ishtoh noo mapper*
I've lost my way.	**Estou perdido(-a).** *ishtoh perdeedoo(-er)*
Can you repeat that, please?	**Importa-se de repetir?** *eemporter-ser der rer-per-teer*
More slowly, please.	**Mais devagar, se faz favor.** *mighsh der-ver-gar ser fash fer-voar*
Thanks for your help.	**Obrigado(-a) pela sua ajuda.** *obrigadoo(-er) payler swer er-zhooder*

Traveling by car De carro

Is this the right road for …?	**Esta é a estrada que vai para …?** *eshter eh er ishtrader ker vigh per-rer*
How far is it to … from here?	**A que distância fica … daqui?** *er ker deeshtawnsyer feeker … der-kee*
Where does this road lead?	**Para onde vai esta estrada?** *per-rer ond vigh eshter ishtrader*
How do I get onto the highway [motorway]?	**Como se vai para a auto-estrada?** *koomoo ser vigh per-rer er owtoshtrader*
What's the next town called?	**Como se chama a cidade mais próxima?** *koomoo ser shamer er sidad mighsh prossymer*
How long does it take by car?	**Quanto tempo leva de carro?** *kwantoo taympoo lever der karroo*

– Desculpe. Como é que se vai para a estação de comboios?
(Excuse me, please. How do I get to the train station?)
– Vire na terceira à esquerda e depois é sempre em frente.
(Take the third left and it's straight ahead.)
– Terceira à esquerda. É longe?
(The third left. Is it far?)
– Dez minutos … a pé. (It's ten minutes … on foot.)
– Obrigado pela sua ajuda. (Thanks for your help.)
– De nada. (You're welcome.)

Location No local

É ...	It's ...
sempre em frente	straight ahead
à esquerda	on the left
à direita	on the right
no outro lado da rua	on the other side of the street
à esquina	on the corner
ao dobrar da esquina	around the corner
na direcção de ...	in the direction of ...
em frente de .../por trás de ...	opposite .../behind ...
a seguir a(o) .../ depois do(-a) ...	next to .../after ...
Desça ...	Go down the ...
a transversal/rua principal	side street/main street
Atravesse ...	Cross the ...
a praça/ponte	square/bridge
Vire na ...	Take the ...
terceira à direita	third turn to the right
Vire à esquerda ...	Turn left ...
depois dos semáforos	after the first traffic light
no segundo cruzamento	at the second intersection [crossroad]

By car De carro

Fica a ... daqui.	It's ... of here.
norte/sul	north/south
deste/oeste	east/west
Apanhe a estrada para ...	Take the road for ...
Não é esta estrada.	You're on the wrong road.
Tem de voltar a ...	You'll have to go back to ...
Siga os sinais para ...	Follow the signs for ...

How far? A que distância?

Fica ...	It's ...
perto/relativamente perto/ muito longe	close/not far/a long way
a 5 minutos a pé	5 minutes on foot
a 10 minutos de carro	10 minutes by car
cerca de 10 km daqui	about 10 kilometers away

TIME ➤ 220; NUMBERS ➤ 216

Road signs Sinais de trânsito

ACCESSO ÚNICO	access only
AFROUXE/REDUZA	slow down
DESVIO	detour [diversion]
DEVAGAR	slow
OBRAS	highway construction
PORTAGEM [PEDÁGIO]	toll
SEM SAÍDA	no through road
SIGA PELA DIREITA	keep right
TRABALHOS	highway construction
TRÂNSITO PROIBIDO	road closed

Town plan O mapa da cidade

aeroporto	airport
cinema	movie theater [cinema]
correios	post office
edifício público	public building
esquadra [delegacia] da polícia	police station
estação	station
estação de metro	subway [metro] station
estacionamento de automóveis	parking lot [car park]
estádio	stadium
igreja	church
informações	information office
paragem de autocarro [parada de ônibus]	bus stop
parque	park
passagem de peões [pedestres]	pedestrian crossing
passagem subterrânea	underpass [subway]
pavilhão desportivo [esportivo]	playing field [sports stadium]
praça [ponto] de táxis	taxi stand [rank]
rota dos autocarros [ônibus]	bus route
rua principal	main [high] street
teatro	theater
zona de peões [pedestres]	pedestrian zone [precinct]

Sightseeing

Tourist information office
Posto de turismo [Informações turísticas]

In Brazil and Portugal, town maps and brochures of the main tourist attractions are available at the airport and in tourist information centers.

Where's the tourist office?	**Onde é o posto deturismo [informações turísticas]?** _ondeh oo poshtoo der tooreeshmoo [infoormer-sawnt tooreeshteekush]_
What are the main points of interest?	**O que há de mais interessante para se ver?** _oo kee ah der mighz eenter-rer-sawnt per-rer ser vair_
We're here for …	**Ficamos aqui …** _feekamooz er-kee_
only a few hours	**só algumas horas** _so algoomuz orush_
a day	**um dia** _oom deeer_
a week	**uma semana** _oomer ser-maner_
Can you recommend …?	**Pode recomendar-me …?** _pod rer-koomayndarmer_
a sightseeing tour	**um circuito turístico** _oom seerkweetoo tooreeshtykoo_
an excursion	**uma excursão** _oomer ayshkoorsawm_
a boat trip/cruise	**uma excursão de barco/um cruzeiro** _oomer ayshkoorsawm der barkoo/oom kroozayroo_
Are these brochures free?	**Estes folhetos são grátis?** _ayshtish foolyaytoosh sawm grateesh_
Do you have any information on …?	**Tem qualquer informação sobre …?** _taym kwalkehr infoormer-sawm soabrer_
Are there any trips to …?	**Há excursões a …?** _ah ayshkoorsoynsh er_

Excursions Excursões

How much does the tour cost?	**Quanto custa a excursão?** _kwantoo kooshter er ayshkoorsawm_
Is lunch included?	**O almoço está incluído?** _oo almoasoo ishtah eenklweedoo_
Where do we leave from?	**De onde é a partida?** _dee ond eh er per-teeder_
What time does the tour start?	**A que horas é a partida?** _er kee oruz eh er per-teeder_
What time do we get back?	**A que horas é o regresso?** _er kee oruz eh oo rer-gresoo_
Do we have free time in …?	**Temos algum tempo livre em …?** _taymooz algoom taympo leevrer aym_
Is there an English-speaking guide?	**Há algum guia que fale inglês?** _ah algoom geeer ker faler eenglaysh_

On the tour De excursão

Are we going to see …?	**Vamos ver …?** _vamoosh vair_
We'd like to have a look at the …	**Gostaríamos de ver …** _gooshter-reeer-moosh der vair_
Can we stop here …?	**Podemos parar aqui …?** _poodaymoosh per-rar er-kee_
to take photographs	**para tirar fotografias** _per-rer teerar footoogrer-feeush_
to buy souvenirs	**para comprar lembranças** _per-rer kawmprar laymbrawnsush_
to use the restrooms [toilets]	**para ir à casa de banho [aos banheiros]** _per-rer eer ah kazer der banyoo [aosh bahnyayroass]_
Would you take a photo of us?	**Importa-se de nos tirar uma fotografia?** _eemporter ser der noosh teerar oomer footoogrer-feeer_
How long do we have here/in …?	**Quanto tempo vamos ficar aqui/em …?** _kwantoo taympoo vamoosh feekar er-kee/aym_
Wait! … isn't back yet.	**Espere! … ainda não voltou.** _ishpehrer. … er-eender nawm voltoh_

Sights Locais de interesse

Guia Quatro Rodas (available from newsstands and bookstores) is the most complete and up-to-date Brazilian guide, providing city maps, road networks, accommodations listings and main sights – with information on means of access, opening times, and telephone numbers.

Where is the …	**Onde fica …?** ond _feeker_
art gallery	**a galeria de arte** er ger-le_reeer_ dart
botanical garden	**o jardim botânico** oo zhur_deem_ boo_tan_nikoo
castle	**o castelo** oo kush_te_loo
cathedral	**a catedral** er ker-ter-_dral_
cemetery	**o cemitério** oo ser-mee_teh_ryoo
church	**a igreja** er eeg_ray_zher
city wall	**as muralhas da cidade** ush moo_ral_yush der si_dad_
downtown area	**o centro da cidade** oo _sayn_troo der si_dad_
harbor	**o porto** oo _poar_too
library	**a biblioteca** er beeblyoo_tek_ker
market	**o mercado** oo mer_ka_doo
monastery	**o mosteiro** oo moosh_tay_roo
museum	**o museu** oo moo_ze_oo
old town	**a parte velha da cidade** er part _vel_yer der si_dad_
opera house	**a ópera** er _o_perer
palace	**o palácio** oo per-_las_syoo
park	**o parque** oo park
parliament building (Port.)	**a assembleia nacional** er er-saym_blay_er ner-syoo_nal_
ruins	**as ruínas** ush rw_ee_nush
shopping area	**a zona comercial** er _zo_aner koomersy_al_
theater	**o teatro** oo ty_a_troo
tower	**a torre** er _toar_rer
town hall	**a câmara municipal [prefeitura]** er _kam_mer-rer moonysy_pal_ [prehfay_too_rer]
university	**a universidade** er ooneeversi_dad_

DIRECTIONS ➤ 94

Admission Entrada

In Portugal, museums are open from 10 a.m. to 6 p.m., and usually closed on Mondays. The tourist guide should be tipped 10–15% in Portugal, R$5–10 in Brazil.

Is the … open to the public?	**… está aberto(-a) ao público?** *ishtah er-behrtoo(-er) ow pooblikoo*
Can we look around?	**Podemos dar uma vista de olhos [olhada]?** *poodaymoosh dar oomer veeshter der ollyoosh [ollyahder]*
What are the hours?	**Quais são as horas de abertura?** *kwighsh sawm uz orush der-er-bertoorer*
When does it close?	**A que horas fecha?** *er kee orush faysher*
When's the next guided tour?	**Quando é a próxima visita guiada?** *kwandoo eh er prossymer veezeeter geeader*
Do you have a guide book (in English)?	**Tem um guia (em inglês)?** *taym oom geeer (aym eenglaysh)*
Can I take photos?	**Posso tirar fotografias?** *possoo teerar footoogrer-feeush*
Is there access for the disabled?	**Há algum acesso para os deficientes?** *ah algoom er-sesoo per-rer oosh der-feesyayntish*
Is there an audioguide in English?	**Há uma gravação da visita guiada em inglês?** *ah oomer grer-ver-sawm der veezeeter geeader aym eenglaysh*

Tickets Bilhetes de entrada

How much is the entrance fee?	**Quanto custa a entrada?** *kwantoo kooshter er ayntrader*
Are there discounts for …?	**Há desconto para …?** *ah dishkontoo per-rer*
children	**crianças** *kryawnsush*
students / groups	**estudantes/grupos** *ishtoodawntish/groopoosh*
senior citizens	**reformados [idosos]** *rer-foormadoosh [eedoasoosh]*
the disabled	**deficientes** *der-feesyayntish*
One adult and two children, please.	**um adulto e duas crianças, se faz favor.** *oom er-dooltoo ee dooush kryawnsush ser fash fer-voar*
I've lost my ticket.	**Perdi meu bilhete.** *perdee meoo billyayt*

– Cinco entradas, se faz favor. Há descontos?
(Five tickets, please. Are there any discounts?)
– Há. Crianças e reformados pagam cinco reais.
(Yes, children and senior citizens pay 5 reais.)
– Então, dois adultos e três crianças.
(Two adults and three children.)
– São vinte e nove reais e cinquenta.
(That's 29 reais 50.)

ABERTO	open
ENTRADA LIVRE	free admission
É PROIBIDA A ENTRADA.	no entry
É PROIBIDO O USO DE FLASH	no flash photography
É PROIBIDO TIRAR FOTOGRAFIAS	no photography
FECHADO	closed
HORAS DE VISITA	hours [visiting hours]
PRÓXIMA VISITA GUIADA ÀS ...	next tour at ...
(LOJA DE) RECORDAÇÕES	gift shop

Impressions Impressões

It's ...	**É ...** _eh_
amazing	**espantoso** _ishpawntoazoo_
beautiful	**lindo** _leendoo_
bizarre/strange	**estranho** _ishtranyoo_
boring	**aborrecido** _er-boorrer-seedoo_
breathtaking	**espantoso** _ishpawntoazoo_
brilliant	**brilhante** _breelyawnt_
great fun	**divertido** _deeverteedoo_
interesting	**interessante** _eenter-rer-sawnt_
magnificent	**magnífico** _magneefykoo_
pretty	**bonito** _booneetoo_
romantic	**romântico** _roomawntykoo_
stunning	**estupendo** _ishtoopayndoo_
superb	**soberbo** _soobairboo_
ugly	**feio** _fayoo_
It's a good value/It's a rip-off.	**Vale a pena/É uma roubalheira.** _valer payner/eh oomer rohber-lyayrer_
I like it.	**Gosto disso.** _goshtoo deesoo_
I don't like it.	**Não gosto disso.** _nawm goshtoo deesoo_

abóbada vault

adro da igreja churchyard

aguarela [aquarela] watercolor

agulha spire

ala wing *(building)*

ameia battlement

antigo ancient

arco arch

arma weapon

arte de gravar carving/engraving

artesanato crafts

azulejos decorated tiles

banhos baths

biblioteca library

claustro cloister

colecção collection

construído em ... built in ...

coro (cadeira) choir *(stall)*

coroa crown

cúpula dome

decorado por ... decorated by ...

descoberto em ... discovered in ...

desenho drawing

destruído por ... destroyed by ...

detalhe detail

doação de ... donated by ...

dourado gilded, gold(en)

edifício building

emprestado a ... on loan to ...

entrada doorway

erigido em ... erected in ...

esboço sketch

escada(ria) staircase

escola de ... school of ...

escultor sculptor

escultura sculpture

exposição display/exhibition

fachada façade

faiança [cerâmica] pottery

fosso moat

friso frieze

fundado em ... founded in ...

gravura carving/engraving

gravura a água-forte etching

gárgula gargoyle

iniciado(-a) em started in

jardim geométrico formal garden

joalharia jewelry

lápide headstone

mobiliário furniture

moeda coin

morreu em ... died in ...

muro wall

mármore marble

nascido(-a) em ... born in ...

no estilo de ... in the style of ...

nível 1 level 1

objeto exposto exhibit

obra de cera waxwork

obra prima masterpiece

olaria pottery

ourivesaria jewelry

ouro gold

painéis panels

palco stage

palestra lecture

parede wall

pedra stone

pedra preciosa gemstone

pedra tumular headstone

pia baptismal font

pilar buttress

pintado por ... painted by ...

pintor(a) painter

pintura painting

pintura a fresco fresco

pintura paisagista landscape (painting)

por ... by ... (person)

portão/porta gate

prata(s) silverware

pátio courtyard

quadro picture/tableau

rainha queen

real royal

reedificado rebuilt

rei king

reinado reign

relógio clock

requerido por ... commissioned by ...

restaurado em ... restored in ...

retábulo altar piece

retrato portrait

rococó rococo

sala de armas armory

salão de recepções stateroom

século/séc. century

talha dourada gilded wooden carving

tapeçaria tapestry

tela canvas

terminado em ... completed in ...

tintas a óleo oils

torre tower

trajo costume

túmulo grave/tomb

varanda balcony

vitral stained glass window

viveu lived

Who?/What?/When?
Quem?/Que?/Quando?

What's that building?	**Que edifício é aquele?**
	keedyfeesyoo eh er-kayl
Who was the …?	**Quem foi …?** *kaym foy*
architect/artist	**o arquitecto/o artista**
	oo urkeetettoo/oo urteeshter
When was it built/painted?	**Quando foi construído/pintado?**
	kwandoo foy konshtrweedoo/peentadoo
What style is that?	**Que estilo é aquele?** *keeshteeloo eh er-kayl*

românico (ca. 11–12)
The romanesque style was characterized by simple lines and round arches; esp. cathedrals in Coimbra and Lisbon, Domus Municipalis in Bragança.

gótico (ca. 12–end 15)
Very complex architectural forms, using pointed arches, rib vaults, and flying buttresses; esp. monastery at Alcobaça, Templo de Elvas, Mosteiro de Santa Maria Vitória in Batalha.

renascença (ca. 15–16)
Derived from the Italian and French Renaissance and characterized by imitating the stability and poise of ancient Roman; esp. churches of Conceição in Tomar, Nossa Senhora de Fora in Lisbon.

barroco/rococó (ca. 17–18)
Large-scale and elaborately decorated architectural style giving an impression of grandeur; esp. (Portugal) Solar de Mateus near Vila Real, convent in Mafra, Bom Jesus staircase near Braga; (Brazil) cities of Ouro Preto, Vila Rica, Tiradentes, and São João del Rey.

neo-clássico (mid ca. 18–mid ca. 19)
The Classical movement brought about a return to classical values such as simplicity and methodical order. esp. Queluz Palace; central Lisbon as rebuilt by Marquês de Pombal with wide, tree-lined avenues and squares.

romântico (end ca. 18–end ca. 19)
Romanticism was marked by idealism, exoticism, fantasy, and an emphasis on content and feeling, rather than on order and form; esp. Palácio da Pena in Sintra, and the Palácio Hotel in Buçaco.

art nouveau (1880s–1910s)
Artistic style orientated towards simplified forms, ranging from the emulation of nature to abstract forms; esp. Lisbon, Coimbra, Leiria.

moderno ca. 20th century
Modern architectural style is most prominent in São Paulo and Brasília (e.g. Congresso Nacional buildings), the Brazilian capital designed by Oscar Niemeyer.

History História

House of Burgundy 1139–1385

After centuries of occupation by the Romans, Visogoths, Moors, and the Spanish, Afonso Henriques proclaimed himself king; Moors are driven from Algarve (1249). The popular revolt (**Revolução de 1385**) ended the Burgundian dynasty when the country's independence was threatened.

Avis dynasty/Spanish rule 1386–1640

Period of great discoveries (**Descobrimentos**), led by Don Henrique (Henry the Navigator); Bartolomeu Dias, Vasco da Gama, Fernão de Magalhães (Magellan). Portugal established trade with India. Brazil was discovered by Pedro Álvares Cabral (1500). But Portugal was overextending itself and the Spanish invaded and occupied – **domínio espanhol** (1580-1640).

Bragança dynasty/Republic 1640–

João IV regained Portugal's independence. An earthquake destroyed Lisbon (1755); British alliance led to defeat of Napoleonic army in the Iberian Peninsula. The decline of the monarch saw independence for Brazil (1822) and a civil war (1828-34). A republic was declared in 1910, leading to the dictatorship under Salazar (1932-70). 1974 brought independence for Portugal's African colonies.

Colonial Brasil ca. 15–ca. 19

There were about 7 million native Indians when the Portuguese colonists (Pedro Álvares Cabral found Brazil in 1500) arrived. The country developed by growing sugar cane and the sale of Indian slaves, hunted by **bandeirantes**.

Império 1822–89

The Brazilian Empire began when Dom Pedro I declared independence; it was followed by civil war, until Dom Pedro II gained control.

República 1889–

A military coup brought a series of Brazilian presidents, supervised by the army. In late 1950s Brasília was built; from early 1960s the economy was hit by chronic inflation. The economy was stabilized in 1994; but Brazil remains a volatile country (of 155 million people) with many social problems.

Places of worship Culto

Although large churches are normally open to the public during the day, services should be respected and permission asked before taking photographs.

Catholic/Protestant church	**a igreja católica/protestante** *er eegrayzher ker-tollikker/prootishtawnt*
mosque	**a mesquita** *er mishkeeter*
synagogue	**a sinagoga** *er seener-gogger*
What time is …?	**A que horas é …?** *er kee oruzeh*
mass/the service	**a missa/o culto** *er meeser/oo kooltoo*

In the countryside No campo

I'd like a map of …	**Queria um mapa …** *ker-reeer oom mapper*
this region	**desta região** *deshter rer-zhyawm*
walking routes	**de itinerários a pé** *deetyner-raryooz er peh*
cycle routes	**de itinerários de bicicleta** *deetyner-raryoosh der beeseekletter*
How far is it to …?	**A que distância fica …?** *er ker deeshtawnsyer feeker*
Is there a right of way?	**É permitida a passagem?** *eh permeeteeder er per-sazhaym*
Is there a trail/scenic route to …?	**Há algum caminho/itinerário turístico para …?** *ah algoom ker-meenyoo/ eetyner-raryoo tooreeshtykoo per-rer*
Can you show me on the map?	**Pode indicar-me no mapa?** *pod eendeekar-mer noo mapper*
I'm lost.	**Estou perdido(-a).** *ishtoh perdeedoo(-er)*

Organized walks Passeios a pé organizados

When does the guided walk start?	**Quando se inicia o passeio a pé com guia?** *kwandoo ser eenyseeer oo per-sayoo er peh kawm geeer*
When will we return?	**Quando é o regresso?** *kwandoo eh oo rer-gresoo*
What is the walk like?	**Que tipo de passeio é?** *ker teepoo der per-sayoo eh*
gentle/medium/tough (hard)	**principiantes/médio/árduo** *preenseepyawntish/medyoo/ardwoo*
I'm exhausted.	**Estou exausto(-a)** *ishtoh eezowshtoo(-er)*
What kind of animal/bird is that?	**Que espécie de animal/pássaro é aquele?** *kee eshpesyer der er-neemal/paser-roo eh er-kayl*
What kind of flower/tree is that?	**Que espécie de flor/árvore é aquela?** *kee eshpesyer der floar/arvoorer eh er-keler*

Geographical features
Pontos de referência geográficos

bridge	**a ponte** *er pont*
cave	**a caverna** *er ker<u>ver</u>ner*
cliff	**a falésia** *er fer-<u>lez</u>yer*
farm	**a quinta [fazenda]** *er <u>keen</u>ter [fa<u>zayn</u>dah]*
field	**o campo** *oo <u>kawm</u>poo*
footpath	**o caminho para peões [pedestres]** *oo ker<u>meen</u>yoo per-rer peeoynsh [pi<u>deh</u>shtrish]*
forest	**a floresta** *er floo<u>resh</u>ter*
hill	**a colina** *er koo<u>lee</u>ner*
lake	**o lago** *oo <u>la</u>goo*
mountain	**a montanha** *er mon<u>tan</u>yer*
mountain pass	**o desfiladeiro** *oo dishfeeler-<u>day</u>roo*
mountain range	**a cordilheira** *er koordee<u>lyay</u>rer*
nature reserve	**a reserva natural** *er rer-<u>zehr</u>ver ner-too<u>ral</u>*
park	**o parque** *oo park*
peak	**o pico** *oo <u>pee</u>koo*
picnic area	**a área para piqueniques** *er <u>ary</u>er <u>per</u>-rer peeker-<u>nee</u>kish*
pond	**a lagoa** *er ler-<u>goh</u>er*
rapids	**os rápidos** *oosh <u>rapi</u>doosh*
ravine	**a ravina** *er rer-<u>vee</u>ner*
river	**o rio** *oo <u>ree</u>oo*
sea	**o mar** *oo mar*
stream	**o ribeiro [riacho]/a corrente** *oo ree<u>bay</u>roo [ree<u>ash</u>oo]/er koo<u>rraynt</u>*
valley	**o vale** *oo <u>va</u>ler*
viewing point	**o miradouro** *oo meerer-<u>doh</u>roo*
village	**a aldeia** *er al<u>day</u>er*
vineyard	**a vinha** *er <u>vee</u>nyer*
waterfall	**a cascata/catarata** *er kush<u>ka</u>tter/ker-ter-<u>ra</u>tter*
wood	**a mata** *er <u>ma</u>tter*

Leisure

Events Espectáculos

Local papers and weekly entertainment guides – such as **Sete** in Portugal and **Veja** in Brazil – will tell you what's on. Regional booklets (**Vejinha**) are also useful in Brazil.

Do you have a program of events?	**Tem um programa dos espectáculos?** *taym oom proogrammer dooz ishpetakooloosh*
Can you recommend a(n) …?	**Pode recomendar-me …?** *pod rer-koomayndar-mer oom(-er)*
Is there a(n) … somewhere?	**Há … em qualquer lado?** *ah … aym kwalkehr ladoo*
ballet/concert	**um bailado [balé]/concerto** *oom bayladoo ['ballet']/konsairtoo*
movie [film]	**um filme** *oom feelmer*
opera	**uma ópera** *oomer operer*

Tickets Bilhetes

Tickets for concerts, theater, and other cultural events in Brazil are available through agencies; they provide credit card reservations and ticket delivery.

When does it start/end?	**A que horas começa/acaba?** *er kee orush koomeser/er-kaber*
Where can I get tickets?	**Onde posso comprar bilhetes?** *ond possoo kawmprar billyaytish*
Are there any seats for tonight?	**Há ainda lugares para hoje à noite?** *ah er-eender loogarish per-rer oazh ah noyt*
I'm sorry, we're sold out.	**Lamento, mas a lotação está esgotada.** *ler-mayntoo mush er looter-sawm ishtah ishgootader*

108

How much are the tickets?	**Quanto custam os bilhetes?** _kwantoo kooshtawm oosh billyaytish_
Do you have anything cheaper?	**Há mais barato?** _ah mighsh ber-rattoo_
I'd like to reserve …	**Queria reservar …** _ker-reeer rer-zervar_
3 for Sunday evening	**tres lugares para domingo à noite** _traysh loogarish per-rer doomeengoo ah noyt_
1 for Friday's matinée	**um lugar para a matinée de sexta-feira** _oom loogar per-rer er mer-teeneh der sa/yshter fayrer_

Qual é … do seu cartão de crédito?	What's your credit card …?
o número	number
o tipo	type
a validade	expiration [expiry] date
Pode levantar [pegar] os bilhetes …	Please pick up the tickets …
até às …	by … p.m.
na bilheteira das reservas	at the reservation desk

May I have a program?	**Pode dar-me um programa?** _pod dar-mer oom proogrammer_
Where's the coatcheck [cloakroom]?	**Onde é o vestuário?** _ond eh oo vishtwaryoo_

> – Teatro Camões. Boa tarde. (Hello, Camões Theater.)
> – Boa tarde. Queria dois bilhetes para a sessão de hoje à noite do "Hamlet".
> (Hello. I'd like two tickets for tonight's "Hamlet".)
> – Com certeza. O número do seu cartão de crédito? (Certainly. What's your credit card number, please?)
> – É zero cinco zero, três seis cinco, sete oito cinco quatro. (It's 050 365 7854.)
> – Obrigada. Pode levantar os seus bilhetes na bilheteira das reservas.
> (Thank you. Please pick up your tickets at the reservation desk.)

RESERVAS	advance reservations
ESGOTADO	sold out
BILHETES PARA HOJE	tickets for today

NUMBERS ➤ 216

Movies [Cinema] Cinema

In Portugal and Brazil, foreign movies (with the exception of those for children) are usually shown in their original language with Portuguese subtitles.

Is there a multiplex movie theater [cinema] near here?	**Há algum cinema (múltiplo) aqui perto?** *ah algoom seenaymer (moolteeploo) er-kee pehrtoo*
What's playing at the movies [on at the cinema] tonight?	**O que há no cinema hoje à noite?** *oo kee ah noo seenaymer oazh ah noyt*
Is the movie dubbed / subtitled?	**O filme é dobrado [dublado]/tem legendas?** *oo feelm eh doobradoo [doobladoo]/ taym ler-zhayndush*
Is the movie in the original English?	**Mostram o filme na versão original inglesa?** *moshtrawm oo feelmer ner versawm ooreezhynal eenglayzer*
Who's the main actor/actress?	**Quem é o actor/a actriz principal?** *kaym eh oo atoar/er atreesh preenseepal*
A ..., please.	**..., se faz favor.** *ser fash fer-voar*
box [carton] of popcorn	**uma embalagem de pipocas** *oomer aymber-lazhaym der peepokkush*
chocolate ice cream [choc-ice]	**um gelado [sorvete] de chocolate** *oom zher-ladoo [soorvait] der shookoolat*
hot dog	**um cachorro quente** *oom ker-shoarroo kaynt*
soft drink	**um refresco [refrigerante]** *oom rer-frayshkoo [rerfrizheranti]*
small/regular/large	**pequeno(-a)/médio(-a)/grande** *per-kaynoo(-er)/medyoo(-er)/grawnd*

Theater Teatro

What's playing at the ... Theater?	**O que está em cena no Teatro ...?** *oo keeshtah aym sayner noo tyatroo*
Who's the playwright?	**Quem é o escritor?** *kaym eh oo eeshkreetoar*
Do you think I'd enjoy it?	**Acha que vou gostar?** *asher ker voh gooshtar*
I don't know much Portuguese.	**Não sei muito português.** *nawm say mweentoo poortoogaysh*

Opera/Ballet/Dance
Ópera/Ballet/Dança

Portugal offers the usual range of nightclubs and discotheques along the coast; alternatively try a **casa de fados**, an intimate, late-night restaurant where your meal is accompanied by the haunting melodies of the **fado**, the national folk song. In Brazil, there are places everywhere to dance and have fun; look for **discotecas**, **danceterias**, and **forrós**. For more information on the famed **Carnaval** ➤ 117.

Where's the opera house?	**Onde fica o teatro de ópera?** *ond feeker oo tyatroo der operer*
Who's the composer/soloist?	**Quem é o compositor/solista?** *kaym eh oo kawmpoozeetoar/sooleeshter*
Is formal dress required?	**O traje é de rigor?** *oo trazher eh der reegoar*
Who's dancing?	**Quem dança?** *kaym dawnser*
I'm interested in contemporary dance.	**Gosto de dança contemporânea.** *goshtoo der dawnser kontaympoorannyer*

Music/Concerts Música/Concertos

Where's the concert hall?	**Onde fica a sala de concertos?** *ond feeker er saler der konsairtoosh*
Which orchestra/band is playing?	**Qual é a orquestra/o grupo que vai tocar?** *kwal eh er orkeshtrer/oo groopoo ker vigh tookar*
What are they playing?	**O que vão tocar?** *oo ker vawm tookar*
Who is the conductor/soloist?	**Quem é o maestro/solista?** *kaym eh oo mer-yeshtroo/sooleeshter*
I like ...	**Gosto de ...** *goshtoo der*
country music	**música country** *moozikker "country"*
folk music	**música popular** *moozikker poopoolar*
jazz	**jazz** *zhaz*
music of the sixties	**música dos anos sesenta** *moozikker doozanoosh ser-saynter*
pop/rock music	**pop/música rock** *pop/moozikker "rock"*
soul music	**música soul** *moozikker "soul"*

Nightlife À noite

What is there to do in the evenings?	**O que há para se fazer à noite?** *oo ker ah per-rer ser fer-zair ah noyt*
Is there a … in town?	**Há … na cidade?** *ah … ner sidad*
Can you recommend a good …?	**Pode recomendar-me um(a) bom/boa …?** *pod rer-koomayndar-mer oom(er) bawm/boaer*
bar	**um bar** *oom bar*
casino	**um casino** *oom ker-zeenoo*
discotheque	**uma discoteca** *oomer deeshkooteker*
gay club	**um clube gay** *oom kloob gay*
nightclub	**um boate** *oom bwaht*
restaurant	**um restaurante** *oom rishtowrawnt*
Is there a floor show/cabaret?	**Tem espectáculo?** *taym ishpetakooloo*
What type of music do they play?	**Que tipo de música tocam?** *ker teepoo der moozikker tokawm*
How do I get there?	**Como se vai para lá?** *koomoo ser vigh per-rer lah*

Admission À entrada

What time does the show start?	**A que horas começa o espectáculo?** *er kee orush koomeser oo ishpetakooloo*
Is evening dress required?	**É preciso traje de noite?** *eh prer-seezoo trazher der noyt*
Is there an admission charge?	**É preciso pagar entrada [ingresso]?** *eh prer-seezoo per-gar ayntrader [eengrehssoa]*
Is a reservation necessary?	**É preciso reservar?** *eh prer-seezoo rer-zervar*
Do we need to be members?	**Precisamos de ser sócios?** *prer-seezamoosh der sair sossyoosh*
How long will we have to stand in line [queue]?	**Quanto tempo vamos ter de estar na fila?** *kwantoo taympoo vamoosh tair der ishtar ner feeler*
I'd like a good table.	**Queria uma mesa boa.** *ker-reeer oomer mayzer boaer*

INCLUI UMA BEBIDA	includes 1 complimentary drink

Children Crianças

Can you recommend
something suitable for children?
**Pode recomendar-me
algo próprio para crianças?**
*pod rer-koomayndar-mer
algoo propryoo per-rer kryawnsush*

Are there changing facilities
here for babies?
É possível mudar fraldas aqui?
eh pooseevell moodar fraldush er-kee

Where are the restrooms
[toilets]?
Onde é a casa de banho [o banheiro]?
*ond eh er kazer der banyoo [oo
bahnyayroo]*

amusement arcade
o salão de jogos
oo ser-lawm der zhoggoosh

fairground
a feira/o parque de diversões
er fayrer/oo park der deeversoynsh

kiddie [paddling] pool
a piscina de bebés [nenês]
er peeshseener der bebesh [naynaysh]

playground
o parque de recreio [playground]
oo park der rer-krayoo ["playground"]

play group
o grupo infantil *oo groopoo eenfawnteel*

puppet show
o espectáculo de marionetes
oo ishpetakooloo der maryoonetish

zoo
o jardim zoológico
oo zhurdeem zoolozhikoo

Babysitting Serviços de babysitter

Can you recommend a
reliable babysitter?
**Pode recomendar-me uma babysitter [babá]
qualificada?** *pod rer-koomayndar mer
oomer "babysitter" [bahba] kwer-lifeekader*

Is there constant supervision?
Há vigilância constante?
ah veezheelawnsyer konshtawnt

Are the helpers properly
trained?
As assistentes são qualificadas?
*ush erseetentish eenfawnteesh sawm
kwer-lifeekadush*

When can I bring them?
Quando é que as posso deixar aí?
kwandoo eh kee ush possoo dayshar er-ee

I'll pick them up at …
Vou buscá-las às … *voh booshkalush ash*

We'll be back by …
Voltamos às … *voltamoosh ash*

Sports Desportos [Esportes]

The Portuguese and Brazilians are avid soccer fans. In Portugal, Porto and Sporting Lisbon attract huge crowds, while Rio boasts **Maracanã**, the largest soccer stadium in the world. Portugal is well known for its splendid golf courses. Volleyball is popular in Brazil.

Spectator Sports De espectador

Is there a soccer [football] game [match] this Saturday?	**Há algum jogo de futebol no sábado?** *ah algoom zhoagoo der footer-bol noo saber-doo*
Which teams are playing?	**Quais são as equipas [os times] que jogam?** *kwighsh sawn uz eekeepush [oosh teemes] ker zhoggawm*
What's the admission charge?	**Quanto é o bilhete de entrada [ingresso]?** *kwantoo eh oo billyayt der ayntrader [der eengrehssoa]*
American football	**o futebol americano** *oo footer-bol er-mer-reekanoo*
athletics	**o atletismo** *oo er-tletteeshmoo*
badminton	**o badminton** *oo badmeenton*
baseball	**o basebol** *oo bayzbol*
basketball	**o basquetebol** *oo bashketbol*
canoeing	**a canoagem** *er ker-nooazhaym*
cycling	**o ciclismo** *oo seekleeshmoo*
field hockey	**o hóquei em campo** *oo okkay aym kawmpoo*
fishing	**a pesca à linha/ao anzol** *er peshker ah leenyer/ow awnzol*
golf	**o golfe** *oo golf*
horseracing	**a corrida de cavalos** *er koorreeder der ker-valoosh*
soccer [football]	**o futebol** *oo footer-bol*
swimming	**a natação** *er ner-ter-sawm*
tennis	**o ténis** *oo teneesh*
volleyball	**o voleibol** *oo vollaybol*

Participation Sports De participante

Where's the nearest …?	**Onde é … mais próximo?** *ond eh … mighsh prossymoo*
golf course	**o campo de golfe** *oo kawmpoo der golf*
sports club	**o clube desportivo [esportivo]** *oo kloob dishpoorteevoo [ishpoorteevoo]*
Where are the tennis courts?	**Onde são os campos [as quadras] de ténis?** *ond sawm oosh kawmpoosh [ush kwadrush] der teneesh*
What's the charge per …?	**Qual é o preço por …?** *kwal eh oo praysoo poor*
day / round / hour	**dia/jogo/hora** *deeer/zhoagoo/orer*
Do I need to be a member?	**Preciso de ser sócio?** *prer-seezoo der sair sossyoo*
Where can I rent …?	**Onde posso alugar …?** *ond possoo er-loogar*
boots	**botas** *bottush*
clubs	**tacos de golfe** *takoosh der golf*
equipment	**o equipamento** *oo eekeeper-mayntoo*
a racket	**uma raquete** *oomer raket*
Are there courses?	**Há cursos?** *ah koorsoosh*
Are there aerobics classes?	**Há aulas de aeróbica?** *ah owlush der er-ehrobyker*
Do you have a fitness room?	**Tem ginásio?** *taym zheenazyoo*
Can I join in?	**Posso jogar também?** *possoo zhoogar tawmbaym*

Lamento, mas não há vagas.	I'm sorry, we're booked.
É preciso deixar um sinal de …	There is a deposit of …
Que número veste?	What size are you?
É preciso uma fotografia de passe [de passaporte].	You need a passport-size photo.

É PROIBIDO PESCAR	no fishing
RESERVADO A SÓCIOS	permit holders only
VESTUÁRIOS	changing rooms

At the beach Na praia

In Portugal, the Algarve offers the best area for beaches, but the **Alentejo** (Atlantic Coast) is becoming more popular. The beaches in the north (**Caminha**, **Apúlia**, **Furadouro**) are good for surfing and body boarding.

Brazil is associated with beaches; **Copacabana** and **Ipanema** in Rio are known the world over. Surfing is popular all along the Brazilian coast; beach volleyball is a popular pursuit for the less adventurous.

The largest beaches have lifeguards, but look for the following swimming flags: red (swimming forbidden), yellow (swim near the beach), green (safe). Avoid taking expensive cameras and any more money than you need to city beaches in Brazil – theft is fairly common.

Is the beach …?	**A praia é …?** er _prigh_er eh
pebbly/sandy	**com seixos/de areia** kawm _say_shoosh/der er-_ray_er
Is there a … here?	**Há … aqui perto?** ah … er-_kee pehr_too
children's pool	**uma piscina para crianças** _oo_mer peesh_see_ner per-_rer_ kry_awn_sush
swimming pool	**uma piscina** _oo_mer peesh_see_ner
indoor/outdoor	**coberta/ao ar livre** koo_behr_ter/ow ar _lee_vrer
Is it safe to swim/dive here?	**Pode-se nadar/mergulhar aqui sem perigo?** _pod_ser ner-_dar_/mergool_yar er-_kee_ saym per-_ree_goo
Is it safe for children?	**É perigoso para as crianças?** eh per-ree_goa_zoo _per_-rer ush kry_awn_sush
Is there a lifeguard?	**Há salva-vidas?** ah sahl-vah-_vee_-dzas
I want to rent a/some …	**Quero alugar …** _keh_roo er-loo_gar_
deck chair	**uma cadeira de encosto** _oo_mer ker_day_rer der ayn_koash_too
fishing equipment	**equipamento para pesca** eekeeper-_mayn_too _per_-rer _pesh_ker
jet-ski	**um jet-ski** oom zhet ski
motorboat	**um barco a motor** oom _bar_koo er moo_toar_
rowboat	**um barco a remos** oom _bar_koo er _re_moosh
sailboat	**um barco à vela** oom _bar_koo ah _ve_ler

umbrella [sunshade]	**um chapéu de sol**
	[guarda sol]
	oom sher-peoo der sol
	[gooarder sol]
surfboard	**uma prancha de surf**
	oomer prawnsher der soorf
water skis	**esquis-aquáticos**
	ishkeesh er-kwatikoosh
windsurfer	**uma prancha à vela**
	oomer prawnsher ah veler
For … hours.	**Por … horas.** *poor … orush*

Carnivals   Os Carnavais

Brazil almost stops when **Carnaval** comes. It starts on the Friday before Ash Wednesday and lasts until Ash Wednesday. Look for parades (**desfiles**) on the streets and carnival balls (**bailes carnavalescos**). The biggest **Carnaval** events are held in Rio, Salvador, and Olinda.
The famed **Carnaval do Rio** sees the spectacularly colorful competition between the various samba schools (**bandas and blocos**) in their parade through the streets of Rio de Janeiro.
Samba and **bossa nova** are the dance styles best known abroad; but regional rhythms like **pagode**, **lambada**, **frevo**, **forró**, **maracatu**, **baião**, **carimbó**, and **bumba-meu boi** with their mixture of African, Indian, and European influences, are also very popular with locals and tourists.
Why not join the rehearsals of the samba schools, especially in Rio before **Carnaval**, and learn to dance?

I'd like to join the samba school.	**Queria um curso de samba.**
	ker-reeer oom koorsoo der samba
Where can I buy tickets for the parade on Saturday?	**Onde é que posso comprar ingressos para o desfile de sábado?** *ond eh ker possoo kawmprar eengrehssoosh parer oo der-zfeeler der saber-doo*
When does the … band start out?	**A que horas sai a Banda de …?** *a kee orush sigh ah banda der*

música popular *moozikker poopoolar* .
Folk music is very popular in Brazil, especially in summer when open-air festivals are held. These are called either the **arraial**, which has groups of folk musicians performing on stage, or the **romaria**, which includes a religious procession. Folk music differs from region to region; in the north, there is the **corridinho**, **dança dos pauliteiros**, **vira**, and **malhão**; while in the south, the **fandango**, the **chula,** and the **marcha** predominate.

Making Friends

Introductions Apresentações

It's polite to shake hands, both when you meet and say good-bye.
In Portuguese, there are a number of forms for "you" (taking different verb forms):

tu is used when talking to a relative, close friend, and a child (and between young people); less commonly used in Brazil

você(s) is slightly more formal, used between people who know each other fairly well; used instead of "tu" in most parts of Brazil

the most formal way of saying "you" is **o(s) senhor(es)** to a man (men) and **a(s) senhora(s)** to a woman (women)

My name is …	**Chamo-me … [Meu nome é …]** _shamoo mer [meoo noamer eh]_
May I introduce …?	**Posso apresentar-lhe …?** _possoo er-prer-zayntarlyer_
John, this is …	**John, apresento-lhe …** _"john" er-prer-zayntoolyer_
Pleased to meet you.	**Muito prazer.** _mweentoo prer-zair_
What's your name?	**Como se chama?** _koomoo ser shammer_
How are you?	**Como está?** _koomoo ishtah_
Fine, thanks. And you?	**Bem, obrigado(-a). E o/a senhor(a)?** _baym obrigadoo(-er). ee oo ser-nyoar (-nyoarer)_
fine	**óptimo(-a)** _ottymoo(-er)_
not bad	**nada mal** _nader mal_
not so good	**adoentado(-a)** _er-dwayntadoo(-er)_

> – Olá, senhor. Como está? (Hello. How are you?)
> – Tudo bem, obrigado. E a senhora?
> (Fine, thanks. And you?)
> – Óptima, obrigada. (Fine, thanks.)

Where are you from? De onde é?

Where are you from?	**De onde é?** *der ond eh*
Where were you born?	**Onde nasceu?** *ond nushseoo*
I'm from …	**Sou …** *soh*
Australia	**da Austrália** *der owshtralyer*
Britain	**da Grã-Bretanha** *der grah brer-tanyer*
Canada	**do Canadá** *doo ker-ner-dah*
England	**da Inglaterra** *der eengler-tehrrer*
Ireland	**da Irlanda** *der eerlawnder*
Scotland	**da Escócia** *der ishkossyer*
the U.S.	**dos Estados Unidos** *doosh ishtadoosh ooneedoosh*
Wales	**do País de Gales** *doo per-eesh der galish*
Where do you live?	**Onde vive?** *ond veev*
What part of … are you from?	**É de que região … ?** *eh der ker rer-zhyawm*
Portugal	**de Portugal** *der poortoogal*
Brazil	**do Brasil** *doo brer-zeel*
Mozambique	**de Moçambique** *der moosawmbeeker*
We come here every year.	**Vimos cá todos os anos.** *veemoosh kah toadoosh ooz anoosh*
It's my/our first visit.	**É a minha/nossa primeira visita.** *eh er meenyer/nosser primayrer veezeeter*
Have you ever been to the U.S./Britain?	**Já esteve nos Estados Unidos/na Grã-Bretanha?** *zhah ishtaiver noosh ishtadoosh ooneedoosh/ner grah brer-tanyer*
Do you like it here?	**Gosta de estar aqui?** *goshter der ishtar er-kee*
What do you think of the …?	**O que acha de …?** *oo ker asher der*
I love the … here.	**Adoro … aqui.** *er-doroo … er-kee*
I don't care for the … here.	**… não me agrada muito.** *nawm mer er-grader mweentoo*
food/people	**a cozinha/o povo** *er koozeenyer/oo poavoo*

119

Who are you with? Com quem está?

English	Portuguese	Pronunciation
Who are you with?	**Com quem está?**	*kawm kaym ishtah*
I'm on my own.	**Estou sozinho(-a)**	*ishtoh sozeenyoo(-er)*
I'm with a friend.	**Estou com um(a) amigo(-a).**	*ishtoh kawm oom(er) er-meegoo(-er)*
I'm with my ...	**Estou com ...**	*ishtoh kawm*
wife/husband	**a minha mulher/o meu marido**	*er meenyer moolyehr/oo meoo mer-reedoo*
family	**a minha família**	*er meenyer fer-meelyer*
children	**os meus filhos**	*oosh meoosh feelyoosh*
parents	**os meus pais**	*oosh meoosh pighsh*
boyfriend/girlfriend	**o meu namorado/a minha namorada**	*oo meoo ner-mooradoo/er meenyer ner-moorader*
my father/son	**o meu pai/filho**	*oo meoo pigh/feelyoo*
my mother/daughter	**a minha mãe/filha**	*er meenyer maym/feelyer*
my brother/uncle	**o meu irmão/tio**	*oo meoo eermawm/teeoo*
my sister/aunt	**a minha irmã/tia**	*er meenyer eermah/teeer*
What's your son's/wife's name?	**Como se chama o seu filho/a sua mulher?**	*koomoo ser shammer oo seoo feelyoo/er swer moolyehr*
Are you married?	**É casado(-a)?**	*eh ker-zadoo(-er)*
I'm ...	**Sou/Estou ...**	*soh/ishtoh*
married/single	**casado(-a)/solteiro(-a)**	*ker-zadoo(-er)/soltayroo(-er)*
divorced/separated	**divorciado(-a)/separado(-a)**	*deevoorsyadoo(-er)/ser-per-radoo(-er)*
engaged	**noivo(-a)**	*noyvoo(-er)*
We live together.	**Vivemos juntos.**	*veevaymoosh zhoontoosh*
Do you have any children?	**Tem/Têm filhos?**	*taym/tayaym feelyoosh*
Two boys and a girl.	**Dois rapazes e uma menina.**	*doysh rer-pazish ee oomer mer-neener*

What do you do? Qual é a sua profissão?

What do you do?	**O que é que faz?** *oo kee eh ker fash*
What are you studying?	**O que é que está a estudar [estudando]?** *oo kee eh ker ishtah er ishtoodar [ishtoodahndoo]*
I'm studying …	**Estudo …** *ishtoodoo*
science	**ciências** *syaynsyush*
the arts	**humanidades [humanas]** *oomer-nidadish [oomahnush]*
I'm in …	**Estou …** *ishtoh*
business	**no comércio** *noo koomehrsyoo*
engineering	**em engenharia** *aym aynzher-nyer-reeer*
sales	**em vendas** *aym vayndush*
Who do you work for?	**Para quem trabalha?** *per-rer kaym trer-balyer*
I work for …	**Trabalho para …** *trer-balyoo per-rer*
I'm (a/an) …	**Sou um/uma …** *soh oom/oomer*
accountant	**contabilista [contador]** *konter-byleeshter [konterdoar]*
housewife	**dona de casa** *donner der kazer*
student	**estudante** *ishtoodawnt*
retired	**reformado(-a) [aposentado(-a)]** *rer-foormadoo(-er) [apoozayntadoo(-er)]*
between jobs	**entre empregos** *ayntrer aympraigoosh*
I'm self-employed.	**Trabalho por conta própria.** *trer-balyoo poor konter propryer*
What are your interests/ hobbies?	**Quais são os seus passatempos?** *kwighsh sawm oosh seoosh paser-taympoosh*
I like …	**Gosto de …** *goshtoo der*
music	**música** *moozikker*
reading	**ler** *lair*
sports	**desporto [esporte]** *dishpoartoo [ishpoorti]*
I play …	**Jogo …** *zhoggoo*
Would you like to play …?	**Gostava de jogar …?** *gooshtaver der zhoogar*
cards/chess	**às cartas/xadrez** *ash kartush/sher-draysh*

What weather! Que tempo!

What a lovely day!	**Que dia lindo!**	*ker deeer leendoo*
What terrible weather!	**Que tempo horrível!** *ker taympoo oorreevell*	
It's hot/cold today!	**Não está mesmo quente/frio hoje!** *nawm ishtah mayshmoo freeoo/ kaynt oazh*	
Is it usually this warm?	**É normalmente assim tão quente?** *eh normalmaynt er-seem tawm kaynt*	
Do you think it's going to ... tomorrow?	**Acha que vai ... amanhã?** *asher ker vigh ... amer-nyah*	
be a nice day	**estar um dia bonito** *ishtar oom deeer booneetoo*	
rain	**chover** *shoovair*	
snow	**nevar** *ner-var*	
What is the weather forecast?	**Quais são as previsões do tempo?** *kwighsh sawm ush prer-veezoynsh doo taympoo*	
It's ...	**Vai ...** *vigh*	
cloudy	**estar enevoado** *ishtar eener-vwadoo*	
foggy	**haver nevoeiro** *er-vair ner-vwayroo*	
frosty	**haver geada** *er-vair zhyader*	
icy	**estar gelado** *ishtar zher-ladoo*	
rainy	**chover** *shoovair*	
snowy	**nevar** *ner-var*	
stormy	**haver trovoadas** *er-vair troovwadush*	
windy	**haver vento** *er-vair vayntoo*	
Has the weather been like this for long?	**O tempo já está assim há muito?** *oo taympoo zhah ishtah er-seem ah mweentoo*	
What's the pollen count?	**Qual é a contagem do pólen?** *kwaleh er kontazhaym doo pollen*	
high/medium/low	**alta/média/baixa** *alter/medyer/bighsher*	

Enjoying your trip?
Que tal a viagem?

Está de férias?	Are you on vacation?
Como veio?	How did you get here?
Onde está a ficar [ficando]?	Where are you staying?
Há quanto tempo está cá [aqui]?	How long have you been here?
Quanto tempo vai ficar?	How long are you staying?
O que é que fez até agora?	What have you done so far?
Para onde vai a seguir?	Where are you going next?
Está a gostar [gostando] das férias?	Are you enjoying your vacation?

I'm here on …	**Estou aqui …** *ishtoh er-kee*
business	**em [a] viagem de negócios** *aym [ah] vyazhaym der ner-gossyoosh*
vacation [holiday]	**de férias** *der fehryush*
We came by …	**Viemos de …** *vyemoosh der*
car/ferry/plane	**carro/ferry-boat [balsa]/avião** *karroo/"ferry-boat" [balser]/er-vyawm*
bus/train	**autocarro [ônibus]/comboio [trem]** *owtokarroo [oanibooss]/kawmboyo [trayn]*
I have a rental [hire] car.	**Aluguei um carro.** *er-loogay oom karroo*
We're staying (in/at) …	**Estamos …** *ishtamoosh*
an apartment	**num apartamento** *noom er-purter-mayntoo*
a hotel/campsite	**num hotel/parque de campismo [camping]** *noom ottel/park der kawmpeeshmoo ["camping"]*
with friends	**em casa de amigos** *aym kazer der er-meegoosh*
Can you suggest …?	**Pode sugerir …** *pod soozher-reer*
things to do	**coisas para fazer** *koyzush per-rer fer-zair*
places to eat	**sítios [lugares] para comer** *seetyoosh [loogarish] per-rer koomair*
We're having a great/ terrible time.	**Estamos a passar [passando] um tempo muito agradável/horrível.** *ishtamoosh er per-sar [persahndoo] oom taympoo mweentoo er-grer-davell/oorreevell*

123

Invitations Convites

Would you like to have dinner with us on …?	**Quer jantar connosco [conosco] no …?** *kehr zhawntar kawnoashkoo noo*
Are you free for lunch?	**Posso convidá-lo(-a) para almoçar?** *possoo konveedaloo(-er) per-rer almoosar*
Can you come for a drink this evening?	**Pode vir hoje à noite tomar uma bebida?** *pod veer oazh ah noyt toomar oomer ber-beeder*
We are having a party. Can you come?	**Vamos dar uma festa. Quer vir?** *vamoosh dar oomer feshter. kehr veer*
May we join you?	**Podemos ir com vocês?** *poodaymoosh eer kawm vossaysh*
Would you like to join us?	**Querem vir conosco?** *kehraym veer kawnoashkoo*

Going out Encontros

What are your plans for …?	**Quais são os seus planos para …?** *kwighsh sawm oosh seoosh planoosh per-rer*
today / tonight	**hoje/hoje à noite** *oazh/oazh ah noyt*
tomorrow	**amanhã** *amer-nyah*
Are you free this evening?	**Está livre hoje à noite?** *ishtah leevrer oazh ah noyt*
Would you like to …?	**Quer …?** *kehr*
go dancing	**ir dançar** *eer dawnsar*
go for a drink	**ir tomar uma bebida** *eer toomar oomer ber-beeder*
go for a meal	**comer alguma coisa** *koomair algoomer koyzer*
go for a walk	**ir dar um passeio** *eer dar oom per-sayoo*
go shopping	**ir às compras** *eer ash kawmprush*
I'd like to go to …	**Quero ir ao/à …** *kehroo eer ow/ah*
I'd like to see …	**Quero ir ver …** *kehroo eer vair*
Do you enjoy …?	**Gosta de …?** *goshter der*

Accepting/Declining Aceitar/Recusar

Great. I'd love to.	**Óptimo! Adorava [adoraria] ir.** *ottymoo. er-dooraver [er-dorareer] eer*
Thank you, but I'm busy.	**Obrigado(-a), mas tenho imenso [muito] que fazer.** *obrigadoo(-er) mush taynyoo eemaynsoo [mweentoo] ker fer-zair*
May I bring a friend?	**Posso trazer um(a) amigo(-a)?** *possoo trer-zair oom(er) er-meegoo(-er)*
Where shall we meet?	**Onde nos vamos encontrar?** *ond noosh vamoosh aynkontrar*
I'll meet you …	**Vou ter consigo [te encontrar] …** *voh tair konseegoo [ti aynkontrar]*
in the bar	**ao bar** *ow bar*
in front of your hotel	**em frente do hotel** *aym fraynt doo ottel*
I'll call for you at 8.	**Vou buscá-lo(-a) às oito.** *voh booshkaloo(-er) ash oytoo*
At about …?	**Por volta das …?** *poor volter dush*
Could we make it a bit later/earlier?	**Pode ser um pouco mais tarde/cedo?** *pod sair oom pohkoo mighsh tard/saydoo*
How about another day?	**E que tal outro dia?** *ee ker tal ohtroo deeer*
That will be fine.	**Está bem.** *ishtah baym*

Dining out/in Jantar fora/em casa

Let me buy you a drink.	**O que quer beber?** *oo ker kehr ber-bair*
Do you like …?	**Gosta de …?** *goshter der*
What are you going to have?	**O que vai tomar?** *oo ker vigh toomar*
Are you enjoying your meal?	**Está a gostar [gostando] do jantar?** *ishtah er gooshtar [gushtahndoo] doo zhawntar*
This is delicious.	**Está delicioso.** *ishtah der-leesyoazoo*
That was a lovely meal.	**Foi um jantar maravilhoso.** *foy oom zhawntar mer-rer-veelyoazoo*

TIME ➤ 220

Socializing Trato social

Do you mind if I ...?	**Importa-se que eu ...?** *eemporter ser kee eoo*
sit here/smoke	**me sente aqui/fume** *mer saynter-kee/foomer*
Can I get you a drink?	**Posso oferecer-lhe uma bebida?** *possoo oofer-rer-sayrlyer oomer ber-beeder*
I'd love to have some company.	**Gostava [gostaria] imenso de ter companhia.** *gooshtaver [gooshtareer] eemaynsoo der ter kawmper-nyeeer*
Why are you laughing?	**Porque se está a rir [está rindo]?** *poorker si ishtah er reer [ishtah rindoo]*
Is my Portuguese that bad?	**O meu português é assim tão mau?** *oo meoo poortoogaysh eh er-seem tawm mow*
Shall we go somewhere quieter?	**Vamos para um sítio [lugar] mais sossegado?** *vamoosh per-rer oom seetyoo [loogar] mighsh soos-er-gadoo*
Leave me alone, please!	**Deixe-me em paz!** *daysh meraym pash*
You look great!	**Está linda!** *ishtah leender*
May I kiss you?	**Posso beijá-la?** *possoo bayzhaler*
Would you like to come back with me?	**Quer voltar comigo?** *kehr voltar koomeegoo*
I'm not ready for that.	**Ainda é muito cedo para isso.** *er-eender eh mweentoo saydoo per-rer eesoo*
I'm afraid we've got to leave now.	**Lamento, mas temos de nos ir já embora.** *ler-mayntoo mush taymoosh der noosh eer zhah aymborer*
Thanks for the evening.	**Obrigado(-a) pela festa.** *obrigadoo(-er) payler feshter*
Can I see you again tomorrow?	**Posso voltar a vê-la amanhã?** *possoo voltar er vayler amer-nyah*
See you soon.	**Até breve.** *er-teh brev*
Can I have your address?	**Pode dar-me o seu endereço/a sua morada?** *pod darmer oo seoo aynder-raysoo/er swer moorader*

Telephoning O telefone

To phone home, dial 00 followed by: 1, Canada; 353, Ireland; 44, United Kingdom; 1, United States. Note that you will usually have to omit the initial 0 of the area code.

Portuguese telephone booths [boxes] are usually blue, marked **Telecom**, and take both coins and cards. In Brazil. you must buy tokens or (in a few state capitals) cards, which are sold at most newsstands, in bars, and small shops near public phones. Local calls are made from yellow phones (**orelhões**) and inter-urban calls from blue ones. Overseas calls can be made from public telephone offices (**estação/central telefônica**) or from your hotel.

Can I have your telephone number?	**Pode dar-me o seu número de telefone?** *pod darmer oo seoo noomeroo der ter-ler-fon*
Here's my number.	**Este é o meu número.** *ayshteh oo meoo noomeroo*
Please call me.	**Telefone-me.** *ter-ler-fon mer*
I'll give you a call.	**Vou telefonar-lhe.** *voh ter-ler-foonarlyer*
Where's the nearest telephone booth [box]?	**Onde é a cabine de telefone [o orelhão] mais próxima?** *ond eh er kabeener der ter-ler-fon [oo ooraylyawn] mighsh prossymer*
May I use your phone?	**Posso telefonar?** *possoo ter-ler-foonar*
It's an emergency.	**É uma emergência.** *eh oomer eemerzhaynsyer*
I'd like to call someone in England.	**Quero telefonar para Inglaterra.** *ker-roo ter-ler-foonar per-rer eengler-tehrrer*
What's the area [dialling] code for …?	**Qual é o indicativo [código] de …?** *kwal eh oo eendiker-teevoo [koadeegoo] der*
I'd like a phone card.	**Queria um credifone [cartão telefônico].** *ker-reeer oom kredifon [kartawm terlerfoneekoo]*
What's the number for Information [Directory Enquiries]?	**Qual é o número das Informações?** *kwal eh oo noomeroo dush infoormer-soynsh*
I'd like the number for …	**Queria o número …** *ker-reeer oo noomeroo*
I'd like to call collect [reverse the charges].	**Queria fazer uma chamada paga [a cobrar] pelo destinatário.** *ker-reeer fer-zair oomer sher-mader pagger [er koobrer] payloo dishteener-taryoo*

On the phone Ao telefone

Hello. This is …	**Estou [Alô]. Fala …**	*ishtoh. [aloh] faler*
I'd like to speak to …	**Queria falar com …**	*ker-reeer fer-lar kawm*
Extension …	**Extensão …**	*ayshtaynsawm*
Speak louder/more slowly, please.	**Fale mais alto/devagar, por favor.**	*faler mighsh altoo/der-ver-gar poor fer-voar*
Could you repeat that?	**Importa-se de repetir?**	*eemporter ser der rer-per-teer*
I'm afraid he's/she's not in.	**Lamento, mas ele/ela não está.**	*ler-mayntoo mush ayl/eler nawm ishtah*
You have the wrong number.	**É engano.**	*eh aynganoo*
Just a moment.	**Só um momento.**	*so oom moomayntoo*
Hold on.	**Não desligue.**	*nawm dershleegi*
When will he/she be back?	**Quando é que ele/ela vai voltar?**	*kwandoo eh kee ayl/eler vigh voltar*
Will you tell him/her that I called?	**Importa-se de dizer-lhe que eu telefonei?**	*eemporter ser der deezairlyer kee eoo ter-ler-foonay*
My name is …	**Chamo-me … [Meu nome é …]**	*shamoomer [meoo naomer eh]*
Would you ask him/her to phone me?	**Importa-se de lhe pedir que me telefone?**	*eemporter ser der lyer per-deer ker mer ter-ler-fon*
Would you take a message, please?	**Posso deixar uma mensagem?**	*possoo dayshar oomer maynsazhaym*
I must go now.	**Tenho de terminar [desligar] agora.**	*taynyoo der termeenar [dershleegar] er-gorer*
Nice to speak to you.	**Foi bom falar consigo [com você].**	*foy bawm fer-lar konseegoo [kon vohsay]*
I'll be in touch.	**Volto a ligar.**	*voltoo er leegar*
Bye.	**Adeus.**	*er-deoosh*

Stores & Services

Stores in Portugal are generally small and individual. However, department store chains appear in major towns and large self-service hypermarkets have developed, particularly on the outskirts of urban areas.

A wide variety of markets exist in Portugal and Brazil; some permanent, others open just one morning a week. There is generally opportunity to bargain over prices.

ESSENTIAL

I'd like …	**Queria …** ker-*reeer*
Do you have …?	**Tem …?** *taym*
How much is this?	**Quanto custa isto?** *kwantoo kooshter eeshtoo*
Thank you.	**Obrigado(-a).** obrig*adoo*(-er)

ABERTO	open
FECHADO	closed

129

Stores and services Lojas e serviços

Where is …? Onde é …?

Where's the nearest …?	**Onde é o/a … mais próximo(-a)?** *ond eh oo/er … mighsh prossymoo(-er)*
Where's there a good …?	**Onde é que há um(a) bom (boa) …?** *ond eh ker ah oom(er) bawm (boaer)*
Where's the main shopping mall [centre]?	**Onde é que é o principal centro comercial?** *ond eh ker eh oo preenseepal sayntroo koomersyal*
How do I get there?	**Como é que vou até lá?** *koomoo eh ker voh er-teh lah*

Stores Lojas

antiques shop	**o antiquário** *oo awnteekwaryoo*
bakery	**a padaria** *er pader-reeer*
bank	**o banco** *oo bawnkoo*
bookstore	**a livraria** *er leevrer-reeer*
butcher	**o talho [açougue]** *oo talyoo [assoaghi]*
camera store	**a loja de artigos fotográficos** *er lozher der urteegoosh footoografikoosh*
clothing store [clothes shop]	**a loja de artigos de vestuário** *er lozher der urteegoosh de vishtwaryoo*
delicatessen	**a charcutaria** *er sharkooter-reeer*
department store	**o grande armazém [a loja de departamentos]** *oo grawnd urmer-zaym [er lozher der der-perrter-mayntoosh]*
drugstore	**a farmácia** *er furmassyer*
fish store [fishmonger]	**a peixaria** *er paysher-reeer*
florist	**a florista** *er flooreeshter*
greengrocer	**a frutaria [quitanda]** *er frooter-reeer [keetahnder]*
health food store	**a loja de produtos dietéticos** *er lozher der proodootoosh dyettettikoosh*
jewelry store	**a joalharia [joalheria]** *er zhooer-lyer-reeer*

liquor store [off-licence]	**a loja de vinhos** *er lozher der veenyoosh*
market	**o mercado** *oo merkadoo*
newsstand [newsagent]	**o quiosque [a banca] de jornais** *oo kyoshk [ah bahnkah] der zhoornighsh*
pharmacy [chemist]	**a farmácia** *er furmassyer*
produce store	**a mercearia** *er mersyer-reeer*
music store	**a loja de discos** *er lozher der deeshkoosh*
shoe store	**a sapataria** *er ser-per-ter-reeer*
souvenir store	**a loja de lembranças** *er lozher der laymbrawnsush*
sporting goods store	**a loja de artigos de desporto [esportivos]** *er lozher der urteegoosh der dishpoartoo [aysporteevoass]*
supermarket	**o supermercado** *oo soopehrmerkadoo*
tobacconist	**a tabacaria** *er ter-ber-ker-reeer*
toy and game store	**o armazém [a loja] de brinquedos** *oo urmer-zaym [er lozher] der breenkaydoosh*

Services Serviços

dentist	**o dentista** *oo daynteeshter*
doctor	**o médico** *oo medikoo*
dry cleaner	**a lavandaria de limpeza a seco** *er ler-vawnder-reeer der leempayzer er saykoo*
hairdresser (women/men)	**o cabeleireiro (de senhoras/homens)** *oo ker-ber-layrayroo (der senyoarush/omaynsh)*
hospital	**o hospital** *oo oshpital*
laundromat	**a lavandaria [lavanderia]** *er ler-vawnder-reeer*
library	**a biblioteca** *er beeblyootekker*
optician	**o oculista** *oo okooleeshter*
post office	**os correios** *oosh koorrayoosh*
travel agency	**a agência de viagens** *er er-zhaynsyer der vyazhaynsh*

Hours Horários de abertura

When does the ... open/close? **Quando é que ... abre/fecha?**
kwandoo eh ker ... abrer/faysher

Are you open in the evening? **Estão abertos ao fim do dia?**
ishtawm er-behrtoosh ow feem doo deeer

Do you close for lunch? **Fecham à hora do almoço?**
fayshawm ah orer doo almoasoo

Where is ...? **Onde é ...** _ond eh_

General hours in Portugal [and Brazil]				
General times for:	Open	Close	Lunch break	Closed
stores	9	7 [6]	1-3 [none]	Sat p.m., Sun
shopping malls	10	12 [10]	none	—
hypermarkets	[9]	[9]	none	[Sun]
post offices	8.30/9 [8]	6	none	Sat p.m., Sun
banks	8.30 [10]	3 [4.30]	none	weekend

cashier [cash desk] — **a caixa** _er kighsher_

escalator — **a escada rolante** _er ishkader roolawnt_

elevator [lift] — **o elevador** _oo eeler-ver-doar_

store directory [guide] — **a planta da loja** _er plawnter der lozher_

It's in the basement. — **É na cave [no subsolo].**
eh ner kav [noo soobsoaloo]

It's on the ... floor. — **É no ... andar.** _eh noo ... awndar_

first [ground (U.K.)] floor — **o rés-do-chão [térreo]**
oo resh doo shawm [tehrayoo]

second [first (U.K.)] floor — **o primeiro andar** _oo primayroo awndar_

ABERTO TODO O DIA	open all day
FECHADO PARA O ALMOÇO	closed for lunch
HORÁRIO DE ABERTURA	hours [business hours]
SAÍDA DE EMERGÊNCIA	emergency exit
ENTRADA	entrance
SAÍDA	exit
SAÍDA DE INCÊNDIO	fire exit
ESCADAS	stairs

Service   Serviço

Can you help me?	**Pode ajudar-me?**
	pod er-zhoo<u>dar</u>mer
I'm looking for …	**Estou à procura de …**
	ish<u>toh</u> ah pro<u>koo</u>rer der
I'm just browsing.	**Estou só a ver [vendo].**
	ish<u>toh</u> so er vair [<u>vehn</u>doo]
It's my turn.	**É a minha vez.** *eh er <u>mee</u>nyer vaysh*
Do you have any …?	**Tem …?** *taym*
I'd like to buy …	**Queria comprar …** *ker-<u>ree</u>er kawm<u>prar</u>*
Could you show me …?	**Podia mostrar-me …?**
	poo<u>dee</u>er moosh<u>trar</u> mer
How much is this/that?	**Quanto custa isto/isso?**
	<u>kwan</u>too <u>koosh</u>ter <u>eesh</u>too/<u>ee</u>soo
That's all, thanks.	**É tudo, obrigado.** *eh <u>too</u>doo obri<u>ga</u>doo*

Bom dia/Boa tarde.	Good morning/afternoon.
Já está a ser [sendo] servido?	Are you being served?
Deseja alguma coisa?	Can I help you?
O que é que deseja?	What would you like?
Vou já verificiar isso.	I'll just check that for you.
É tudo o que deseja?	Is that everything?
Mais alguma coisa?	Anything else?

– Deseja alguma coisa? (Can I help you?)
  – Não, obrigada. Estou só a ver.
  (No, thanks. I'm just browsing.)
– Esteja à sua vontade. (Fine.)
  – Se faz favor. (Excuse me.)
– Sim, o que é que deseja? (Yes, what would you like?)
  – Quanto custa isso? (How much is this?)
– Hm, vou verificar … São trinta euros.
  (Hm, I'll check that for you … 30 euros.)

PROMOÇÃO	special offer
SALDO	clearance [sale]
SELF-SERVICE	self-service
SERVIÇO AOS CLIENTES	customer service

133

Preferences Preferências

I don't want anything too expensive.	**Não quero nada muito caro.** *nawm kehroo nader mweentoo karoo*
Around … euros/reais.	**Por volta de … euros [reais].** *poor volter der … ayoorosh [reh-ighsh]*
I'd like something …	**Queria uma coisa …** *ker-reeer oomer koyzer*
It must be …	**Tem que ser …** *taym ker sair*
big/small	**grande/pequeno(-a)** *grand/per-kaynoo(-er)*
cheap/expensive	**barato(-a)/caro(-a)** *ber-ratoo(-er)/karoo(-er)*
dark/light	**escuro(-a)/claro(-a)** *ishkooroo(-er)/klaroo(-er)*
light/heavy	**leve/pesado(-a)** *lev/per-zadoo(-er)*
oval/round/square	**oval/redondo(-a)/quadrado(-a)** *oval/rer-dondoo(-er)/kwer-dradoo(-er)*
genuine/imitation	**autêntico(-a)/de imitação** *owtayntikoo(-er)/der eemeeter-sawm*
Do you have anything …?	**Tem alguma coisa … ?** *taym algoomer koyzer*
larger	**maior** *mighor*
better quality	**de melhor qualidade** *der melyor kwer-lidad*
cheaper	**mais barata** *mighsh ber-rater*
smaller	**mais pequena [menor]** *mighsh per-kayner [meenor]*

Qual é que queria …?	Which … would you like?
a cor/o feitio	color/shape
a qualidade/a quantidade	quality/quantity
De que género queria?	What kind would you like?
Quanto é que queria gastar?	What price range are you thinking of?

Can you show me …?	**Pode-me mostrar …?** *pod mer mooshtrar*
this/that	**este/esse** *ayss/aysht*
these/those	**estes/esses** *ayshtish/aysish*

COLOR ➤ 143

Conditions of purchase
Condições de compra

Is there a guarantee?
Tem garantia?
taym ger-rawnteeer

Are there any instructions with it?
Vem com instruções?
vaym kawm eenshtroosoynsh

Out of stock Esgotado

Lamento, mas não temos.	I'm sorry, we don't have any.
Está esgotado.	We're out of stock.
Posso-lhe mostrar outra coisa/ um género diferente?	Can I show you something else/ a different kind?
Quer que mande vir?	Shall we order it for you?

Can you order it for me?
Pod-me encomendar?
pod mer aynkoomayndar

How long will it take?
Quanto tempo é que demora?
kwantoo tempoo eh ker der-morer

Is there another store that sells ...?
Em que outro lado [Aonde mais] é que eu podia encontrar ...?
aym ker ohtroo ladoo [aond maysh] eh ker eoo poodeeer aynkoontrara

Decisions Decisões

That's not quite what I want.
Não é bem o que quero.
nawm eh baym oo ker kehroo

No, I don't like it.
Não, não gosto. *nawm nawm goshtoo*

It's too expensive.
É caro demais. *eh karoo der-mighsh*

I'll take it.
Levo. *levoo*

– Bom dia, senhora. Queria uma sweatshirt.
(Hello. I'd like a sweatshirt.)
– Com certeza. Que género queria?
(Certainly. What kind would you like?)
– Cor-de-laranja, por favor. E tem que ser grande.
(Orange, please. And it has to be large.)
– Aqui. São cinquenta reais. (Here you are. 50 reais.)
– Hm, não é bem o que quero. Muito obrigada.
(Hm, that's not quite what I want. Thanks anyway.)

Paying Pagamento

Small businesses may not accept credit cards; however, large stores, restaurants and hotels accept major credit cards, traveler's checks and Eurocheques – look for the signs on the door. Tax can be reclaimed on larger purchases in Portugal when returning home (if outside the EU).

Where do I pay?	**Onde é que pago?** _ond eh ker pagoo_
How much is it?	**Quanto custa?** _kwantoo cushter_
Could you write that down?	**Podia escrever-me isso num papel?** _poodeeer ishkrer-ver mer eesoo noom per-pell_
Do you accept traveler's checks [cheques]?	**Aceita cheques de viagem?** _er-sayter shekish der vyazhaym_
I'll pay …	**Pago …** _pagoo_
by cash	**a dinheiro** _er deenyayroo_
by credit card	**com o cartão de crédito** _kawm oo kertawm der kreditoo_
I don't have any small change.	**Não tenho mais traco [trocado].** _nawm taynyoo mighsh troakoo [trookadoo]_
Sorry, I don't have enough money.	**Desculpe, não tenho dinheiro que chegue.** _dishkoolp nawm taynyoo deenyayroo ker shayger_
Please give me a receipt.	**Dava-me um recibo, se faz favor.** _daver mer oom rer-seeboo ser fash fer-voar_
I think you've given me the wrong change.	**Acho que o troco [trocado] que me deu não está certo.** _ashoo ker oo troakoo [trookadoo] ker mer deoo nawm ishtah sehrtoo_

Como deseja pagar?	How are you paying?
Esta transacção não foi autorizada.	This transaction has not been approved/accepted.
Este cartão não é válido.	This card is not valid.
Posso usar outra forma de identificação?	May I have additional identification?
Não tem troco [trocado]?	Do you have any small change?

PAGUE AQUI POR FAVOR please pay here

Complaints Reclamações

This doesn't work.	**Isto tem um defeito.** *eeshtoo taym oom der-faytoo*
Where can I make a complaint?	**Onde é que posso fazer uma reclamação?** *ond eh ker possoo fer-zair oomer rer-kler-mer-sawm*
Can you exchange this, please?	**Podia-me trocar isto, se faz favor?** *poodeeer mer trookar eeshtoo ser fash fer-voar*
I'd like a refund.	**Queria um reembolso.** *ker-reeer oom rer-aymbolsoo*
Here's the receipt.	**Está aqui o recibo.** *ishtah er-kee oo rer-seeboo*
I don't have the receipt.	**Não tenho o recibo.** *nawm taynyoo oo rer-seeboo*
I'd like to see the manager.	**Queria falar com o/a gerente.** *ker-reeer fer-lar kawm oo/er zher-raynt*

Repairs/Cleaning Consertos/Limpeza

This is broken. Can you repair it?	**Isto está partido [quebrado]. Pode consertar?** *eeshtoo ishtah purteedoo [kaybradoh]. pod konsertar*
Do you have … for this?	**Tem … para isto?** *taym … per-rer eeshtoo*
a battery	**uma pilha** *oomer peelyer*
replacement parts	**sobressalentes** *soobrer-ser-layntish*
There's something wrong with the …	**Há aqui qualquer coisa que não está bem …** *ah er-kee kwalkehr koyzer ker nawm ishtah baym*
I'd like this …	**Queria isto …** *ker-reeer eeshtoo*
cleaned/pressed	**limpo/engomado [passado]** *leempoo/ayngoomadoo [persadoo]*
Can you … this?	**Pode … isto?** *pod … eeshtoo*
alter/mend	**modificar/consertar** *moodifikar/konsertar*
When will it be ready?	**Quando é que está pronto?** *kwandoo eh ker ishtah prontoo*
This isn't mine.	**Isto não me pertence.** *eeshtoo nawm mer pertaynser*

TIME ➤ 220; DATES ➤ 218

Bank/Currency exchange
Banco/Câmbio

Currency exchange offices (**câmbio**) can be found in most Portuguese and Brazilian tourist centers; they generally stay open longer than banks, especially during the summer season.

You can also change money at travel agencies and hotels, but the rate will not be as good.

Remember your passport when you want to change money.

Where's the nearest …?	**Onde é … mais próximo?** *ond eh … mighsh prossymoo*
bank	**o banco** *oo bawnkoo*
currency exchange office [bureau de change]	**o câmbio** *oo kawmbyoo*

CAIXAS	cashiers
TODAS AS TRANSACÇÕES	all transactions
DIVISAS [MOEDAS] ESTRANGEIRAS	foreign currency

Changing money Trocar dinheiro

Can I exchange foreign currency here?	**Posso trocar divisas [moedas] estrangeiras aqui?** *possoo trookar [mooedush] deeveezush ishtrawnzhayrush er-kee*
I'd like to change some dollars/ pounds into euros/reais.	**Queria trocar dólares/libras em euros/ reais.** *ker-reeer trookar doller-rish/ leebrush aym ayoorosh/reh-ighsh*
I want to cash some traveler's checks [cheques].	**Quero cobrar [trocar] cheques de viagem.** *kehroo koobrar [trookar] sheckish der vyazhaym*
What's the exchange rate?	**A como [Quanto] está o câmbio?** *er koomoo [kwahntoo] ishtah oo kawmbyoo*
How much commission do you charge?	**Quanto cobram de comissão?** *kwantoo kobrawm der koomeesawm*
I've lost my traveler's checks.	**Perdi o meu livro de cheques.** *perdee oo meoo leevroo der sheckish*
These are the numbers.	**São estes os números.** *sawm ayshtish oosh noomeroosh*

Security Segurança

Podia deixar-me [Posso] ver … ?	Could I see …?
o seu passaporte	your passport
um documento de identificação	some identification
o seu cartão de banco	your bank card
Qual é a sua morada [endereço]?	What's your address?
Onde está a ficar [ficando]?	Where are you staying?
Preencha este impresso, se faz favor.	Fill out this form, please.
Assine aqui, se faz favor.	Please sign here.

ATMs (Cash machines) Multibancos

Can I withdraw money on my credit card here?	**Posso levantar [sacar] dinheiro aqui com o meu cartão de crédito?** _possoo ler-vawntar [serkar] deenyayroo er-kee kawm oo meoo kertawm der kreditoo_
Where are the ATMs (cash machines)?	**Onde são os multibancos [as caixas automáticas]?** _ond sawm os mooltibawnkoosh [ush kayshush owtomateekush]_
Can I use my … card in the ATM?	**Posso usar o meu cartão … no multibanco [na caixa automática]?** _possoo oozar oo meoo kertawm … noo mooltibawnkoo [ner kaysher owtomateeker]_
The ATM [cash machine] has eaten my card.	**O multibanco [a caixa automática] ficou com o meu cartão.** _oo mooltibawnkoo [er kaysher owtomateeker] feekoh kawm oo meoo kertawm_

MULTIBANCO [CAIXA AUTOMÁTICA]	automated teller (ATM)/ cash machine

In 2002 the currency in most EU countries, including Portugal, changed to the euro (€), divided into 100 cents (**cêntimos**). The currency in Brazil is the real (R$, plural **reais**), divided into 100 **centavos**.

Portugal	*Coins*: 1, 2, 5, 10, 20, 50 cêntimos; €1, 2
	Notes: €5, 10, 20, 50, 100, 200, 500
Brazil	*Coins*: 1, 5, 10, 25, 50 centavos; 1 R$
	Notes: 1, 2, 5, 10, 20, 50, 100 R$

Pharmacy Farmácia

Pharmacies are easily recognized by their sign: a green or red cross, usually lit up.

If you are looking for a pharmacy at night, on Sundays or holidays, you'll find the address of all-night pharmacies (**farmácia de serviço**) listed in the newspaper and displayed in all pharmacy windows. In Portugal, many pharmacies sell only pharmaceutical products, though some now sell cosmetics – also available in a **perfumaria**. Household and toilet articles can be bought from a **drogaria**. In Brazil, you can normally find medicines, perfume, cosmetics and household articles.

Where's the nearest (all-night) pharmacy?	**Onde fica a farmácia de serviço [de plantão] mais próxima?** *ond feeker er furmassyer der serveesoo [der plawntawm] mighsh prossymer*
What time does the pharmacy open/close?	**A que horas é que a farmácia abre/fecha?** *er ker orush eh ker er furmassyer abrer/faysher*
Can you make up this prescription for me?	**Pode aviar-me esta receita?** *pod er-vyar mer eshter rer-sayter*
Shall I wait?	**Fico à espera?** *feekoo ah ishpehrer*
I'll come back for it.	**Venho buscá-la mais tarde.** *vaynyoo booshkaler mighsh tard*

Dosage instructions Instruções sobre as doses

How much should I take?	**Quanto é que devo tomar?** *kwantoo eh ker dayvoo toomar*
How often should I take it?	**Quantas vezes é que devo tomar?** *kwantush vayzish eh ker dayvoo toomar*
Is it suitable for children?	**É próprio para crianças?** *eh propryoo per-rer kryawnsush*

Tome ... comprimidos	Take ... pills/tablets
Tome ... colheres de chá	Take ... teaspoons
antes/depois das refeições	before/after meals
com água	with water
inteiros	whole
De manhã/à noite	in the morning/at night
Durante ... dias	for ... days

Asking advice Pedindo conselho

What would you recommend for (a/an) …?	**O que é que me recomenda para …?** *oo ker eh ker mer rer-koomaynder per-rer*
cold	**uma constipação [um resfriado]** *oomer kawnshteeper-sawm [oom raysfryadoa]*
cough	**a tosse** *er toss*
diarrhea	**a diarreia** *er dyer-rrayer*
hangover	**uma ressaca** *oomer rer-saker*
insect bites	**as picadas de insecto** *ush peekadush der eensettoo*
motion [travel] sickness	**o enjoo** *oo aynzhohoo*
sore throat	**a dor de garganta** *er doar der gurgawnter*
sunburn	**uma queimadura de sol** *oomer kaymer-doorer der sol*
upset stomach	**uma indisposição gástrica** *oomer eendeeshpoozysawm gashtriker*
Can I get it without a prescription?	**Posso comprar sem receita médica?** *possoo kawmprar saym rer-sayter mediker*
Can I have some …?	**Pode arranjar-me [arrumar-me] …?** *pod r-rrawnzher mer [arroomar mi]*
antiseptic cream	**uma pomada antiséptica** *oomer poomader awntysettiker*
(soluble) aspirin	**aspirina (solúvel)** *ushpeereener (sooloovell)*
condoms	**preservativos** *prer-zerver-teevoosh*
cotton [cotton wool]	**algodão** *algoodawm*
gauze [bandage]	**uma ligadura [atadura]** *oomer leeger-doorer [atadoorah]*
insect repellent	**um repelente para insectos** *oom rer-per-laynt per-er eensettoosh*
painkillers	**um analgésico** *oom er-nalzhezykoo*

141

Toiletries Produtos de higiene e cosméticos

I'd like …	**Queria …** ker-_reeer_
aftershave	**uma loção para depois da barba [loção após barba]** _oo_mer loo_sawm_ per-rer der-_poysh_ der _barb_er [loo_sawm_ a_posh_ _barb_er]
deodorant	**um desodorizante [desodorante]** oom der-zoodooreez_awnt_ [dayzoadoa_rahn_ti]
razor blades	**lâminas de barbear** _lam_eenush der burb_yar_
sanitary napkins [towels]	**pensos [absorventes] higiénicos** _payn_soosh [erbzor_ven_tish] eezhy_en_nikoosh
soap	**um sabonete** oom ser-boo_nayt_
sun block	**um protector solar** oom prote_ttoar_ soo_lar_
suntan cream	**um creme de bronzear** oom _krem_mer der bronz_yar_
tampons	**tampões higiénicos** ter-m_poynsh_ eezhy_en_nikoosh
tissues	**lenços de papel** _layn_soosh der per-_pell_
toilet paper	**papel higiénico** per-_pell_ eezhy_en_nikoo
toothpaste	**uma pasta de dentes** _oo_mer _pash_ter der _dayn_tish

Haircare Produtos para o cabelo

comb	**o pente** oo _paynt_
conditioner	**o amaciador [condicionador] para cabelo** oo er-mer-syer-_doar_ [koondeesyooner_door_] per-rer ker-_bay_loo
hair spray	**a laca [laquê] para o cabelo** er _lak_ker [la_kay_] _per_-rer oo ker-_bay_loo
shampoo	**o shampoo [xampu]** oo shawm_poa_ [shahn_poo_]

For the baby Para o bebé [nenê]

baby food	**a comida de bebé [nenê]** er koo_mee_der der be_beh_ [nay_nay_]
baby wipes	**os toalhetes de limpeza para o bebé [nenê]** oosh twal_yay_tish der leem_pay_zer _per_-rer oo be_beh_ [nay_nay_]
diapers [nappies]	**as fraldas** ush _fral_dush

Clothing Vestuário

You'll find that airport boutiques offering tax-free shopping may have cheaper prices but less selection.

General Generalidades

I'd like …	**Queria …** *ker-reeer*
Do you have any …?	**Tem … ?** *taym*

ROUPA DE CRIANÇAS	childrenswear
ROUPA DE HOMEM	menswear
ROUPA DE SENHORA	ladieswear

Color Cor

I'm looking for something in …	**Estou à procura de uma coisa …** *ishtoh ah prokoorer der oomer koyzer*
beige	**em beige [bege]** *aym bayzher*
black	**em preto** *aym praytoo*
blue	**em azul** *aym er-zool*
brown	**em castanho [marrom]** *aym kushtanyoo [marrawn]*
green	**em verde** *aym vaird*
gray	**em cinzento [cinza]** *aym seenzayntoo [seenzer]*
orange	**em cor-de-laranja** *aym koar der ler-rawnzher*
pink	**em cor-de-rosa** *aym koar der rozzer*
purple	**em roxo** *aym roashoo*
red	**em vermelho** *aym vermaylyoo*
white	**em branco** *aym brawnkoo*
yellow	**em amarelo** *aym er-mer-relloo*
light …	**claro …** *klaroo*
dark …	**escuro …** *ishkooroo*
I'd like a darker/lighter shade.	**Queria um tom mais escuro/mais claro.** *ker-reeer oom tawm mighzishkooro/mighsh klaroo*
Do you have the same in …?	**Tem o mesmo em …?** *taym oo mayshmoo aym*

143

Clothes and accessories
Roupas e acessórios

belt	**o cinto** *oo seentoo*
bikini	**o bikini [biquini]** *oo beekeenee*
blouse	**a blusa** *er bloozer*
bra	**o soutien [sutiã]** *oo sootyah*
briefs	**as calcinhas** *ush kalseenyush*
coat	**o casaco comprido** *oo ker-zakoo kawmpreedoo*
dress	**o vestido** *oo vishteedoo*
handbag	**a mala de mão [bolsa]** *er maller der mawm [boalsah]*
hat	**o chapéu** *oo sher-peoo*
jacket	**o casaco (curto)** *oo ker-zakoo (koortoo)*
jeans	**os jeans** *oosh zheenss*
leggings	**as perneiras** *ush pernayrush*
pants	**as calças** *ush kalsush*
pantyhose [tights]	**o collant** *oo kollah*
raincoat	**a gabardine** *er ger-bardeener*
scarf	**o lenço de pescoço** *oo laynsoo der pishkoasoo*
shirt	**a camisa** *er ker-meezer*
shorts	**os calções** *oosh kalsoynsh*
skirt	**a saia** *er sigher*
socks	**as peúgas [meias curtas]** *ush pyoogush [mayass koortush]*
stocking	**a meia** *er mayer*
suit	**o fato [terno]** *oo fattoo [tehrnoa]*
sweatshirt	**o sweatshirt [a blusa de moleton]** *oo "sweatshirt" [er bloozer dzhi mooleton]*
sweater	**a camisola [o suéter]** *er kermeezoa [oo "sweater"]*
swimming trunks	**os calções de banho** *oosh kalsoynsh der banyoo*
swimsuit	**o fato [maiô] de banho** *oo fattoo [mighoa] der banyoo*
trousers	**as calças** *ush kalsush*

Shoes Sapatos

boots	**as botas**	ush _bottush_
flip-flops	**os chinelos de borracha**	oosh shee_nel_loosh der boo_rra_sher
running [training] shoes	**os sapatos de ténis [tênis]**	oosh ser-_pa_ttoosh der tenish [_tay_nish]
sandals	**as sandálias**	ush saw_nda_lyush
shoes	**os sapatos**	oosh ser-_pa_toosh
slippers	**as chinelas [pantufas]**	ush shee_ne_lush [pern_too_fersh]

Walking/Hiking gear Equipamento desportivo

knapsack	**a mochila**	er moo_shee_ler
walking boots	**as botas para caminhar**	ush _bott_ush per-rer ker-mee_nya_r
waterproof jacket [anorak]	**o impermeável [a jaqueta impermeável]**	oo eempermy_a_vell [er zha_kay_ter eempermy_a_vekk]
windbreaker [cagoule]	**a cagoule [o quebra-vento]**	er ker-_gool_ [oo _kay_brer vehntoo]

Fabric Tecido

I'd like something in …	**Queria uma coisa de …**	ker-_reeer_ _oo_mer _koy_zer der
cotton	**algodão**	algoo_dawm_
denim	**ganga [brim]**	_gaw_nger [breen]
lace	**renda**	_ray_nder
leather	**cabedal [couro]**	ker-be_dal_ [_koa_roo]
linen	**linho**	_lee_nyoo
wool	**lã**	lah
Is this …?	**Isto é …?**	_eesh_too eh
pure cotton	**de algodão puro**	der algoo_dawm_ _poo_roo
synthetic	**sintético**	seen_tett_ikoo
Is it hand/machine washable?	**Isto é para lavar à mão/na máquina?**	_eesh_too eh _per_-rer ler-_var_ ah mawm/ner _makinner_

Does it fit? Serve?

Can I try this on?	**Posso provar isto?** _possoo proovar eeshtoo_
Where's the fitting room?	**Onde é que é o gabinete de provas [vestuário]?** _ond eh ker eh oo ger-beenayt der provush [vishtwaryoo]_
It fits well. I'll take it.	**Serve-me bem. Levo.** _sehrv mer baym. levoo_
It doesn't fit.	**Não me serve.** _nawm mer sehrv_
It's too ...	**É ... demais** _eh ... der-mighsh_
short/long	**curto(-a)/comprido(-a)** _koortoo(-er)/kawmpreedoo(-er)_
tight/loose	**apertado(-a)/largo(-a)** _er-pertadoo(-er)/largoo(-er)_
Do you have this in size ...?	**Tem isto no tamanho ...?** _taym eeshtoo noo ter-manyoo_
What size is this?	**Que tamanho é este?** _ker ter-manyoo eh aysht_
Could you measure me, please?	**Podia-me tirar as medidas, se faz favor?** _poodeeer mer teerar ush mer-deedush ser fash fer-voar_
I don't know Portuguese/Brazilian sizes.	**Não conheço os tamanhos portugueses/brasileiros.** _nawm koonyaysoo oosh ter-manyoosh poortoogaysish/brazillayrooss_

Size Tamanho

	Dresses/Suits						Women's shoes			
American	8	10	12	14	16	18	6	7	8	9
British	10	12	14	16	18	20	$4^{1/2}$	$5^{1/2}$	$6^{1/2}$	$7^{1/2}$
Continental	36	38	40	42	44	46	37	38	40	41

	Shirts				Men's shoes							
American } **British**	15	16	17	18	5	6	7	8	$8^{1/2}$ 9	$9^{1/2}$	10	11
Continental	38	41	43	45	38	39	41	42	43	43	44	44 45

1 centimeter (cm.) = 0.39 in.	1 inch = 2.54 cm.
1 meter (m.) = 39.37 in.	1 foot = 30.5 cm.
10 meters = 32.81 ft.	1 yard = 0.91 m.

Health and beauty Saúde e beleza

Tipping: in Brazil, 10% is normal; in Portugal, €1–2.

I'd like a …	**Queria …** *ker-reeer*
facial	**uma limpeza de pele** *oomer lymperzer der pehler*
manicure	**uma manicure** *oomer maneekoorer*
massage	**uma massagem** *oomer mer-sazhaym*
waxing	**uma depilação à cera** *oomer der-peeler-sawm er sayrer*

Hairdresser Cabeleireiro

I'd like to make an appointment for …	**Queria fazer uma marcação para …** [**Queria marcar um horário para …**] *ker-reeer fer-zair oomer murker-sawm per-rer* [*ker-ree-er murker oom oraryoo per-rer*]
I'd like a …	**Queria …** *ker-reeer*
cut	**um corte** *oom kort*
cut and blow-dry	**um corte e brushing [escova]** *oom kort ee brasheeng [ishkover]*
shampoo and set	**lavar e mise [pentear]** *ler-var ee meez [pehntiah]*
trim	**acertar as pontas [aparar]** *er-sertar ush pontush [erperah]*
I'd like my hair …	**Queria …** *ker-reeer*
highlighted	**mechas** *meshush*
permed	**uma permanente** *oomer permer-naynt*
Don't cut it too short.	**Não corte muito curto.** *nawm kort mweentoo koortoo*
A little more off the …	**Tire um bocadinho …** *teer oom booker-deenyoo*
back/front	**atrás/à frente** *er-trash/ah fraynt*
neck/sides	**no pescoço/dos lados** *noo pishkoasoo/doosh ladoosh*
top	**no cimo [em cima]** *noo seemoo [aym seemer]*
That's fine, thanks.	**Está muito bem, obrigado(-a).** *ishtah mweentoo baym obrigadoo(-er)*

Household articles Artigos para a casa

I'd like a(n)/ some …	**Queria …** *ker-reeer*
alumin[i]um foil	**papel de alumínio** *per-pell der er-loomeenyoo*
bottle opener	**um abre-garrafas [abridor de garrafas]** *oom abrer ger-rrafush [abreedoar der ger-rrafush]*
can [tin] opener	**um abre-latas [abridor de latas]** *oom abrer lattush [abreedoarder lattush]*
clothespins [pegs]	**molas [prendedores] para a roupa** *mollush [prehnderdoarish} per-rer er rohper*
corkscrew	**um saca-rolhas** *oom saker roalyush*
cups	**as chávenas [xícaras]** *ush shavnush [sheekarass]*
forks	**os garfos** *oosh garfoosh*
glasses	**os copos** *oosh kopoosh*
knives	**as facas** *ush fakush*
light bulb	**uma lâmpada eléctrica** *oomer lawmper-der eelettrikker*
matches	**fósforos** *foshfooroosh*
paper napkins	**guardanapos de papel** *gwerder-napoosh der per-pell*
plates	**os pratos** *oosh pratoosh*
scissors	**uma tesoura** *oomer ter-zohrer*
spoons / teaspooons	**as colheres/as colheres de chá** *ush koolyehrish/ush koolyehrish der shah*

Cleaning items Artigos de limpeza

bleach	**a lixívia [o alvejante]** *er leesheevyer [oo alvayzhanti]*
dishcloth	**o pano da louça** *oo panoo der lohser*
dishwashing detergent [washing-up liquid]	**o detergente para a louça** *oo der-terzhaynt per-rer er lohser*
garbage bags	**os sacos para o lixo** *oosh sakoosh per-rer oo leeshoo*
laundry soap [washing powder]	**o detergente em pó para a roupa** *oo der-terzhaynt aym po per-rer er rohper*

Jeweler Joalharia

Could I see …?	**Podia mostrar-me** *poodeeer mooshtrar mer*
this/that	**isto/aquilo** *eeshtoo/er-keeloo*
It's in the window/ display case.	**Está na montra/na vitrine.** *ishtah ner montrer/ner veetreener*
I'd like a(n)/some …	**Queria …** *ker-reeer*
alarm clock	**um despertador** *oom dishperter-doar*
battery	**uma pilha** *oomer peelyer*
bracelet	**uma pulseira** *oomer poolsayrer*
brooch	**um broche** *oom brosh*
chain	**um fio para o pescoço [uma corrente]** *oom fyoo per-rer oo pishkoasoo [oomer koraynti]*
clock	**um relógio** *oom rer-lozhyoo*
earrings	**uns brincos** *oomsh breenkoosh*
necklace	**um colar** *oom koolar*
ring	**um anel** *oom er-nell*
watch	**um relógio de pulso** *oom rer-lozhyoo der poolsoo*

Materials Materiais

Is this real silver/gold?	**Isto é prata/ouro verdadeiro?** *eeshtoo eh pratter/ohroo verdadayroo*
Is there any certification for it?	**Tem garantia?** *taym gerernteeer*
Do you have anything in …?	**Tem alguma coisa em …?** *taym algoomer koyzer aym*
copper	**cobre** *kobrer*
crystal	**cristal** *kreeshtal*
cut glass	**vidro facetado** *veedroo fer-setadoo*
diamonds	**brilhantes** *breelyawntish*
gold	**ouro** *ohroo*
goldplate	**dourado** *dohradoo*
platinum	**platina** *pler-teener*
silver	**prata** *pratter*
silverplate	**casquinha [folheado a prata]** *kushkeenyer [foalyahdoo er pratter]*

Newsstand [Newsagent]/ Tobacconist Quiosque/Tabacaria

Foreign newspapers can usually be found at train stations, airports, and on newsstands in major cities.

Newsstands (**Quiosques** or **Tabacarias**) can be found inside coffeehouses, in the middle of traffic circles [roundabouts], and on street corners. Cigarettes can be bought at newsstands, and in hotels and bars. Foreign brands are heavily taxed.

Do you sell English-language books/newspapers?	**Vende livros/jornais em inglês?** _vaynder_ _leevroosh/zhoornighsh_ aym een_glay_sh
I'd like a/some…	**Queria …** ker-_reeer_
book	**um livro** oom _leev_roo
candy [sweets]	**rebuçados [balas]** rer-boo_sa_doosh [_ba_lush]
chewing gum	**uma pastilha elástica [goma de mascar]** _oo_mer push_tee_lyer eelash_ti_kker [_goa_mer der mersh_kar_]
chocolate bar	**um chocolate** oom shookoo_lat_
cigarettes (pack of)	**(um maço de) cigarros** (oom _ma_ssoo der) seegar_roosh_
dictionary	**um dicionário** oom deesyoo_na_ryoo
English–Portuguese	**inglês–português** een_glay_sh poortoo_gay_sh
envelopes	**envelopes** aynver-_lo_pish
guidebook of …	**um guia de …** oom _geeer_ der
lighter	**um isqueiro** oom ish_kay_roo
magazine	**uma revista** _oo_mer rer-_vee_shter
map of the town	**um mapa da cidade** oom _ma_per der si_dad_
matches	**fósforos** _fosh_fooroosh
newspaper	**um jornal** oom zhoor_nal_
American/English	**americano/inglês** er-meree_ka_noo/een_glay_sh
pen	**uma caneta** _oo_mer ker-_nay_ter
postcard	**um postal** oom poosh_tal_
stamps	**selos** _say_loosh

Photography Fotografia

I'm looking for ...	**Estou à procura de [procurando]** ...*ishtoh ah pro<u>koo</u>rer der [prokoor<u>ah</u>ndoo]*
a(n) ... camera	**uma máquina fotográfica** ... <u>oo</u>mer <u>ma</u>kinner footoogra<u>fi</u>kker
automatic	**automática** owt<u>oo</u>mattikker
compact	**compacta** kaw<u>mpa</u>kter
disposable	**descartável** dishker<u>ta</u>vell
I'd like a ...	**Queria** ker-<u>ree</u>er
battery	**uma pilha** <u>oo</u>mer <u>pee</u>lyer
electronic flash	**um flash electrónico** oom flash eele<u>tro</u>nnikoo
filter	**um filtro** oom <u>fee</u>ltroo
lens	**uma objectiva** <u>oo</u>mer obzhe<u>ttee</u>ver
lens cap	**uma tampa para a objectiva** <u>oo</u>mer <u>ta</u>wmper per-rer er obzhe<u>ttee</u>ver

Film / Processing Filme/Revelação

I'd like a ... film.	**Queria um filme** ... ker-<u>ree</u>er oom <u>fi</u>lmer
black and white	**a preto e branco** er <u>pray</u>too ee <u>braw</u>nkoo
color	**a cores** er <u>ko</u>arish
24/36 exposures	**24/36 fotografias** <u>veen</u>tee <u>kwa</u>troo/<u>tree</u>nter ee saysh footoogrer-<u>fee</u>ush
I'd like this film developed, please.	**Queria mandar revelar este filme, se faz favor.** ker-<u>ree</u>er mawn<u>da</u>r rer-ver-<u>la</u>r aysht <u>fi</u>lmer ser fash fer-<u>voa</u>r
Could you enlarge this, please?	**Podia ampliar isto, por favor?** poo<u>dee</u>er awmply<u>a</u>r <u>ee</u>shtoo poor fer-<u>voa</u>r
How much do ... exposures cost?	**Quanto é que custam ... revelações?** <u>kwa</u>ntoo eh ker <u>koo</u>shtawm ... rer-ver-ler-<u>soy</u>nsh
When will my photos be ready?	**Quando é que as fotografias estão prontas?** <u>kwa</u>ndoo eh ker ush footoogrer-<u>fee</u>ush ish<u>ta</u>wm <u>pro</u>ntush

Police Polícia

To get the police in an emergency, ☎ 112 (Portugal). For Brazil, numbers vary by state, but can be found in telephone kiosks.

In Brazil, the first place to report a theft is to the 'tourist police' (**polícia de turismo**), who speak English (telephone number shown in main hotels).

Beware of pickpockets, particularly in crowded places. Report all thefts to the local police within 24 hours for your own insurance purposes.

Where's the nearest police station?	**Onde é a esquadra [delegacia] da polícia mais próxima?** *ond eh er ishkwadrer [dehlay-gasyer] der pooleesyer mighsh prossymer*
Does anyone here speak English?	**Há aqui alguém que fale inglês?** *ah er-kee algaym ker faler eenglaysh*
I want to report …	**Quero dar parte de …** *kehroo dar part der*
an accident/attack	**um acidente/um ataque** *oom aseedent/oom er-tacker*
a mugging/rape	**um assalto/uma violação [um estupro]** *oom er-saltoo/oomer vyooler-sawm [oom ishtooproo]*
My son/daughter is missing.	**Desapareceu o meu filho/a minha filha.** *der-zer-per-reseoo oo meoo feelyoo/er meenyer feelyer*
Here's a photo of him/her.	**Aqui está um retrato dele/dela.** *er-kee ishtah oom rer-tratoo dayl/deler*
I need an English-speaking lawyer.	**Preciso de um advogado que fale inglês.** *prer-seezoo doom er-dvoogadoo ker faler eenglaysh*
I need to make a phone call.	**Preciso de fazer um telefonema.** *prer-seezoo der fer-zair oom ter-ler-foonaymer*

É capaz de fazer uma descrição?	Can you describe him/her?
o homem/a mulher	male/female
de cabelos louros/castanhos	blond(e)/brunette
ruivo(-a)/grisalho(-a)	red-headed/gray
com o cabelo comprido/curto/	long/short hair/
a ficar calvo [ficando careca]	balding
com cerca … de altura	approximate height …
(com uns) … anos	aged (approximately) …
Ele/Ela trazia vestido [estava vestindo] …	He/She was wearing …

Lost property/Theft Perda/Roubo

I want to report a theft/break-in.	**Quero dar parte de um roubo.** _kehroo dar part der oom rohboo_
My car's been broken into.	**O meu carro foi assaltado.** _oo meoo karroo foy er-saltadoo_
I've been robbed/mugged.	**Fui roubado(-a)/assaltado(-a).** _fwee rohbadoo(-er)/er-saltadoo(-er)_
I've lost my …	**Perdi …** _perdee_
My … has been stolen.	**Roubaram-me …** _rohbarawm mer_
camera	**a máquina fotográfica** _er makinner footoografiker_
(rental) car	**o carro (alugado)** _oo karroo (er-loogadoo)_
credit cards	**os cartões de crédito** _oosh kertoynsh der kreditoo_
handbag	**a mala de mão [bolsa]** _er maler der mawm [boalsah]_
money	**o dinheiro** _oo deenyayroo_
passport	**o passaporte** _oo passer-port_
purse	**o porta-moedas** _oo porter mooedush_
wallet	**a carteira (de documentos)** _er kurtayrer (der dookoomayntoosh)_
watch	**o relógio** _oo rer-lozhyoo_
I need a police report for my insurance claim.	**Preciso de um documento para reclamar o seguro.** _prer-seezoo der oom dookoomayntoo per-rer rer-kler-mar oo ser-gooroo_

O que é que falta?	What's missing?
Quando é que foi roubado?	When was it stolen?
Quando é que foi?	When did it happen?
Onde é que está a ficar [ficando]?	Where are you staying?
De onde é que foi tirado?	Where was it taken from?
Onde é que estava nessa altura?	Where were you at the time?
Vamos arranjar-lhe um intérprete.	We're getting an interpreter for you.
Vamos investigar o assunto.	We'll look into the matter.
Por favor preencha este impresso.	Please fill out this form.

Post office Correios

Post offices in Portugal are indicated by CCT (**Correios e Telecomunicações**). Main offices operate until 10 p.m. and on Saturday and Sunday until 6 p.m. Red mailboxes are for **correio normal** (normal mail) and blue for **correio azul** (express mail).

In Brazil, post offices bear the sign ECT (**Empresa Brasileira de Correios e Telégrafos**); they are generally open 8 a.m. to 6 p.m. Monday through Friday, and till noon on Saturday. Streetcorner mailboxes are yellow.

General queries Perguntas gerais

Where is the nearest/ main post office?	**Onde é que é o correio mais próximo/central?** *ond eh ker eh oo koorrayoo mighsh prossymoo/sayntral*
What time does the post office open/close?	**A que horas é que o correio abre/fecha?** *er ker orush eh ker oo koorrayoo abrer/faysher*
Where's the mailbox [postbox]?	**Onde é que é a caixa do correio?** *ond eh eh er kighsher doo koorrayoo*
Where's the general delivery? [poste restante]?	**Onde é que é a posta restante?** *ond eh ker eh er poshter rishtawnt*
Is there any mail for me? My name is …	**Há algum correio [correspondência] para mim? Chamo-me …** *ah algoom koorrayoo [koorrayspondaynsee-er] per-rer meem? shamoomer*

Buying stamps Comprar selos

A stamp for this postcard/ letter, please.	**Um selo para este postal/esta carta, se faz favor.** *oom sayloo per-rer aysht pooshtal/eshter karter ser fash fer-voar*
A …-cent/reais stamp, please.	**Um selo de … cêntimos [reais], se faz favor.** *oom sayloo der … sentimosh [reh-ighsh] ser fash fer-voar*
What's the postage for a postcard/letter to …?	**Qual é o porte para um postal/uma carta para …?** *kwal eh oo port per-rer oom pooshtal/oomer karter per-rer*

– Se faz favor, queria mandar estes postais
aos Estados Unidos.
(Hello. I'd like to send these postcards to the U.S.)
– *Quantos são? (How many?)*
– Nove, se faz favor. (Nine, please.)
– *São cinquenta cêntimos vezes nove: quatro euros cinquenta, por favor. (That's 50 cents times nine: 4 euros 50, please.)*

154

Sending packages
Mandar embrulhos [pacotes]

I want to send this package [parcel] by …	**Queria mandar este embrulho [pacote] por …** ker-*reeer* mawn*dar eshter* aym*brool*yoo [per-*kot*] poor
airmail	**via aérea** *veeer* er-*ehryer*
special delivery [express]	**correio expresso** koo*rrayoo* aysh*presoo*
registered mail	**correio registado** koo*rrayoo* rer-zheesht*adoo*
It contains …	**Contém …** kawm*taym*

> **Por favor preencha a declaração da alfândega.** Please fill out the customs declaration form.
> **Qual é o valor?** What is the value?
> **O que é que tem dentro?** What's inside?

Telecommunications Telecomunicações

I'd like a phone card, please.	**Queria um credifone [cartão telefônico], se faz favor.** ker-*reeer* oom kredi*fon* [kar*tawn* teeleefohn*neekoo*] ser fash fer-*voar*
10/20/50 units	**10/20/50 unidades** desh/veent/seen*kwaynter* ooni*dadish*
Do you have a photocopier?	**Tem uma fotocopiadora?** taym *oomer* fotokopyer-*doarer*
I'd like … copies.	**Queria … cópias.** ker-*reeer* … *kopyush*
I'd like to send a message by e-mail/fax.	**Queria mandar uma mensagem por e-mail/ fax.** ker-*reeer* mawn*dar oomer* mayn*sadzaym* per eemail/fax
What's your e-mail address?	**Qual é o seu e-mail?** kwal eh oo *seoo* eemail
Can I access the Internet here?	**Tenho acesso à internet daqui?** *taynoo* as*sessoo* ah eenter*net* da*kee*
What are the charges per hour?	**Qual é o custo por hora?** kwal eh oo *cushtoo* poor *horer*
How do I log on?	**Como é que obtenho acesso?** *koomoo* eh ker ob*taynoo* as*sessoo*

Souvenirs Lembranças

Typical local souvenirs Lembranças regionais

Souvenirs you might want to take home from Portugal include pottery (**cerâmica**), leather goods (**artigos de couro**), tiles (**azulejos**), copperware (**artigos de cobre**), especially the famous **cataplana**. Wooden painted cocks (**galos de Barcelos**) are a national symbol going back to an ancient legend. And don't forget some of the famous Portuguese port wine (**vinho do porto**) or the various regional sweet brandies.

Popular Brazilian souvenirs include antique furniture (**mobiliário antigo**), baskets (**cestos**), coffee (**café**), dresses (**vestidos**), dolls with regional costumes (**bonecas em trajes típicos**), embroidery (**bordados**), gemstones (**pedras semi-preciosas**), hammocks (**redes**), Indian crafts (**artesanato indígena**), bow and arrow (**arco e flexa**), jacaranda-wood salad bowls and trays (**tigelas e travessas de jacarandá**), pictures (**quadros**), religious objects (**objectos religiosos**), silverware (**artigos de prata**), soapstone goods (**artigos em pedra-sabão**), statues (**estátuas**), tapestry (**tapeçaria**), woodprints (**xilogravuras**).

Afro-Brazilian craft music instruments provide alternative ideas as presents: **berimbau** (stretched metal strip, played with a stick), **bongô** (bongo drums), **atabaque** (larger than the bongo with a single drum).

Gifts Presentes

bottle of wine	**a garrafa de vinho** *er ger-rrafer der veenyoo*
box of chocolates	**a caixa de chocolates** *er kighsher der shookoolattish*
calendar	**o calendário** *oo ker-layndaryoo*
key ring	**a argola para chaves [o chaveiro]** *er urgoller per-rer shavish [oo shavayroo]*
postcards	**postais** *pooshtaighsh*
scarf	**um lenço** *oom lensoo*
souvenir guide	**o guia turístico** *oo geeer tooreeshtykoo*
dish cloth	**o pano da louça** *oo panoo der lohser*
T-shirt	**a camiseta/T-shirt** *er ker-meesayter/"T-shirt"*

Music A música

I'd like a …	**Queria …** _ker-reeer_
cassette	**uma cassete** _oomer kasset_
compact disc	**um disco compacto [CD]** _oom deeshkoo kompaktoo ["CD"]_
videocassette	**uma cassete [fita] de vídeo** _oomer kasset [feeter] der veedyoo_
Who are the popular native singers/bands?	**Quem são os cantores/os conjuntos populares nacionais?** _kaym sawm oosh kawntoarish/oosh konzhoontoosh poopoolarish ner-syoonighsh_

Toys and games Brinquedos e jogos

I'd like a toy/game …	**Queria um brinquedo/um jogo …** _ker-reeer oom breenkaydoo/oom zhoagoo_
for a boy	**para um rapaz** _per-rer oom rer-pash_
for a 5-year-old girl	**para uma menina de cinco anos** _per-rer oomer mer-neener der seenkoo anoosh_
chess set	**um jogo de xadrez** _oom zhoagoo der sher-draysh_
doll/electronic game	**uma boneca/um jogo electrónico** _oomer booneker/oom zhoagoo eelettronikoo_
pail and shovel [bucket and spade]	**um balde e uma pá** _oom baldee-oomer pah_
teddy bear	**um urso de peluche [de pelúcia]** _oom oorsoo der per-loosh [der perloosyer]_

Antiques Antiguidades

How old is this?	**Qual é a data disto?** _kwal eh er datter deeshtoo_
Do you have anything from the … era?	**Tem alguma coisa do período …?** _taym algoomer koyzer doo per-reeoodoo_
Can you send it to me?	**Pode mandar-mo [mandar para mim]?** _pod mawndarmoo [mawndar per-rermeem]_
Will I have problems with customs?	**Vou ter problemas com a alfândega?** _voh tair prooblaymush kawm er alfawnder-ger_
Is there a certificate of authenticity?	**Há um certificado de autenticidade?** _ah oom serteefeekadoo dowtaynteesidad_

Supermarket Supermercado

Large shopping centers like **Amoreiras** (Lisbon), **Brasília** and **Gaishopping** (Porto) are flourishing in Portugal. Regional chains operate in Brazilian states. Some accept credit cards. Shopping centers now stay open until late at night, including Saturdays and Sundays.

At the supermarket No supermercado

Excuse me. Where can I find …?	**Desculpe. Onde é que posso encontrar …?** *dishkoolp. ond eh ker possoo aynkontrar*
Do you sell …?	**Vende …?** *vaynder*
Where are the carts [trolleys]/baskets?	**Onde é que estão os carrinhos/os cestos?** *ond eh ker ishtawm oosh ker-rreenyoosh/sayshtoosh*
Is there a … here?	**Há aqui …?** *ah er-kee*
delicatessen	**uma charcutaria** *oomer sharkooter-reeer*
pharmacy	**uma farmácia** *oomer furmassyer*
bakery	**uma padaria** *oomer pader-reeer*
fish counter	**uma banca de peixe** *oomer bawnker der paysh*

PÃO E BOLOS	bread and cakes
PRODUTOS DE LIMPEZA	cleaning products
LACTICÍNIOS	dairy products
PEIXE FRESCO	fresh fish
CARNE FRESCA	fresh meat
FRUTAS E HORTALIÇAS	fruit and vegetables
COMIDA CONGELADA	frozen foods
ARTIGOS PARA A CASA	household goods
CRIAÇÃO	poultry
VINHOS	wines and spirits

Weights and measures

- **1 kilogram** or **kilo (kg.)** = **1000 grams (g.)**; **100 g.** = 3.5 oz.; **1 kg.** = 2.2 lb; 1 oz. = **28.35 g.**; 1 lb. = **453.60 g.**
- **1 liter (l.)** = 0.88 imp. quart or 1.06 U.S. quart; 1 imp.quart = **1.14 l.**; 1 U.S. quart = **0.951 l.**; 1 imp. gallon = **4.55 l.**; 1 U.S. gallon = **3.8 l.**

Food hygiene Higiene alimentar

EXPOR ATÉ ...	display until ...
COMER DENTRO DE ...	eat within ... days
DIAS DEPOIS DE ABRIR	of opening
MANTER REFRIGERADO	keep refrigerated
PODE IR AO MICROONDAS	microwaveable
AQUECER ANTES DE COMER	reheat before eating
DATA DE VENDA	sell by ...
PRÓPRIO PARA VEGETARIANOS	suitable for vegetarians
USAR ATÉ ...	use by ...

At the minimart Na loja da esquina

I'd like some of that/those.
Queria disso/desses.
ker-reeer deesoo/daysish

That's all, thanks.
É tudo, obrigado(-a).
eh toodoo obrigadoo(-er)

I'd like a(n)/some ...
Queria ... *ker-reeer*

kilo of apples
um quilo de maçãs
oom keeloo der mer-sash

half-kilo of tomatoes
meio quilo de tomates
mayoo keeloo der toomattish

100 grams of cheese
100 gramas de queijo
saym gramush der kayzhoo

liter of milk
um litro de leite *oom leetroo der layt*

half-dozen eggs
meia dúzia de ovos
mayer doozyer der ovoosh

slices of ham
umas fatias de fiambre [presunto] *oomush fer-teeush der fyawmbrer [prer-zoomtoo]*

bottle of wine
uma garrafa de vinho
oomer ger-rrafer der veenyoo

carton of milk
um pacote de leite *oom per-kot der layt*

jar of jam
um frasco de doce
oom frashkoo der doass

can of cola
uma lata de cola *oomer latter der koller*

– Queria meio kilo desse queijo, se faz favor.
(I'd like half a kilo of that cheese, please.)
– Este? (This one?)
– Sim, esse, se faz favor.
(Yes, that one, please.)
– Com certeza. É tudo?
(Certainly. Anything else?)
– E quatro fatias de fiambre, se faz favor.
(And four slices of ham, please.)
– Aqui tem. (Here you are.)

Provisions/Picnic Víveres/Piquenique

apples	**as maçãs** *ush mer-sash*
butter	**a manteiga** *er mawntayger*
cheese	**o queijo** *oo kayzhoo*
cold meats	**as carnes frias [os frios]** *ush karnish freeush [oosh freeoosh]*
cookies [biscuits]	**as bolachas** *ush boolashush*
eggs	**os ovos** *oosh ovoosh*
grapes	**as uvas** *ush oovush*
ice cream	**o sorvete** *oo soorvayt*
instant coffee	**o café instantâneo** *oo ker-feh eenshtawntanyoo*
loaf of bread	**o pão** *oo pawm*
margarine	**a margarina** *er murger-reener*
milk	**o leite** *oo layt*
mustard	**a mostarda** *er mooshtarder*
oranges	**as laranjas** *ush ler-rawnzhush*
rolls	**os pãezinhos** *oosh paynzeenyoosh*
sausages	**as salsichas** *ush salseeshush*
six-pack of beer	**a embalagem de seis cervejas** *er aymber-lazhaym der saysh servayzhush*
soft drink	**a bebida gasosa [o refrigerante]** *er ber-beeder ger-zozer [oo rerfrizheranti]*
sugar	**o açúcar** *oo er-sookar*
winebox	**o pacote de vinho** *oo per-kot der veenyoo*
yogurt	**o yogurte** *oo yogoort*

VEGETABLES/FRUIT ➤ 47

Health

Before you leave home, make sure your health insurance policy covers any illness or accident while you are abroad. If not, ask your insurance representative or travel agent for details of special health insurance.
In Portugal, EU citizens with a Form E111 are eligible for free medical treatment. This only applies to clinics that belong or are connected to the national health service.
If you need to see a doctor, you'll probably have to pay the bill on the spot; save all receipts for reimbursement. Main hotels and tourist offices in Portugal and Brazil have a list of English-speaking doctors. In Brazil, you will only be hospitalized free of charge if you catch an infectious disease.

Doctor (general) Médico (generalidades)

Where can I find a doctor/dentist?	**Onde é que posso encontrar um médico/um dentista?** _ond eh ker possoo aynkontrar oom medikoo/oom daynteeshter_
Where's there a doctor who speaks English?	**Onde é que há um médico que fale inglês?** _ond eh ker ah oom medikoo ker faler eenglaysh_
What are the office [surgery] hours?	**A que horas é que há consulta?** _er ker orush eh ker ah konsoolter_
Could the doctor come to see me here?	**O médico podia vir cá ver-me [aqui me ver]?** _oo medikoo poodeeer veer kah vair mer [er-kee mer vair]_
Can I make an appointment for …?	**Queria marcar uma consulta para …** _ker-reeer merkar oomer konsoolter per-rer_
tomorrow	**amanhã** _amer-nyah_
as soon as possible	**o mais cedo possível** _oo mighsh saydoo pooseevell_
I've got an appointment with Doctor …	**Tenho consulta marcada com o Dr. …** _taynyoo konsoolter merkader kon oo dohtoar_

- Queria marcar uma consulta para o mais cedo possível.
(I'd like to make an appointment for as soon as possible.)
- É urgente? (Is it urgent?)
- Sim. (Yes.)
- Bem, posso arranjar-lhe uma vaga às dez e quinze amanhã com o Dr. Martin.
(Right, I can fit you in to see Dr. Martin at 10:15 tomorrow morning.)
- 10:15. Muito obrigado. (10:15. Thank you.)

Accident and injury Acidente e ferimento

My ... is hurt.	**A minha ... está magoada [machucada].** er _meenyer_ ... ish_tah_ mer-gw_ader_ [mershook_ader_]
wife/daughter/friend *(female)*	**mulher/filha/amiga** mool_yehr_/_feelyer_/er-_meeger_
My ... is hurt.	**O meu ... está magoado [machucado].** oo _meoo_ ... ish_tah_ mer-gw_adoo_ [mershook_adoo_]
husband/son/baby	**marido/filho/bebé** mer-_reedoo_/_feelyoo_/bebeh
friend *(male)*	**amigo** er-_meegoo_
He/She is ...	**Ele/Ela está ...** ayl/_eler_ ish_tah_
bleeding	**a sangrar [sangrando]** er sawn_grar_ [sawn_grahndoo_]
(seriously) injured	**(gravemente) ferido(-a)** (grav_maynt_) fer-_reedoo_(-er)
unconscious	**inconsciente** _een_konshsyaynt
I have a(n) ...	**Tenho ...** _taynyoo_
blister/boil	**uma bolha/um furúnculo** oomer bo_alyer_/oom foo_roon_kooloo
bruise	**uma nódoa negra [uma escoriação]** _oomer_ _nod_wer _naygrer_ [oomer ishkoreea_sawm_]
burn	**uma queimadura** _oomer_ kaymer-_doorer_
cut	**um corte** oom kort
insect bite	**uma picada de insecto** _oomer_ peek_ader_ der _eensetto_
lump	**um alto [caroço]** oom _altoo_ [ka_ro_soo]
rash	**uma erupção cutânea** _oomer_ eeroop_sawm_ koo_tannyer_
sprained muscle	**uma distensão muscular** _oomer_ deeshtayn_sawm_ _mooshkoolar_

162

Symptoms Sintomas

I've been feeling ill for … days.	**Há … dias que me sinto doente.** *ah … deeush ker mer seentoo dooaynt*
I feel …	**Sinto-me …** *seentoo mer*
faint	**a desmaiar [desmaiando]** *er dishmighar [dishmighahndoo]*
feverish/shivery	**febril/com arrepios** *fer-brill/kawm er-rrer-pyoosh*
I've been vomiting.	**Tenho estado a vomitar [vomitando].** *taynyoo ishtadoo er voomeetar [vomeetahndoo]*
I have diarrhea.	**Tenho diarréia.** *taynyoo dyer-rrayer*
My … hurts.	**Dói-me o …** *doymer oo*
It hurts here.	**Dói-me aqui.** *doymer erkee*
I have (a/an) …	**Tenho tido …** *taynyoo teedoo*
backache	**dor nas costas** *doar nush koshtush*
cold	**uma constipação [um resfriado]** *oomer konshteeper-sawm [oom raysfryadoa]*
cramps	**cólicas** *kollikush*
earache/headache	**dor de ouvidos/cabeça** *doar der ohveedoosh/ker-bayser*
sore throat	**dor de garganta** *doar der gurgawnter*
stiff neck	**um torcicolo** *oom toorsykolloo*
stomachache	**dor de estômago** *doar der ishtoamer-goo*
I have sunstroke.	**Apanhei uma insolação.** *er-per-nyay oomer ensoler-sawm*

Health conditions Estados de saúde

I'm …	**Sou …** *soh …*
deaf/diabetic	**surdo/diabético** *soordoo/dyer-bettikoo*
epileptic/handicapped	**epilético/deficiente** *epylettikoo/der-feesyaynt*
I have …	**Tenho …** *taynyoo*
arthritis/asthma/high blood pressure	**artrite/asma/tensão alta** *ertreet/ashmer/taynsawm alter*
I'm (… months) pregnant.	**Estou grávida (de … meses).** *ishtoh graveeder (der … mayzish)*
I had a heart attack … years ago.	**Tive um ataque de coração há … anos.** *teev oom er-tack der koorer-sawm ah … anoosh*

163

Doctor's inquiries O interrogatório do médico

Há quanto tempo se sente assim?	How long have you been feeling like this?
É a primeira vez que tem isto?	Is this the first time you've had this?
Está a tomar [tomando] outros remédios?	Are you taking any other medication?
É alérgico a alguma coisa?	Are you allergic to anything?
Está vacinado contra o tétano?	Have you been vaccinated against tetanus?
Tem apetite?	Is your appetite okay?

Examination O exame

Vou tirar-lhe a temperatura/ a tensão arterial.	I'll take your temperature/ blood pressure.
Arregace a manga, se faz favor.	Roll up your sleeve, please.
Dispa-se da cintura para cima, se faz favor.	Please undress to the waist.
Deite-se, por favor.	Please lie down.
Abra a boca.	Open your mouth.
Respire fundo.	Breathe deeply.
Tussa, se faz favor.	Cough, please.
Onde é que lhe dói?	Where does it hurt?
Dói-lhe aqui?	Does it hurt here?

Diagnosis Diagnóstico

Quero que tire uma radiografia.	I want you to have an x-ray.
Quero uma amostra de sangue/ de fezes/de urina.	I want a specimen of your blood/stool/urine.
Quero que vá ver um especialista.	I want you to see a specialist.
Quero que vá para o hospital.	I want you to go to the hospital.
Está partido [quebrado]/ deslocado.	It's broken/dislocated.
Tem uma rotura [ruptura].	It's torn.

Tem ...	You have (a/an) ...
uma apendicite	appendicitis
uma cistitite [cistite]	cystitis
uma gripe	flu
uma intoxicação alimentar	food poisoning
uma fractura	fracture
uma gastrite	gastritis
uma hérnia	hernia
uma inflamação de ...	inflammation of ...
sarampo	measles
uma pneumonia	pneumonia
uma ciática	sciatica
uma amigdalite	tonsilitis
um tumor	tumor
uma doença venérea	venereal disease
Está infectado.	It's infected.
É contagioso.	It's contagious.

Treatment Tratamento

Vou dar-lhe ...	I'll give you ...
um antiséptico/um analgésico	an antiseptic/a pain killer
Vou receitar ...	I'm going to prescribe ...
uma dose de antibióticos	a course of antibiotics
supositórios	some suppositories
É alérgico a algum remédio?	Are you allergic to any medication?
Tome ...	Take ...
um comprimido ...	one pill ...
de 2 em 2 horas	every two hours
... vezes ao dia	... times a day
antes/depois de cada refeição	before/after each meal
de manhã/à noite	in the morning/at night
em caso de dor	in case of pain
durante ... dias	for ... days
Gostava [gostaria] que voltasse daqui a ... dias.	I'd like you to come back in ... days.
Consulte um médico quando chegar a casa.	Consult a doctor when you get home.

Parts of the body Partes do corpo

appendix	o apêndice	oo er-payndiss
arm	o braço	oo brassoo
back	as costas	ush koshtush
bladder	a bexiga	er ber-sheeger
bone	o osso	oo oasoo
breast	a mama [o seio]	er mammer [oo sayoo]
chest	o peito	oo paytoo
ear	o ouvido	oo ohveedoo
eye	o olho	oo oalyoo
face	a cara [o rosto]	er karer [oo rostoo]
finger	o dedo	oo daydoo
foot	o pé	oo peh
gland	a glândula	er glawndooler
hand	a mão	er mawm
head	a cabeça	er ker-bayser
heart	o coração	oo koorer-sawm
jaw	o maxilar	oo maksylar
joint	a articulação	er urtykooler-sawm
kidney	o rim	oo reem
knee	o joelho	oo zhooaylyoo
leg	a perna	er pehrner
lip	o lábio	oo labyoo
liver	o fígado	oo feeger-doo
mouth	a boca	er boaker
muscle	o músculo	oo mooshkooloo
neck	o pescoço	oo pishkoasoo
nerve	o nervo	oo nairvoo
nose	o nariz	oo ner-reesh
rib	a costela	er kooshteler
shoulder	o ombro	oo awmbroo
skin	a pele	er pell
stomach	o estômago	oo ishtoamer-goo
thigh	a coxa	er koasher
throat	a garganta	er gurgawnter
thumb	o polegar	oo poolgar
toe	o dedo do pé	oo daydoo doo peh
tongue	a língua	er leengwa
tonsils	as amígdalas	ush er-meegder-lush

Gynecologist O ginecologista

I have …	**Tenho …** *taynyoo*
abdominal pains	**dores abdominais** *doarish ubdoomynighsh*
period pains	**dos períodos menstruais** *doosh per-reeoodoosh maynshtrooighsh*
a vaginal infection	**uma infecção na vagina** *oomer eenfeksawm ner ver-zheener*
I'm on the Pill.	**Estou a tomar [tomando] a pílula.** *ishtoh er toomar [toomahndoo] er peelooler*

Hospital O hospital

Please notify my family.	**Por favor informe a minha família.** *poor fer-voar eenform er meenyer fer-meelyer*
What are the visiting hours?	**Quais são as horas de visita?** *kwighsh sawm erz orush der veezeeter*
I'm in pain.	**Estou com dores.** *ishtoh kawm doarish*
I can't eat/sleep.	**Não consigo comer/dormir.** *nawm konseegoo koomair/doormeer*
When will the doctor come?	**Quando é que vem o médico?** *kwand eh ker vaym oo medikoo*
Which section [ward] is … in?	**Em que enfermaria é que está …?** *aym ker aynfermer-reeer eh ker ishtah*

Optician O oculista

I'm near- [short-] sighted/ far- [long-] sighted.	**Tenho vista curta/vista cansada.** *taynyoo veeshter koorter/veeshter kawnsader*
I've lost …	**Perdi …** *perdee*
one of my contact lenses	**uma das minhas lentes de contacto** *oomer dush meenyush layntish der kontaktoo*
my glasses	**os óculos** *ooz okooloosh*
Could you give me a replacement?	**Podia arranjar-me outro(-a)?** *poodeeer er-rrawnzharmer ohtroo(-er)*

Dentist Dentista

If you need to see a dentist, you'll probably have to pay the bill on the spot; save all receipts for reimbursement.

I have (a) toothache.	**Tenho dores de dentes.**	_taynyoo doarish der dayntish_
This tooth hurts.	**Dói-me este dente.**	_doymer aysht daynt_
I don't want it extracted.	**Não o quero arrancar.**	_nawm oo kehroo er-rrawnkar_
I've lost a filling.	**Perdi um chumbo [uma obturação].**	_perdee oom shoomboo [oomer oobtoorer-sawn]_
Can you repair this denture?	**Pode consertar esta dentadura?**	_pod konsertar eshter daynter-doorer_

Vou dar-lhe uma injecção/ uma anestesia local.	I'm going to give you an injection/ a local anesthetic.
Precisa de uma obturação/ uma coroa.	You need a filling/cap (crown).
Vou ter que arrancá-lo.	I'll have to take it out.
Só posso fazer um conserto temporário.	I can only fix it temporarily.
Volte dentro de … dias.	Come back in … days.
Não coma nada durante … horas.	Don't eat anything for … hours.

Payment and insurance Pagamento e seguro

How much do I owe you?	**Quanto lhe devo?**	_kwantoo lyer dayvoo_
I have insurance.	**Tenho um seguro.**	_taynyoo oom ser-gooroo_
Can I have a receipt for my health insurance?	**Pode dar-me [Podia me dar] um recibo para o seguro de saúde?**	_pod dar-mer [poodeeer mer dar] oom rer-seeboo per-rer oo ser-gooroo der ser-ood_
Would you fill out this health insurance form?	**Não se importa de preencher o impresso do seguro de saúde?**	_nawm ser eemporter der pryaynshair oo eempresoo doo ser-gooroo der ser-ood_
Can I have a medical certificate?	**Pode passar-me [Podia me passar] um atestado médico?**	_pod per-sar-mer [poodeeer mer per-sar] oom er-tishtadoo medikoo_

Most terms in this dictionary are either followed by an example
or cross-referenced to pages where the word appears in a phrase.
In addition, the notes below provide some basic grammar guidelines.

Nouns

Nouns are either masculine (m) or feminine (f). Normally, nouns that
end in a vowel add **-s** to form the plural (pl). The articles they take (a,
an, the, some) depend on their gender:

masculine	**o carro**	the train	*feminine*	**a casa**	the house
	um carro	a train		**uma casa**	a house
	os carros	the trains		**as casas**	the houses
	uns carros	some trains		**umas casas**	some houses

Nouns that end in a consonant vary in the plural. For those that end in **r**
or **s**, add **-es**; for those ending in **l**, take off the **l** and add **-is**; for those
ending in **m**, take off the **m** and add **-ns**:

cor	color	**cores**	colors
canal	canal	**canais**	canals
fim	end	**fins**	ends

Adjectives

Adjectives agree in gender and number with the noun they describe. In
this dictionary the feminine form (where it differs from the masculine)
is shown in brackets, e.g.

small **pequeno(-a)** = *masculaine form* **pequeno**, *feminine form* **pequena**

If the masculine form ends in **-e** or with a consonant, the feminine
usually keeps the same form:

o mar (m) **azul** the blue sea **a flor** (m) **azul** the blue flower

Verbs

Verbs are generally shown in the infinitive (to say, to eat, etc.) Here are
three of the main categories of regular verbs in the present tense:

	falar (to speak)	**comer** (to eat)	**cobrir** (to cover)
	ends in **-ar**	ends in **-er**	ends in **-ir**
eu	falo	como	cubro
tu	falas	comes	cobres
el/ela	fala	come	cobre
nós	falamos	comemos	cobrimos
vós	falais	coméis	cobris
eles/elas	falam	comem	cobrem

Negatives are generally formed by putting **não** before the verb:

É novo. It's new. **Não é novo.** It's not new.

a few alguns (algumas) 15
a little um pouco 15
a lot muito 15
a.m. da manhã
abbey abadia f
able, to be (*also* ➤ **can, could**) ser capaz
about (*approximately*) cerca de
above (*place*) acima/por cima de
abroad no estrangeiro
abscess abcesso m
accept, to aceitar 136; **do you accept …?** aceitam …?
access acesso m 100
accessories acessórios mpl
accident (*road*) desastre [acidente] m 92; 152
accidentally sem querer 28
accommodations alojamento m
accompaniments acompanhamentos mpl 38
accompany, to acompanhar
accountant contabilista [contador] m
ace (*cards*) ás m
activities actividades fpl
acne acne m
across do outro lado
acrylic acrílico(-a)
actor/actress actor m/actriz f 110
adaptor adaptador m
address morada f, endereço m 84, 93, 126
adhesive bandage penso m rápido [bandaid] 141
adjoining room quarto m contíguo [conjugado] 22
admission charge entrada f/ bilhete m 114
adult (*noun/adj.*) o/adulto(-a) 81, 100
advance, in antecipadamente 21
aerial (*car/TV*) antena f
aerobics aeróbica f
after (*time*) depois de 13; (*place*) 95
aftershave loção f para depois da barba [loção f após barba] 142
after-sun lotion loção f para depois do sol 142
age: what age? que idades?

aged, to be com … anos 152
ago há 13
agree: I agree concordo
air conditioning ar m condicionado 22, 25
air mattress colchão m pneumático 31
air pump máquina f pneumática [bomba f de ar] 87
air-freshener purificador m do ar
airline companhia f de aviação
airmail via f aérea 155
airport aeroporto m 96
aisle seat lugar m na coxia [no/de corredor] 74
alarm clock despertador m 149
alcoholic drink bebida f alcoólica
all: I like all these gosto de todos estes; **I like it all** gosto de tudo f
allergic, to be ser alérgico 164
allergy alergia f
allowance que m é permitido 67
allowed: is it allowed? é permitido?
almost quase
alone só
alphabet alfabeto m
already já 28
also também 19
alter, to modificar 137
alumin[i]um foil papel m de alumínio 148
always sempre 13
am: I am here ((eu)estou aqui (*temporary situation*); **I am a man** (eu) sou um homem (*permanent situation*)
ambassador embaixador m
amber (*light*) amarelo
ambulance ambulância f 92
American (*noun/adj.*) americano(-a) 150; **~ football** futebol m americano
amusement arcade salão m de jogos 113
anesthetic anestésico [anestésico] m
anchor, to ancorar
anchorage ancoradouro m
and e 19
angling pesca f à linha
Angola Angola
announcement: what was that announcement? o que é que anunciaram?

another outro(-a) 21, 125
antibiotic antibiótico m
antifreeze anticongelante m
antique antiguidade f 157; **~ shop** antiquário m 130
antiseptic cream pomada f antiséptica 141
any algum(a)
anyone else mais alguém 93
anyone: does anyone speak English? há alguém que fale inglês?
anything cheaper algo mais barato 21
anything else? mais alguma coisa?
apartment apartamento m 28
apologies desculpas 10
apologize: I apologize peço desculpa
apology desculpa f
apples maçãs fpl 160
appointment, to make an fazer uma marcação [marcar um horário] 147
approximately aproximadamente
archery tiro m ao arco
architect arquitecto(-a) 104
architecture arquitectura f
are you …? (formal) senhor é …?; (informal) você é …?
area área f
area code indicativo [código] m 127
Argentina Argentina f
armbands (swimming) braçadeiras fpl
around (time) cerca de 13; (place) à volta de
arrange: can you arrange it? pode arranjar isso?
arrest, to be under estar preso
arrive, to chegar 68, 70, 71, 76
art arte f
art gallery galeria f de arte 99
artificial sweetener adoçante 38
artist artista m/f 104
as soon as possible o mais cedo possível
ashore, to go ir para terra
ashtray cinzeiro m 39
ask: please ask her to call me back peça-lhe por favor que me telefone de volta; **I asked for …** pedi … 41
asleep, to be estar adormecido
aspirin aspirina f 141

at (place) em 12; (time) às 13
at least pelo menos 23
athletics atletismo m 114
ATM (automated teller machine) multibanco m 139
attack (assault/medical) ataque m 152, 163
attendant empregado(-a)
attractive atraente
aunt tia f 120
Australia Austrália f 119
Australian (noun) australiano(-a)
authentic: is it? é autêntico?
authenticity autenticidade f 157
automatic (car) automático(-a) 86; (camera) 151
avalanche avalanche f
away longe 12
awful horrível

B **baby** bebé [nenê] m/f 39, 142, 162; **~ food** comida f de bebé [nenê] 142; **~ products** produtos para o bebé [nenê]; **~ seat** cadeira f de bebé [nenê]; **~sitter** baby-sitter [ama] f 113; **~ wipes** toalhetes mpl de limpeza para o bebé [nenê] 142
baby's bottle biberão m [mamadeira f]
backpacking turismo m de pé descalço [de mochileiro]
bad mau (má) 14
badminton badminton
baked cozido no forno 52
bakery padaria f 130, 158
balcony varanda f 29; (theater) balcão m
ball bola f
ballet ballet [balé] m 108, 111
ballroom sala f de baile
bananas bananas fpl
band (musical) grupo m/ banda f 111; conjunto m 157
bandage ligadura [atadura] f 141
bank banco m 130; 138; **~ account** conta f bancária; **~ card** cartão m de banco 139
bar bar m 26, 112
barber barbeiro m

barge (*longboat*) barcaça f
baseball basebol m
basement cave f [subsolo m] 132
basin bacia
basket cesto m 158
basketball basquetebol m 114
bath banho m
bath: to take a tomar banho
bath towel toalha f de banho
bathing hut (*cabana*) barraca f
bathroom casa f de banho [banheiros mpl] 26, 29
battery pilha f 137, 149, 151; (*car*) bateria f 88
battle site campo m de batalha 99
be able, to poder/ser capaz de
be back, to voltar
be, to (*also ➤ am, are*) ser; (*temporary state*) estar, (*situated*) ficar
beach praia f 116
beard barba f
beautician instituto m de beleza
beautiful bonito(-a) 14; lindo(-a) 101; lindo(-a)/maravilhoso(-a)
because porque 15; ~ **of** por causa de 15
bed cama f 21; ~ **and breakfast** quarto e pequeno-almoço [pernoite e café da manhã] 24; **I'm going to** ~ vou para a cama
bedding roupa de cama 29
bedroom quarto m de dormir 29
bee abelha f
beer cerveja f 40, 49
before (*time*) antes de 13, 221
begin, to (*also ➤ start*) começar
beginner o/principiante m/f
beginning começo m
beige beige [bege] 143
belong: this belongs to me isto pertence-me
below 15°C abaixo de 15°C
belt cinto m 144
beneath por baixo de
berth beliche m 74, 77
best melhor
better melhor 14
between entre

bib babete [babador] m
bicycle (*also ➤ cycle*) bicicleta f 83; ~ **rental** aluguer [aluguel] m de bicicletas 83; ~ **parts** 82
bidet bidé m
big grande 14, 134
bigger maior 24
bikini bikini [biquini] m 144
bin liner saco m para o lixo
binoculars binóculo m
biscuits biscoitos mpl
bishop (*chess*) bispo m
bite (*insect*) picada f (de insecto)
bitten: I've been bitten by a dog fui mordido por um cão
bitter azedo(-a) 41
bizarre estranho(-a) 101
black preto 143
black and white film (*camera*) filme m a preto e branco 151
black coffee bica [cafezinho] f 40
blanket cobertor m 27
bleach lixívia f [alvejante m] 148
bleeding, to be estar a sangrar [sangrando] 92, 162
bless you bem haja [te abençoe]
blind (*window*) estore m 25
blocked, to be estar entupido(-a) 25; **the drain is** ~ o cano m (do esgoto) está entupido; **the road is** ~ a estrada f está bloqueada
blood group grupo m sanguíneo
blouse blusa f 144
blow-dry brushing [escova] m 147
blue azul 143
blush (*rouge*) rouge m
board, on bordo f
boarding (*plane*) a bordo
boarding pass cartão m de embarque
boat barco m 81; ~ **trip** passeio m de barco 81
boiled cozido 52
book livro m 150
book, to reservar
booked, to be não haver vagas/estar superlotado 115
booking reserva f
booking office bilheteira f

book of tickets bilhetes mpl 79; caderneta f de bilhetes

bookmaker agenciador m de apostas

bookstore livraria f 130

boots botas fpl 115, 145

border (country) fronteira f

boring aborrecido(-a) 101

born: I was born in nasci em

borrow: may I borrow …? posso pedir-lhe emprestado …?

botanical garden jardim m botânico 99

botany botânica f

bother: sorry for the bother desculpe a maçada [incomodar]

bottle garrafa f 37, 159; ~ **opener** abre-garrafas [abridor de garrafas] m 148

bottle of wine garrafa f de vinho 156

bow (ship) proa f

box of chocolates caixa f de chocolates 156

box office bilheteira f

boxing box m

boy rapaz m 120, 157

boyfriend namorado 120

bra soutien m 144

bracelet pulseira f 149

brake travão [freio] m 90

brass latão m

Brazil Brasil m 119

Brazilian (n) brasileiro(-a)

bread pão 38

break, to (trip) interromper

breakdown: we've broken down avariámos [quebramos] 28

break, to partir [quebrar] 28

break-in assalto m

breakage quebra f

breakdown a(s) avaria(s) f 88; **to have a ~** ter uma avaria [seu carro quebrou] 88

breakfast pequeno-almoço [café da manhã] m 26, 27

breathe, to respirar 92, 164

breathtaking espantoso(-a) 101

bridge ponte f 107; (cards) bridge m

briefcase pasta f

briefs calcinhas fpl 144

brilliant brilhante 101

bring, to trazer

Britain Grã-Bretanha f 119

British (noun/adj.) britânico(-a)

brochure folheto m

broken, to be estar partido(-a) 25, 137, 164

bronze (adj.) de bronze

brooch broche m 149

broom vassoura f

brother irmão 120

brown castanho 143

browse, to estar a ver [vendo] 133

brush escova f

bubble bath banho m de espuma

bucket (pail) balde m 157

buffet car vagão-restaurante m

build, to construir 104

building edifício m

built construído 104

bureau de change câmbio m 138

burger hambúrguer m 40; ~ **stand** casa f de hambúrgueres 35

burglary (also ➤ theft) roubo m

burnt, to be (food) estar queimado; **it's burned** está queimado

bus autocarro m 70, 78, 79; (long-distance) camioneta f 78; ~ **route** rota f dos autocarros; ~ **station** estação f de autocarros 78; de camionetas 78; ~ **stop** paragem [parada] f de autocarro 65, 96

business: on ~ em negócios 66; ~ **class** (em) navigator/business 68; ~ **trip** viagem f de negócios 123; ~**man** homem m de negócios; ~**woman** mulher f de negócios

busy, to be (occupied) estar ocupado(-a) 125

but mas 19

butane gas gás m butano 31

butcher shop talho [açouague] m 130

butter manteiga f 38, 160

button botão m

buy, to comprar 80

by (time) até 13; ~ **car** de carro 17, 94; ~ **credit card** com cartão de crédito 17

bye! adeusinho! [adeus!]

bypass desvio m

cabana barraca f
cabin cabina f [camarote m] 81
cable car funicular m
café café m 35, 40
cake bolo m 40; **cake shop** pastelaria [confeitaria] f
calendar calendário m 156
call: last call (*boarding*) última chamada
call, to chamar 92, 128; ligar 128; telefonar 127; **I'll ~ back;** eu telefono de volta; **~ for someone** ir buscar alguém 125; **I'll ~ round** dou uma saltada [um pulo]; **call collect, to** chamada f paga pelo destinatário [a cobrar] 127; **~ the police!** chame a polícia! 92, 224;
camcorder câmara f vídeo
camel hair pêlo m de camelo
camera máquina f fotográfica 151, 153; **~ case** estojo m para a máquina; **~ store** loja f de artigos fotográficos 130
campbed colchão m de campismo [camping]/cama f portátil 31
camping campismo [camping] 30; **~ equipment** material m de campismo [camping] 31
campsite parque m de campismo [camping] 30
can lata f 159; **~ opener** abre-latas [abridor de latas] m 148
can I? posso? 18
can I have? pode dar-me? 18
can you help me? pode ajudar-me? 18
can you recommend ...? pode recomendar-me ...? 97, ;112
Canada Canadá m 119
Canadian (*noun/adj.*) canadiano(-a) [canadense]
canal canal m
cancel, to cancelar 68
cancer (*disease*) cancro [câncer] m
candles velas fpl
candy rebuçados mpl [balas fpl] 150
canoe canoa f
canoeing fazer canoagem
canyon desfiladeiro m
cap touca f
capital city capital f

captain (*boat*) comandante m
car (*automobile*) carro m/automóvel m 86–9, 153; (*train compartment*) compartimento m 75; **by ~** de carro 95; **~ alarm** alarme m do carro; **~ ferry** ferry-boat [balsa] m 81, **~ park** parque m de estacionamento 26, 87; estacionamento m de automóveis 96; **~ pound** depósito m dos carros rebocados; **~ rental** aluguer [aluguel] m de carros 70, 86; **~ repairs** oficina f de reparações [mecânica]; **~ wash** lavagem f de carros
carafe jarro 37
cardphone credifone [cartão telefônico] m
cards as cartas 121
careful: be careful! tenha cuidado!
carousel carrossel m
carpet (*rug*) tapete m; (*fitted*) alcatifa f
carrier bag saco m
carry-cot porta-bebés [-nenês] m
carton pacote m 159
cartoon banda f desenhada [desenho m animado]
cash dinheiro m 136; **~ card** cartão m de multibanco [de caixa automática] 139; **~ desk** caixa f 132
cash, to cobrar 138
cashmere cachemira [casimira] f
casino casino m 112
cassette cassete f 157
castle castelo m 99
casualty deptartment (*hospital*) urgências fpl
cat gato(-a)
catch, to (*bus*) apanhar (o autocarro/o ônibus)
cathedral catedral f 99
cause, to causar 94
cave caverna f 107
CD CD m, disco m compacto
CD-player tocador m de discos compactos
cemetery cemitério 99
cent cêntimo m
central heating aquecimento m central
center of town centro m da cidade 21
ceramics cerâmica f
certificate certificado m 157, 168

certification contraste m 149
chain fio m para o pescoço 149
chair cadeira f
change *(coins)* trocado 87, 136; **keep the ~** guarde o troco 84; *(bus)* mudar 79; *(clothes)* trocar (de roupa) *(money)* trocar 136, 138; *(reservation)* mudar 68; *(trains)* mudar/fazer transbordo 75, 80; **~ lanes** mudar de faixa; **where can I ~ the baby?** onde é que posso mudar as fraldas do bebé [nenê]?
changing facilities sítio [lugar] onde se pode mudar fraldas
changing rooms vestiários mpl
channel *(sea)* canal m
chapel capela f
charcoal carvão m 31
charge tarifa f 30, 115
charter flight vôo m charter
cheap barato(-a) 14, 134
cheaper mais barato(-a) 21, 24 109, 134
check *(bill)* conta f; **put it on the check** ponha na conta
check, to verificar; **please check the …** por favor verifique …
checkbook [cheque book] livro [talão] m de cheques
check guarantee card cartão m de garantia
check in, to registar [fazer o check in] 68
check-in desk registo m 69
check out, to *(hotel)* pagar a conta
checked *(patterned)* xadrez
checkers *(draughts)* damas fpl
checkout *(supermarket)* caixa f
cheers! à sua saúde!
cheese queijo m 48, 160
chemical toilet fossa f séptica
chemist farmácia f 130, 140
chess xadrez m 121; **~ set** jogo m de xadrez 157
chewing gum pastilha f elástica [goma de mascar] 150
chickenpox varicela f
child criança f; menino(-a); filho m, filha f
child's seat cadeirinha f de criança 39; *(in car)* cadeira f de criança
childcarer [childminder] ama f

children crianças fpl 24, 39. 66, 74, 81, 100, 113; filhos(-as) mpl/fpl 120
children's meals refeições de crianças
chips batatas fpl fritas (às rodelas) 160
chocolate chocolate m; *(drink)* chocolate m quente 40; **~ bar** chocolate m 150; **chocolate ice cream [choc-ice]** gelado [sorvete] m de chocolate 110
chop *(meat)* costeleta f
christian *(noun/adj.)* cristão(-ã); **~ name** nome m próprio
church igreja f 96, 99, 105
cigarette machine máquina f de cigarros
cigarettes: pack of ~s maço m de cigarros mpl 150
cigars charutos mpl
cinema cinema m 96, 110
circle *(theater)* balcão m
city wall muralhas fpl da cidade 99
class *(travel)* classe f 68
clean *(adj.)* limpo(-a) 14, 39, 41
clean, to limpar 137
cleaned: I'd like my shoes cleaned queria os meus sapatos limpos
cleaner *(person)* empregado(-a) da limpeza; *(product)* produto m de limpeza
cleaning limpeza f; **~ utensils** utensílios mpl de limpeza
cleansing lotion loção f de limpeza
cleansing solution *(contact lenses)* líquido m de limpeza (para lentes)
cliff falésia m 107
cling film papel m aderente
cloakroom bengaleiro m, vestiário m 109
clock relógio m 149
close *(near)* perto
close, to fechar 100, 140
clothes roupa f 144; **~ dryer** centrifugador m; **~ line** corda f da roupa; **~ pins [pegs]** molas [prendedores] para a roupa 148
clothing store loja f de artigos de vestuário 130

A-Z

cloudy, to be estar nublado 122
clown palhaço m
clubs (golf) tacos mpl de golfe 115
coach (train compartment) compartimento m 75
coast costa f
coat casaco m (comprido) 144; ~check bengaleiro m, vestiário m 109; ~ hanger cabide m
cockroach barata f
code (area/dialing) indicativo [código] m 127
coffee café m 40
coil (contraceptive) dispositivo m intrauterino
coin moeda f
cola cola f 40
cold frio(-a) 14, 24, 41, 122; (flu) constipação f [resfriado m] 141
cold meats carnes fpl frias [frios] 160
collapse: he's collapsed ele desmaiou
collect, to vir buscar
college colégio m, faculdade f
color cor f 134, 143
color film filme m a cores 151
comb pente m 142
come back, to (return) voltar 36; vir buscar 140
comedy comédia f
comforter edredão m
commission comissão f 138
communion comunhão f
compact (camera) compacto(-a) 151
compact disc disco m compacto [CD] 157
company (business) companhia f; (companionship) 126
compartment (train) compartimento m
compass compasso m 31
complaint (hotel) reclamação f 41; to make a ~ fazer uma reclamação 137
computer computador m
concert concerto m 108, 111; ~ hall sala f de concertos 111
concession desconto m
concussion, to have a ter um traumatismo cerebral

conditioner (hair) amaciador [condicionador] m para o cabelo 142
condoms preservativos mpl
conductor (orchestra) o/maestro m/f 111
conference conferência f
confirm, to confirmar 22, 68
confirmation confirmação f
connection (transport) ligação f
conscious, to be consciente, estar
constipation prisão f de ventre
consulate consulado m
consultant (medical) o(-a) especialista
contact, to contactar 28
contain, to conter 69, 155
contraceptive contraceptivo m
convenient conveniente
convertible (car) descapotável [conversível] m
cook cozinheiro(-a)
cook, to cozinhar
cook book livro m de cozinha
cookies bolachas fpl 160
cooking (cuisine) cozinha f
coolbox geladeira f
copper cobre m 149
copy (photocopies) cópia f 155
corked (wine) sabe a rolha
corkscrew saca-rolhas m 148
corn plaster adesivo m para calos
corner esquina f 95
correct (also ▶ right) correcto(-a)
cosmetics cosméticos mpl
cot cama f de bebé [nenê] 22
cottage chalé m
cotton algodão m 145; ~ [wool] algodão m 141
cough tosse f 141; ~ syrup xarope m para a tosse
could I have ...? podia ter ...?
counter balcão m
country (nation) país m
country music música f country 111
countryside campo m
couple (pair) par m
courier (guide) guia m
course (meal) prato m
courthouse palácio m de justiça
cousin primo(-a) m/f

cover (*lid*) tampa f
cover charge entrada f
craft shop loja f de artigos regionais
crash: I've had a crash tive um desastre [acidente]
creaks, the bed a cama range
credit card cartão m de crédito 42, 136, 153; ~ number número m do cartão de crédito 109
credit status crédito m
credit, in com saldo positivo
crockery louça f 29, 148
cross (*crucifix*) crucifixo m
cross, to (*road*) atravessar 95
crossing (*boat*) travessia f
crossroad cruzamento m
crowded com muita gente
cruise cruzeiro
crutches canadianas f
crystal cristal m 149
cuisine cozinha f 119
cup chávena f 39, 148
cupboard armário m
curlers rolos mpl para o cabelo
currency moeda f 67, 138
currency exchange (office) bureau m de change / câmbio m 73
curtains cortinados [cortinas fpl] mpl
cushion almofada f
customs alfândega f 67; ~ declaration declaração f da alfândega 155
cut and blow-dry corte m e brushing [escova] 147
cut glass vidro m facetado 149
cycle helmet capacete m
cycle path via f para ciclistas
cycling ciclismo m 114
cyclist ciclista m/f

D daily diariamente
damage danos mpl
damaged, to be estar avariado 28; ser danificado(-a) 71
damp (*adj.*) húmido(-a)
dance (*performance*) dança f 111
dancing, to go ir dançar 124
dangerous perigoso
dark escuro(-a) 14, 24, 134, 143

daughter filha f 120
dawn madrugada f
day dia m 97; (*ticket*) para o dia
day trip excursão f de um dia
dead morto(-a); (*battery*) descarregado(-a) 88
dear (*formal greeting*) caro(-a); (*informal*) querido(-a)
decide: we haven't decided yet ainda não decidimos
deck (*ship*) convés m
deck chair uma cadeira f de encosto 116
declare, to declarar 67
deduct, to (*money*) deduzir
deep profundo(a)
deep-freeze congelador m
defrost, to descongelar
degrees (*temperature*) graus mpl
delay atraso m 70
delicatessen charcutaria f 130
delicious delicioso(-a) 14
deliver, to entregar
denim ganga f [brim m] 145
dental floss fio m dental
dentist dentista m 131, 168
deodorant desodorizante [desodorante] m 142
depart, to (*train, bus*) partir
department (*store*) secção f
department store grande armazém m [loja f de departamentos] 130
departure (*train*) partida f 76; ~ lounge sala f de embarque
depend: it depends on depende de
deposit sinal m 24, 83, 115; to pay a ~ deixar um sinal
describe, to descrever 152
design (*dress*) de marca
designer costureiro m
destination destino m
details pormenores mpl
detergent detergente m
develop, to (*photos*) revelar 151
diabetes diabetes m
diabetic, to be ser diabético(-a) 39
diamonds brilhantes mpl; (*cards*) ouros

A-Z

diapers fraldas fpl 142
diarrhea diarreia f 141
dice dados mpl
dictionary dicionário m 150
diesel gasóleo [diesel] m 87
diet, I'm on a estou a fazer dieta
different, something alguma coisa diferente
difficult difícil 14
digital digital
dine, to jantar m
dining car serviço m de restaurante 75, 77
dining room sala f de jantar 26
dinner jacket smoking m
dinner jantar m, almoço m; to have ~ jantar
direct directo(-a) 75
direct, to indicar
direct-dial telephone telefone m de ligação directa
direction direcção f; in the ~ of ... na direcção de
director (film) realizador m; (company) director m
directory (telephone) lista f telefónica
Directory Assistance Informações fpl 127
dirty sujo(-a) 14, 28
disabled (person) deficiente 22, 100
disco discoteca f 112
discount: can you offer me a discount? pode fazer-me um desconto?; is there a ~ for children? há desconto para crianças?
disgusting horroroso(-a)
dish (meal) prato m
dish cloth pano m da louça 148
dishes louça f 29, 148
dishwashing liquid/detergent detergente m para a louça 148
display case vitrina f 149
disposable (camera) descartável 151
distilled water água f destilada
district (city/town) bairro m
disturb, don't não incomodar
dive, to mergulhar 116
diversion desvio m
divorced, to be estar divorciado(-a) 120
do: things to do coisas para fazer 123

do you accept ...? aceita ...? 136
do you have ...? tem ...? 37
dock doca f
doctor médico m 131, 161, 165, 224
does anyone here speak English? há aqui alguém que fale inglês?
dog cão m
doll boneca f 157
dollar dólar m 67, 138
door porta
dosage dose f
double bed cama f de casal 21
double room quarto m duplo 21
down abaixo
downstairs em baixo 12
downtown area baixa f/centro m da cidade 99
dozen dúzia f 159
drain esgoto m
drama drama m
draught (wind) corrente f de ar
dress vestido m 144
drink (n) bebida f 70, 124, 125, 126
drinking water água m potável 30
drip: the faucet [tap] drips a torneira pinga
drive, to guiar/conduzir 93
driver condutor m
driver's license carta f de condução [carteira f de motorista] 93
drop off, to (someone) deixar 83, 113
drowning: someone is drowning está uma pessoa a afogar-se [se afogando]
drugstore farmácia f 130
drunk bêbedo(-a) [bêbado(-a)]
dry cleaner lavandaria [lavanderia] f de limpeza a seco 131
dry clothes, to secar roupa
dry cut corte a seco
dry-clean, to limpar a seco
dual freeway [carriageway] via f rápida
due, to be (payment) ser devido
dummy (pacifier) chupeta f
during durante
dustbin lixeira f 30
dusty poeirento(-a)
duty: to pay duty pagar direitos (alfandegários) 67

duty-free goods artigos mpl isentos de taxas

duty-free store 'duty-free-shop' m

duty-free shopping compras fpl duty-free 67

 E each: how much each? quanto é cada?

ear drops gotas fpl para os ouvidos

earlier mais cedo 147

early cedo 13

earrings brincos mpl 149

east leste m 95

easy fácil 14

eat, to comer 41; **places to eat** sítios [lugares] para comer

eaten: have you eaten? já comeu?; **we've already eaten** já comemos

economical económico(-a)

economy class (em) classe económica 68

eggs ovos mpl 160

either ... or ou ... ou

elastic *(adj.)* elástico(-a)

electric blanket cobertor m eléctrico

electric fire radiador m

electric meter contador m da electricidade 28

electric shaver máquina f de barbear

electrical items artigos m eléctricos

electrical store loja f de artigos eléctricos

electrician electricista m

electricity electricidade f

electronic game jogo m electrónico 157

elevator elevador m 26, 132

else, something outra coisa

embark, to *(boat)* embarcar

embarkation point cais m de embarque

embassy embaixada f

emerald esmeralda f

emergency emergência f 127; **it's an ~** é uma emergência; **~ exit** saída f de emergência; **~ room** *(hospital)* urgências fpl

empty vazio(-a) 14

enamel esmalte m

end, to acabar/terminar

end: at the end ao fim de

engaged, to be estar noivo(-a) 120

engine motor m

engineer mecânico(-a)

England Inglaterra f 119

English inglês m/inglesa f 11, 110, 150

English-speaking que fale inglês 152

enjoy, to apreciar 110; gostar de 124, 125

enlarge, to *(photos)* ampliar 151

enough bastante 15; que chegue 136

enquiry desk balcão m de informações

ensuite bathroom casa f de banho privativa [banheiros mpl privativos]

entertainment: what entertainment is there? que espectáculos é que há?; **~ guide** guia m de espectáculos

entirely completamente

entrance fee bilhete m de entrada/entrada 100

entry visa visto m de entrada

envelopes envelopes mpl 150

epileptic epiléptico

equally em partes iguais

equipment *(sports)* equipamento m 115

error erro m

escalator escada f rolante 132

essential essencial 89

estate car carrinha f [minivan m]

EU (European Union) UE f (União Europeia)

euro euro m 139

Eurocheck Eurocheque m

Europe Europa f

evening dress traje m de noite 112

events espectáculos mpl 108

every day todos os dias

every week todas as semanas 13

example, for por exemplo

except excepto

excess baggage excesso m de bagagem 69

exchange rate câmbio m 138

exchange, to trocar 138

excluding meals sem refeições

excursion excursão f 97

excuse me *(apology)* desculpe 10; *(attention)* desculpe/se faz favor/com licença 10, 94

exhausted, to be estar exausto(-a) 106

A-Z

exhibition exposição f
exit saída f 70; **at the ~** à saída f
expected, to be ser necessário
expensive caro(-a) 14, 134
expire: when does it expire? quando é que caduca?
expiration date validade 109
exposure (*photos*) fotografias fpl 151
extra (*additional*) mais/extra 23
extremely extremamente 17
eyeliner lápis m para os olhos
eyeshadow sombra f para os olhos

F **fabric** (*material*) tecido m
facial limpeza de pele 147
facilities serviço(s) 22, 30
facilities (*food*) instalações fpl
factor ... (*sunscreen*) factor ... m
fairground parque m de diversões/feira 113
fall: he's had a fall ele deu uma queda
family família f 66, 74, 120
famous famoso(-a)
fan (*electric*) ventoinha f, [ventilador m] 25
fan: I'm a fan of ... sou um(a) fã de ...
far longe; **how ~ is it?** fica longe?; **is it ~?** é longe?
farce farsa f
fare bilhete m
farm quinta f 107
fashionable, to be estar à moda
fast depressa 93; **you were driving too ~** estava a guiar [guiando] depressa demais
fast food refeições mpl rápidas; **~ restaurant** restaurante m de comidas rápidas [cadeia de fast food] 35
fat (*noun*) gordura f; (*adj*) gordo (-a)
father pai m 120
faucet torneira f 25
fault: it's my/your fault é minha/sua culpa
faulty com defeito; **to be ~** ter defeito
favorite preferido(-a)
fax fax m 155
feed, to alimentar/dar de comer

feeding bottle biberão m [mamadeira f]
feel sick, to sentir-se mal
female mulher f 152
fence cerca f
ferry ferry-boat m [balsa f] 81
festival festival m
few poucos(-as) 15
fiancé(e) noivo(-a) m/f
field campo m 107
fight (*brawl*) briga f
fill out, to (*form*) preencher 155
filling (*sandwich*) recheio m
film (*camera*) filme m 151
film speed sensibilidade f
filter filtro m 151; **~ paper** (*coffee*) filtro m de papel
filter-tipped com ponta de filtro
find out: could you find that out? pode descobrir isso?
fine (*penalty*) multa f 93; (*well*) bem/óptimo(-a) 118
fire: there's a fire! há fogo!
fire alarm alarme m de incêndio
fire department [**brigade**] bombeiros mpl 92
fire escape saída f de incêndio
fire extinguisher extintor m de incêndio
firelighters acendedores mpl 31
fireplace lareira f
first o/primeiro(-a) 68, 75, 81; **I was ~** cheguei primeiro
first class (**em**) primeira classe 68, 74
first floor rés-do-chão m
first-aid kit estojo m de primeiros socorros
fish counter banca f do peixe 158
fish store peixaria f 130
fishing, to go ir pescar
fishing rod cana [vara] f de pesca
fit, to (*clothes*) servir 146
fitting room gabinete m de provas 146
fix, to: can you fix it? pode arranjar isso?
flag bandeira f
flannel (*face*) toalha f de rosto; (*material*) flanela f
flash (*photography*) flash m 151
flashlight lanterna f 31
flat (*tire*) furo m 83, 88

flavor: what flavors do you have? que sabores é que tem?

flea pulga f [brechó m]

flea market feira f

flight voo [vôo] m 70; ~ attendant comissário m/hospedeira f de bordo [aeromoça]; ~ number número m do voo 68

flip-flops chinelos mpl [sandálias fpl] de borracha, [havaianas fpl] 145

flippers (swimming) barbatanas [nadadeiras fpl] fpl

flood inundação f

floor (level) andar m 132

floor mop esfregão f

floor show espectáculo m

florist florista f 130

flour farinha f

flower flor f 106

fluent: to speak fluent Portuguese falar um português fluente

flush: the toilet won't flush retrete f não faz descarga

fly (insect) mosca f

fly, to voar

foggy, to be haver nevoeiro 122

folding chair/table cadeira f/mesa f portátil

folk art arte f popular

folk music música f popular 111

follow, to seguir; (pursue) ir atrás de

food alimentos mpl 39; comida f 41

football futebol m 114

footpath caminho m para peões [pedestres] 107

for a day para um dia 86

for a week para uma semana 86

forecast previsão f 122

foreign estrangeiro(-a); ~ currency divisas fpl estrangeiras 138

forest floresta f 107

forget, to esquecer 42

fork garfo m 39, 41, 148; (in road) bifurcação f

form impresso m 23, 153, 168

formal dress traje m de rigor 111

fortnight quinze dias

fortunately felizmente 19

forward: please forward my mail por favor remeta o meu correio

forwarding address morada f [endereço m] (de envio)

foundation (make-up) base f

fountain fonte f

four-door car carro m de quatro portas 86

four-wheel drive tracção f às 4 rodas 86

foyer (hotel/theater) átrio m / foyer m

frame (glasses) armação f

free (available, not busy) livre 36, 124; (no charge) grátis

French (language) francês m

frequent: how frequent? qual é a frequência?

frequently muitas vezes

fresh fresco(-a) 41

fried frito

friendly simpático

fries batatas fpl fritas 38, 40

frightened, to be estar assustado(-a)

fringe franja f

from de 12; from ... to das ... às 13

front door porta f (principal) 26; ~ key chave f da porta (da frente)

frozen congelado

fruit juice sumo [suco] m de fruta 40

fruiterer frutaria f

fuel (gasoline/petrol) combustível m 86

full cheio(-a) 14

full board (American Plan [A.P.]) pensão completa 24

full insurance seguro m contra todos os riscos 86

fun, to have divertir-se

funny (amuzing) divertido; (odd) estranho

furniture mobília f

fuse fusível 28; ~ box quadro m da electricidade 28; ~ wire fio m do fusível

G gallon galão m

gambling jogo m

game (toy) jogo m 157

garage garagem [oficina] f 88

A-Z

garbage bags sacos mpl para o lixo 148
garden jardim m
gardener jardineiro m
gardening jardinagem f
gas (gasoline) f 87, 88 ~ can lata f
gas: I smell gas! gás: cheira a gás!
gas bottle botija f [botijão m] de gás 28
gasoline gasolina f 87
gate (airport) porta f/gate f 70
gay club clube m gay 112
generous: that's very generous isso é muito generoso
genuine autêntico 134
geology geologia
get, to (find) apanhar 84
get by: may I get by? posso passar?
get out, to (vehicle) sair
gift presente m, oferta f 67, 156
girl menina f 120
girlfriend namorada f 120
give, to dar
give way, to (on the road) dar prioridade 93
glass copo m 39, 148
gliding vôo m planado
gloomy lúgubre
glove luva f
go ir; let's ~! vamos!; where does this bus ~? para onde vai este autocarro?
go away! vá-se embora!
go back, to (turn around) voltar atrás/virar para trás
go for a walk, to ir passear (a pé) 124
go out, to (in evening) sair
go shopping, to ir às compras 124
goggles óculos mpl de protecção
gold ouro m 149; ~ plate em dourado 149
golf golfe m 114; ~ course campo m de golfe 115
good bom (boa) 14, 35, 42; ~ afternoon boa tarde 10; ~ evening boa tarde 10; ~ morning bom dia 10; ~ night boa noite 10
good value, to be valer a pena 101
good-bye adeus 10

gorge desfiladeiro m
grade (fuel) grau m/tipo m
grammar gramática f
gram grama m 159
grandparents os avós mpl
grapes uvas fpl 160
grass relva [grama] f
gratuity gratificação f
gray cinzento(-a) 143
greasy (hair) oleoso(-a)
great fun divertido(-a) 101
green verde 143
greengrocer frutaria f
grilled grelhado
grocery store mercearia f 130
ground (camping) terreno 31
groundsheet plástico m de estender no chão 31
group grupo m 66, 100
guarantee garantia f 135
guide (person) guia m/f 98
guidebook guia m 150
guided tour visita f guiada 100
guitar guitarra f
guy rope (tent) corda f de firmar (de tenda) [de barraca] 31

H hair cabelo m 147; ~ brush escova f de cabelo; ~ dryer secador m de cabelo; ~ gel geleia f para o cabelo; ~ mousse mousse f para o cabelo; ~ clip clipe m; ~ spray laca f para o cabelo 142
haircut corte m de cabelo 147
hairdresser (ladies/men) cabeleireiro m (senhoras/homens) 131, 147
half board (Modified American Plan [M.A.P.]) meia-pensão 24
half fare meio-bilhete m
hammer martelo m 31
hand cream creme m para as mãos
hand luggage bagagem de mão 69
hand towel toalha f de mãos
hand washable para lavar à mão
handbag mala f de mão 144, 153
handicap (golf) handicap m
handicrafts artesanato
handkerchief lenço m
handle pega f

182

hanger cabide 27
hangover ressaca f 141
happen: what happened? o que aconteceu?
harbor porto m 99
hard shoulder (road) berma f [acostamento m]
hardware store loja f de ferragens 130
hat chapéu m 144
have, to ter; **do you ~ any ...?** tem ...?
haversack mochila f (de campismo [camping])
hayfever febre f dos fenos [rinite f alérgica]
headband bandelette f [faixa f para o cabelo]
heading, to be (in a direction) ir (a caminho de) 83
health food store loja f de produtos dietéticos 130
hear, to ouvir
hearing aid aparelho m de ouvir
hearts (cards) copas
heater aquecedor m 25
heating aquecimento m 25
heavy pesado(-a) 14, 134
height altura f
helicopter helicóptero m
hello olá
help ajuda f 94
help, to ajudar 18; **can you ~ me?** pode ajudar-me? 92
helper vigilante m/f 113
hemorrhoids hemorróides [hemorróidas] mpl
her ela/sua/dela 16
here aqui 12,17
hers sua/dela 16; **it's ~** é dela
high altura f/altitude f
high tide maré f alta
highlight, to fazer mechas 147
highway auto-estrada f 94
hike (walk) passeio m a pé 106
hiking fazer longas caminhadas a pé
hill colina f 107
him ele 16
hire, for para alugar
his seu/dele 16; **it's ~** é dele
history história f

hitchhike, to pedir boleia [carona]
hitchhiking à boleia [carona] 83
HIV-positive HIV positivo
hobby (pastime) passatempo m 121
hold, to (contain) conter
hole (in clothes) buraco m
holiday resort estância f de férias
home: casa f; **to go ~** ir para casa
homosexual (adj.) homosexual
honeymoon, to be on estar em lua-de-mel
horse cavalo m
horseracing corrida f de cavalos 114
hospital hospital m 131
hot quente 24; (weather) 122
hot chocolate chocolate m quente 40
hot dog cachorro m 110
hot spring nascente f de água quente
hot water água f quente 25; **~ bottle** botija [garrafa] f de água quente
hotel hotel m 21; **~ reservation** reservas fpl de hotel 21
hour hora f 97; **in an ~** daqui a uma hora 84
house casa f
household articles artigos para a casa mpl 148
housewife dona f de casa 121
how? como? 17
how are you? como está? 118
how far? a que distância? 94, 106
how long? quanto tempo? 23, 75, 76, 78, 88, 94, 98, 135
how many? quantos(-as)? 15, 80
how much? quanto? 15, 21, 84, 109
how often? quantas vezes 140
how old? que idade?
however contudo
hungry, to be fome, ter
hurry, to be in a estar com pressa
hurt, to be estar ferido(-a) 92
husband marido m 120
hypermarket hipermercado m

 I'd like ... queria ... 18, 36, 37, 40

I'd like to reserve ... queria reservar ... 74
I'll have ... quero ...
I've lost ... perdi ...
ice gelo m 38
ice cream gelado m 40, sorvete m; **~ parlor** gelataria [sorveteria] f 35; **~ cone** cone m de gelado [sorvete]
ice pack pacote m de gelo; ice pack
ice rink rinque m de patinagem [patinação] no gelo
ice hockey hóquei m no gelo
icy, to be estar gelado 122
identification identificação f 136
ill, to be estar doente 152
illegal, to be ser ilegal
illness doença f
imitation de imitação 134
immediately imediatamente 13
impressive impressionante
in (place) em 12; (time) em 13
included: is ... included? ... está incluído(-a)? 86, 98
inconvenient, it's é inconveniente
indicate, to fazer sinal
indoor dentro de casa; **~ pool** piscina f coberta 116
inexpensive barato(-a) 35
inflammation inflamação f
informal (dress) de passeio
information informação f 97; **~ desk/office** 73, 96
injured, to be estar ferido(-a) 92
innocent inocente
insect insecto m 25; **~ bite** picada f de insecto 141; **~ repellent** repelente m de insectos 141
inside dentro de
inside lane faixa f da direita
insist: I insist insisto
insomnia insónia f
instant coffee café m instantâneo 160
instead of em vez de
instructions instruções fpl 135
instructor instrutor m
insulin insulina f

insurance seguro m 86, 89, 93; **~ certificate** apólice f de seguro 93; **~ claim** reclamação f ao seguro 153; **~ company** companhia f de seguros 93
interest (hobby) passatempo m 121
interest rate taxa f de juros
interesting interessante 101
international internacional
International Student Card Cartão m Internacional de Estudante 29
interpreter tradutor(a) 93; intérprete m/f 153
intersection cruzamento m
interval intervalo m
into para
invitation convite m 124
invite, to convidar 124
Ireland Irlanda f 119
Irish (adj.) irlandês m, irlandesa f
iron (clothing) ferro m de engomar
iron, to engomar, passar a ferro
is there ...? há ...?
is this seat taken? este lugar está ocupado? 77
island ilha f
it is ... é/está ... 17
Italian cuisine cozinha f italiana
itch: it itches faz comichão
itemized bill conta f detalhada 32, 42

J **jack** (cards) valete m
jacket casaco m(curto) 144
jam doce m
jammed, to be estar empenado(-a) 25
jar frasco m 159
jeans jeans mpl 144
jellyfish alforreca [agua viva] f
jet lag: I have ~ estou com decalagem horária
jewelry store/jeweler joalharia f 131, 149
Jewish (adj.) judeu (judia)
job: what's your job? qual é o seu emprego
jogging pants calças fpl de jogging
jogging, to go ir fazer jogging
join: may we join you podemos ir com vocês? 124
joint (meat) peça f (de carne)
joint passport passaporte m em conjunto 66

joke piada f
joker *(cards)* joker m, diabo m
journalist jornalista m/f
journey viagem f 123
judo judo m
jug *(water)* jarro m
jumper camisola f [suéter m]
jumper cables [jump leads] cabos mpl
da bateria
junction *(intersection)* cruzamento m

K kaolin caolina f
keep: keep the change
guarde o troco
kerosene querosene m
ketchup ketchup m
kettle chaleira f
key chave f 27, 71, 88;
~ ring argola f para chaves 156
kiddie pool piscina f de bebés
[nenês] 113
kilo(gram) quilo m 159
kilometer quilómetro m
kind *(pleasant)* amável
kind: what kind of ...? que espécie
de ...?
king *(cards, chess)* rei m
kiosk quiosque m
kiss, to beijar 126
kitchen cozinha f 29; ~ paper towels
papel m da cozinha
knapsack mochila f 31, 145
knickers calcinhas fpl
knife faca f 39, 148
know: I don't know não sei

L label etiqueta f
lace renda f
ladder escada f de mão
ladies room *(toilet)* toalete m das senhoras
lake lago m 107
lamp candeeiro m [luminária f] 25;
lampdina f
land, to aterrar 70
landlord/landlady senhorio(-a)
[locador(-a)] m/f
lane faixa f, via f
large grande 40, 110
last último(-a) 14, 68, 75, 80, 81

last, to *(time)* durar
late tarde 14; *(delayed)*
atrasado(-a) 70
later mais tarde 125, 147
laugh, to rir 126
laundromat lavandaria
[lavanderia] f 131
laundry service serviço de lavandaria
[lavanderia] 22
lavatory casa f de banho
[banheiros mpl]
lawn relvado [gramado] m
lawyer advogado m 152
laxative laxante m
lead, to *(road)* ir 94
lead-free *(petrol/gas)* sem chumbo 87
leaflet folheto m 97
leak, to *(roof/pipe)* pingar; *(car)* perder
learn, to *(language/sport)* aprender
leather cabedal [couro] m 145
leave from, to *(transport)* partir/sair 78
leave me alone! deixe-me em paz! 126
leave, to partir 68, 70, 76, 81, 98; *(drop
off)* deixar 86; *(place)* ir embora 126
lecturer conferente m
left, on the à esquerda 76, 95
left-hand side lado m esquerdo
left-handed canhoto
left-luggage office *(baggage check)*
depósito m de bagagem 71, 73
legal, to be legal, ser
leggings perneiras fpl 144
lemon limão 38
lemonade limonada f 40
lend: could you lend me ...? podia-me
emprestar ...?
length (of) comprimento m (de)
lens objectiva f 151; ~ cap tampa f para
a objectiva 151
lesbian club clube m de lesbianas
[lésbicas]
less menos 15
lesson lição
letter carta f 154
letterbox caixa f do correio
level *(flat)* nivelado 31
library biblioteca f 99, 131
license plate number matrícula [placa] f
23, 88, 93

lie down, to deitar-se
lifeboat barco m salva-vidas
lifeguard banheiro m/salva-vidas m 116
life jacket colete m salva-vidas
life preserver [belt] cinto m salva-vidas [segurança] 81
lift (hitchhiking) boleia 83
light (shade) claro(-a) 14, 134, 143; (weight) 14, 134
light (bicycle) luz f 83; (cigarette) lume [fogo] m 126; (electric) luz f 25
lightbulb lâmpada f (eléctrica) 25, 148
lighter isqueiro m 150
lightning relâmpago m
like this (similar to) como isto
like: I'd like queria
line (queue) fila f; **to wait in line** estar na fila 112
line (subway [metro]) linha f 80
line (profession) profissão f
line: an outside ~ (telephone) ligue-me à rede
linen linho m 145
lipsalve bâton m para o cieiro
lipstick bâton m
liqueur licor m
liquor store loja f de vinhos 131
liter litro m 87, 159
little pouco
live, to viver; **~ together** viver juntos 120
living room sala f de estar 29
loaf of bread pão m 160
lobby (theater/hotel) foyer m/átrio m
local regional 35, 37
lock fechadura f 25; (canal) comporta f
locked, to be fechar (à chave) 26; **it's locked** está fechado à chave
locker cacifo m com fecho
lollipop chupa-chupa [pirulito] m
London Londres
long (clothing) comprido(-a) 146; (time) muito
long-distance bus autocarro m de longo curso 78
long-distance call chamada f de longa distância

look, to: I'm just looking estou só a ver [vendo]
look, to have a (check) dar uma vista de olhos [dar uma olhada]
look after: please look after my case for a minute por favor tome conta da minha mala por um minuto
look for, to procurar 18
look forward: I'm looking forward to it estou ansioso(-a) por
look like: what does your luggage look like? como é a sua bagagem? 71
loose (clothing) largo(-a) 146
lose, to perder 28, 153; **I've lost ...** perdi ... 71
loss perdas 71
lost, to be estar perdido
lost-and-found [lost property office] perdidos mpl e achados
lotion loção f
lots muitos
loud, it's too está demasiado [muito] alto
louder mais alto 128
love: I love Portuguese food adoro a comida portuguesa; **I love you** amo-te [eu te amo]
low-fat magro
lower (berth) inferior 74
lubricant lubrificante m
luggage bagagem f 67, 69, 71
luggage allowance peso m permitido
luggage carts [trolleys] carrinhos mpl 71
luggage locker cacifo m de bagagem 71, 73
luggage tag etiqueta f de bagagem
luggage ticket talão m de bagagem 71
lumpy (mattress) aos altos e baixos
lunch almoço m 98
luxury luxo m

M madam senhora f
magazine revista f 150
magician mágico m
magnetic north norte m magnético
magnificent magnífico(-a) 101
maid empregado(-a) m/f da limpeza
maiden name nome m de solteira
mail (post) correio m 27, 155

mailbox caixa f do correio 154
main principal 130; **~ course** prato m principal, **~ street** rua f principal 95
mains *(electricity)* rede f
main street rua f principal 96
make *(brand)* marca f
make-up maquilhagem [maquiagem] f
make: to make tea/coffee fazer chá/café
male homem m 152
mallet maço m
man homem m
manager gerente m/f 25, 41, 137
manicure manicure f 147
manual *(gears)* manual m de instruções
many muitos(-as) 15
map mapa m 94, 106, 150
margarine margarina f 160
market mercado m 99, 131
market day dia m de mercado
married, to be ser casado(-a) 120
mascara rímel m
mask *(diving)* máscara f (de mergulho)
mass missa f 105
massage massagem f 147
match *(game)* jogo m 114
matches *(box)* fósforos mpl 31, 148, 150
material material m
matinée matinée f 109
matter: it doesn't ~ não importa; **what's the ~?** qual é o problema?
mattress colchão m 31
may I …? posso …? 37
maybe talvez
me mim 16
meal refeição f 38, 42, 125
mean, to significar 11
measure, to medir 146
measurement tamanho m
meat carne f 41
medicine remédio m
medium *(regular size)* médio(-a) 40; *(steak)* meio-passado
meet, to encontrar(-se) 125; **pleased to meet you** muito prazer 118
meeting place ponto m de encontro
member *(club)* membro m/sócio m 112, 115
men *(toilets)* toaletes dos homens

mend, to consertar 137
mention: don't ~ it não tem de quê 10
menu menu m
message mensagem 27, 128
metal metal m
meter *(taxi)* taxímetro m
methylated spirits álcool m (desnaturado) 31
metro *(subway)* metro 80; **~ station** estação f de metro 80, 96
Mexico México f
mezzanine *(theater)* balcão m
microwave *(oven)* microondas m
midday meio-dia m
migraine enxaqueca f
mileage quilometragem f 86
milk leite m 160
milk of magnesia leite m de magnésia
mince carne f picada
mind: do you mind? importa-se? 77, 126
mine meu/minha 16; **it's ~** é meu/minha
mineral water água f mineral 40
minibar mini-bar m [frigobar] 32
minibus autocarro [micro ônibus] m
minimum *(n)* mínimo m
minister pastor m
minivan carrinha f [minivan m]
minute minuto m 76
mirror espelho m
Miss Menina [Senhorita] f
miss, to perder; **have I missed the bus to …?** perdi o autocarro [ônibus] para …?
missing, to be faltar; *(person)* desaparecer 152
mistake engano m 41, 42
misunderstanding, there's a houve um mal-entendido
mobile home casa f ambulante; mobile home
modern moderno(-a) 14
modern art arte f moderna
moisturizer *(cream)* creme m hidratante
moisturizing cream creme m hidratante
monastery mosteiro m 99
money dinheiro m 42, 139, 153
money order vale m postal

money belt cinto m porta-moedas
monthly *(ticket)* mensal 79
monument monumento m
mooring ancoradouro m
moped acelera f/ lambreta 83
more mais 15, 67; **I'd like some ~** queria mais
moslem *(adj.)* muçulmano(-a)
mosquito mosquito m; **~ bite** picada f de mosquito
mother mãe f 120
motion sickness enjoo m 141
motorbike motocicleta f 83; **~ parts** 82
motorboat um barco m a motor 116
motorway *(highway)* auto-estrada f 94
mountain montanha f 107; **~ bike** bicicleta f de montanha; **~ pass** desfiladeiro m 107; **~ range** cordilheira f 107
mountaineering montanhismo m
mousetrap ratoeira f
moustache bigode m
mouth ulcer afta f
move, to mudar(-se) 25
movie filme m 108, 110
movie theater cinema m
Mozambique Moçambique 119
Mr. sr. m
Mrs. senhora f
much muito 15
mug *(drinking)* caneca f
mugged, to be ser assaltado 153
mugging assalto m 152
mumps papeira [caxumba] f
museum museu 99
music música f 111
music box caixa f de música
musical *(entertainment)* comédia f musical 108
musician músico m
Muslim *(person)* muçulmano(-a)
must: I must eu devo
mustard mostarda f 38, 160
my meu/minha 16
myself: I'll do it ~ faço isso eu mesmo

 nail *(body)* unha f; **~ polish** verniz [esmalte] m de unhas; **~ scissors** tesoura f de unhas
name nome m 22, 36, 93, 118, 120; **my ~ is** chamo-me [meu nome é …] 118; **what's your ~?** como se chama? 118
napkin guardanapo m 39
narrow estreito(-a) 14
national nacional
nationality nacionalidade f
natural history ciências fpl naturais
nature reserve reserva f natural 107
nausea náusea f
navy blue azul marinho
nearby perto(-a) 21
nearest mais próximo(-a) 80, 88, 92, 130
necessary necessário(-a) 89
neck *(clothing)* gola f
necklace colar m 149
need: I need to … precisar de … 18
needle agulha f
neighbor vizinho(-a)
nephew sobrinho m
never nunca 13
never mind não tem importância 10
new novo(-a) 14
New Zealand Nova Zelândia f
newsagent *(newsdealer)* vendedor m de jornais 150
newspaper jornal m 150
newsstand [newsagent] quiosque m [banca f] de jornais 131
next próximo(-a) 14, 68, 75, 78, 80, 81, 87
next stop! na próxima paragem! [parada] 79
next to ao lado de; a seguir a 95
niece sobrinha f
night, per por noite
night porter porteiro m
nightclub nightclub m 112
nightdress camisa f de noite
no não 10
no one ninguém 16, 92
noisy barulhento(-a) 14
non-alcoholic não-alcoólica
non-smoking *(adj.)* não-fumadores [não-fumantes] 36, 69
none nenhum(a) 15

normal normal 67
north norte m 95
Northern Ireland Irlanda f do Norte
not that one esse(-a) não 16
not yet ainda não 13
note nota f
notebook caderno m
nothing to declare nada a declarar
nothing else mais nada 15
nothing for me nada para mim
notice board quadro m de avisos
now agora 13, 84
nudist beach praia f de nudismo
number *(telephone)* número m de
telefone 84; **sorry, wrong ~** desculpe, é
engano no número
number plate *(car)* placa f de matrícula
nurse enfermeiro(-a)
nut *(bolt)* porca f
nylon nylon m

O **observatory** observatório m
occupied ocupado(-a) 14
of de
of course com certeza 19
off-licence loja f de vinhos 131
off-peak estação baixa
office escritório m
often muitas vezes 13
oil óleo m
oily *(hair)* oleoso(-a)
okay O.K. 10
old velho(-a) 14
old town parte f velha da cidade
old-fashioned antigo(-a) 14
olive oil azeite m
omelet omeleta f
on, to be *(showing at cinema)* estar em cena
on: ~ board *(transport)* a bordo 74;
~ foot a pé 17, 95; **~ the left** à esquerda
12; **~ the other side (of)** do outro lado
(de) 95; **~ the right** à direita 12; **~ the
spot** no local
once a week uma vez por semana 13
one um(a) 216
one-way ticket bilhete m de ida 68, 74, 79
open, to abrir 132, 140

open aberto(-a) 14;
~ to the public aberto(-a)
ao público 100; **~ to
traffic** aberto(-a) ao
trânsito
open-air pool piscina f ao
ar livre 116
opening hours horas fpl de
funcionamento 100
opera ópera f 108, 111; **~ house** teatro
m de ópera 99, 111
operation operação f
operator telefonista f
opposite em frente de 12
optician oculista m 131
or ou 19
orange *(fruit)* laranja f 160;
(color) cor-de-laranja 143
orchestra orquestra f 111; *(theater)* plateia f
order, to encomendar 37, 41, 89, 135;
(call) chamar 32
organized walk/hike passeio a pé
organizado 106
ornithology ornitologia f
others outros(-as)
our(s) nosso(-a) 16
out: he's *(not here)* ele não está
outdoor ao ar livre; **~ pool** piscina f ao
ar livre 116
outside fora de; lá fora 36
outside lane faixa f da esquerda
oval oval 134
oven forno m
over para/do outro lado
over there ali 76
overcharged, I've been levaram-me
dinheiro a mais
overdone *(adj.)* cozido(-a) demais 41
overheat aquecer demais
overnight só uma noite 23
owe: how much do I ~ you? quanto
lhe devo?
own: on my ~ sozinho(-a)

P **p.m.** da tarde/da noite
pacifier chupeta f
pack of cards baralho m de
cartas
pack, to fazer as malas 69
package embrulho m [pacote m] 155

A-Z

packed lunch farnel m
pack [packet] pacote m
paddling pool piscina f de bebés [nenês] 113
padlock cadeado m
pain killers analgésico m 141
paint, to pintar
painted pintado 104
painter o/pintor(a)
painting quadro m
pajamas pijama m
palace palácio m 99
panty hose collant m 144
paper papel m
paper napkins guardanapos mpl de papel 148
paraffin parafina f 31
parcel embrulho m [pacote m] 155
pardon? como?
parents pais mpl 120
park parque m 96, 99, 107
park, to estacionar
parking estacionamento m 87; ~ **lot** parque m de estacionamento 26, 87; estacionamento m de automóveis 96; ~ **meter** parquímetro m 87; ~ **space** parque/lugar m de estacionamento; ~ **token/disk** bilhete m/ticket m de estacionamento
partner (boyfriend/girlfriend) companheiro m/companheira f
parts (car components) peças fpl 89
party (social) festa f 124; (group) grupo m
pass carreiro m/atalho m
pass, to passar 77; ~ **through** estar de passagem 66
passenger passageiro (-a)
passport passaporte m 66, 69, 153; ~ **control** controle m de passaportes 66
pastry shop pastelaria [confeitaria] f
patch, to remendar
path caminho m
pavement, on the no passeio
pay, to pagar 42, 87, 136; ~ **a fine** pagar uma multa 93; ~ **by credit card** pagar com cartão de crédito
pay phone telefone m público

payment pagamento m 32
peak pico m 107
pearl pérola f
pebbly (beach) de seixos 116
pedestrian crossing passagem f de peões [pedestres] 96
pedestrian zone [precinct] zona f de peões [pedestres] 96
pedicure pedicure f
pen caneta f 150
pencil lápis m
penicillin penicilina f
penknife canivete m
penpal correspondente m/f
people pessoas fpl 92
people carrier (minivan) carrinha f [minivan m]
pepper pimenta f 38
per: ~ day por dia 30, 83, 86, 87, 115; ~ **hour** por hora 87, 115; ~ **night** por noite 21; ~ **week** por semana 83, 86
performance sessão f
perhaps talvez 19
period período m
perm (hair) permanente f
perm, to fazer uma permanente 147
permit permissão f
personal stereo Walkman ® m
pet (animal) animal m de estimação
pewter peltre m
pharmacy farmácia f 140, 158
phone telefone m; ~ **call** telefonema m 152; ~ **card** credifone m [cartão m telefónico] 127, 155
photo fotografia f; **passport-sized ~** fotografia de passe [de passaporte] 115; **to take a ~** tirar uma fotografia
photocopier fotocopiadora f 155
photographer fotógrafo m
photography fotografia f 151
phrase frase f 11; ~ **book** livro m de frases 11
piano piano m
pick up, to ir buscar 28, 113; (collect) levantar 109
pickup truck camioneta f de caixa aberta
picnic piquenique m; ~ **area** área f para piqueniques 107
piece peça f 69

pill, on the *(contraceptive)* estar a tomar [tomando] a pílula
pillow almofada f 27; **~ case** fronha f
pilot light piloto m
pink cor-de-rosa 143
pint meio-litro m
pipe cachimbo m
pitch *(camping)* lote m; **~ charge** preço m do lote
pity: it's a pity é uma pena
pizzeria pizzaria f 35
place lugar m
place a bet, to fazer uma aposta
plain *(not patterned)* liso(-a)
plane avião m 68
plans planos mpl 124
plant planta f
plastic bag saco m de plástico
plastic wrap papel m aderente
plate prato m 39, 148
platform linha [plataforma] f 73, 76
platinum platina f 149
play, to *(sport)* jogar 121; *(drama)* estar em cena 110; *(instrument)* tocar
playground parque m infantil [playground] 113
playgroup grupo m infantil 113
playing cards cartas de jogar
playing field campo m de jogos
playwright escritor(a) m/f 110
please se faz favor [por favor] 10
pliers alicate m
plug *(electric)* ficha [tomada] f (eléctrica)
plumber canalizador [encanador] m
pocket dictionary dicionário m de algibeira [de bolso]
point to, to mostrar 11
poison veneno m 141
poisonous venenoso
police polícia f 92, 152; **~ report** documento m da polícia 153; **~ station** esquadra [delegacia] f da polícia 96, 152
pollen count contagem f do pólen 122
polyclinic policlínica f
polyester poliéster m
pond lagoa f 107
pony ride passeio m de pónei
pop music música f pop

popcorn pipocas fpl 110
popular popular 157
port *(harbor)* porto m
porter porteiro m 27; carregador m 71
Portugal Portugal 119
Portuguese *(adj.)* português m 11, 110, 126; *(person)* português m/portuguesa f
possible: as soon as ~ o mais depressa possível
possibly possivelmente
post *(mail)* correio m; **~ office** correios mpl 96, 131, 154
post, to *(mail, to)* pôr no correio
postbox *(mailbox)* caixa f do correio 154
postcard postal m, [cartão postal] 150, 154, 156
poster cartaz
postman carteiro m
potatoes batatas fpl
pottery cerâmica f
pound *(sterling)* libra f (esterlina) 67, 138
powder puff borla f de pó de arroz
power failure corte m de energia
power point tomada f
premium *(petrol/gas)* super 87
prescription receita f 140, 141
present *(gift)* presente m
press, to engomar
pretty bonito(-a) 101
priest padre m
primus stove fogão m portátil (a petróleo)
prison prisão f
private bathroom casa f de banho privativa [banheiros mpl privativos]
probably provavelmente
prohibited: is it ~? é proibido?
pronounce, to pronunciar 11
properly como deve ser
protestant protestante
public building edifício m público 96
public holiday feriado m nacional
pullover pullover [pulôver] m
pump bomba f 83; *(gas)* bomba f de gasolina

puncture (tyre) furo m
83, 88
puppet show espectáculo
m de marionetas/
fantoches 113
pure puro(-a)
pure cotton de algodão puro
purple roxo 143
purpose objectivo m
purse porta-moedas m 153
pushchair cadeira f de bebé [nenê]
put: where can I put …? onde posso
pôr …?
put aside, to (in shop) pôr de lado
put up: can you put me up for the night?
pode-me arranjar alojamento para esta
noite?
putting course relva [grama] f de golfe

Q **quality** qualidade f 134
quantity quantidade f 134
quarantine quarentena f
quartz de quartzo
quay cais m
queen (cards, chess) rainha f
question pergunta f
queue, to estar na fila/bicha 112
quick rápido(-a) 14
quickly rapidamente 17
quiet sossegado(-a) 14
quieter mais sossegado(-a) 24, 126

R **rabbi** rabino m
race (cars/horses) corrida f; **track**
[~course] hipódromo m
racing bike bicicleta f de corrida
racket (tennis, squash) raquete f 115
radio rádio m
rail station estação f de caminho de
ferro [estação f(ferroviária)]
railroad caminho m [estrada f] de ferro
rain, to chover 122
raincoat gabardine f 144
rape violação f [estupro m] 152
rare (unusual) raro(-a); (steak)
mal-passado(-a)
razor navalha f; **~ blades** lâminas fpl
de barbear 142
re-enter, to voltar a entrar

read, to ler
ready, to be estar pronto(-a) 89, 137,
151; **are you ready?** está pronto?
real (genuine) de lei 149
real estate agent agente m imobiliário
receipt factura [recibo m] f 32, 89, 136,
137, 151
reception (desk) recepção f
receptionist recepcionista m/f
reclaim tag talão m da reclamação 71
recommend, to recomendar 21, 35, 141;
can you ~ …? pode recomendar-me …?
97; **what do you ~?** que recomenda? 37
red vermelho 143; **~ wine** vinho m tinto 40
reduction desconto m 24, 74
refreshments serviço m de bar
refrigerator frigorífico m [geladeira f] 30
refund reembolso m 137
refuse tip lixeira f
region região f 106
register receipt recibo m
registration form ficha (de registo)
registration number matrícula [placa] f
23, 88, 93
registration plate placa f de matrícula
regular (gas/petrol) normal 87; (size)
médio(-a) 110
religion religião f
remember: I don't ~ não me lembro
rent, to alugar 86; **for ~** para alugar
rental car carro m alugado 153
repair, to arranjar 89; consertar 137
repairs reparações fpl 89, consertos
mpl 137
repeat, to repetir 94, 128; **please repeat
that** repita, se faz favor 11
replacement part sobresselente m 137
report, to dar parte 152
representative guia m 27
required, to be ser necessário 112
reservation marcação f, reserva f 22, 68,
77, 112
reservation desk bilheteira f das
reservas 109
reserve, to reservar 36, 74, 109
rest, to descansar
restaurant restaurante m 35

restrooms casa f de banho [banheiros mpl] 26, 29; lavaros mpl; wc mpl pislicos

return, to *(come back)* voltar, regressar 75; *(surrender)* devolver

reverse the charges, to *(call collect)* chamada f paga pelo destinatário [a cobrar] 127

revolting horrível 14

right *(correct)* certo(-a), correcto(-a) 14, 77, 79, 94; **~ of way** prioridade 93; permitida a passagem 106; **on the ~** à direita 76, 95; **~-hand drive** condução f à direita

ring anel m 149

river rio m 107

river cruise cruzeiro m no rio 81

road estrada f 94, 95; **~ accident** acidente m rodoviário; **~ assistance** assistência f na estrada; **~ signs** sinais mpl de trânsito 96

roasted assado(-a)

robbed, to be ser roubado(-a) 153

robbery roubo m

rock climbing alpinismo m

rock concert concerto m de música rock

rocks rochas fpl

roller blades patins m em linha

rolls pãezinhos mpl 160

romance *(film/play)* romance m

romantic romântico(-a) 101

roof *(house/car)* telhado / tejadilho m

roof-rack porta-bagagens m

rook *(chess)* torre f

room quarto m 21; **~ service** serviço m de quarto 26

rope corda f

round redondo(-a) 134

round *(golf)* jogo m / round m 115; **it's my ~** é a minha rodada

roundabout rotunda f

round-trip ticket bilhete m de ida e volta 65, 68, 74, 79, 81

route caminho m 106

rowing remo m

rowboat barco m a remos 116

rude, to be ser malcriado(-a)

ruins ruínas fpl 99

run into, to *(crash)* chocar 93

run out, to *(fuel)* acabar-se 88

rush hour hora f de ponta [do rush]

S safe *(lock box)* cofre m; *(not dangerous)* sem perigo 116

safety segurança f 65

safety pins alfinetes mpl de dama [gancho]

sailboard windsurf m

sailboarding fazer windsurf

sailboat um barco m à vela 116

salad salada f

sales rep delegado [representante] m de vendas

sales tax IVA 24; **sales tax receipt** factura f com IVA

salt sal m 38, 39

same mesmo(-a); **the ~ again** torne a dar-me o mesmo

sand areia f; **sandy** *(beach)* de areia 116

sandals sandálias fpl 145

sandwich sandes f [sanduíche f] 40

sanitary napkins pensos mpl higiénicos [toalhas fpl higiénicas] 142

satellite TV satélite de TV [TV parabólica]

satin cetim m

satisfied: I'm not satisfied with this não estou satisfeito(-a) com isto

sauce molho 38

saucepan tacho m [caçarola f] 29

sauna sauna f 22

sausage salsicha f 160

saw *(tool)* serra f

say, to dizer; **how do you say …?** como se diz …?; **what did he say?** o que é que ele disse?

scarf lenço m de pescoço 144

schedule horário m 75

scheduled flight voo m previsto

school escola f

scientist cientista m / f

scissors tesoura f 148

scooter scooter f

Scotland Escócia f 119

Scottish escocês(-esa)

A-Z

scouring pad esfregão m
screw parafuso m
screwdriver chave f de parafusos
scrubbing brush escova f
scuba-diving mergulho m
sculptor escultor(a)
sea mar m 107
seafront zona f de cidade à beira-mar
seasick, I feel sinto-me enjoado(-a)
season ticket passe m
seat lugar m 74, 77, 109
second class (em) segunda (classe) 74
secondhand de segunda-mão
secondhand shop loja f de segunda-mão
secretary secretária f
security guard segurança m
sedative sedativo m
see, to ver 24, 37, 93; ~ someone again voltar a ver alguém 126
self-catering férias independentes 28
self-employed, to be ser trabalhador independente 121
self-service auto-serviço 87
sell, to vender
send, to mandar 88, 155
senior citizen reformado(-a) [idoso(-a)] 74
separated, to be estar separado(-a) 120
separately separado 42
serious grave/sério(-a)
service (religious) culto m
service charge serviço m
service station (gas station) bombas fpl de gasolina 87
set menu ementa turística 37
sex (act) sexo m
shade tom m 143
shady com sombra
shallow pouco fundo
shampoo shampoo [xampu] m 142
shape feitio m
share, to (room) partilhar
sharp afiado
shatter, to (glass) estilhaçar-se
shaver máquina f de barbear [barbeador m eléctrico]; ~ socket tomada f para a máquina de barbear

shaving brush pincel m da barba
shaving cream creme m da barba
she ela
sheath (contraceptive) preservativo m
sheet (bed) lençol m 28
shelf prateleira f
ship navio m 81
shirt camisa f 144
shock (electric) choque m eléctrico
shoe: shoes sapatos mpl 145; ~ cleaning service serviço m de limpeza de sapatos; ~ laces atacadores [cordões] mpl de sapatos; ~maker sapateiro m; ~ polish pomada f de calçado; ~ repair conserto m de sapatos; ~ store sapataria f 131; shop loja f
shop assistant empregado(-a)
shopkeeper dono(-a) da loja
shopping area zona f comercial 99
shopping basket cesto m das compras
shopping mall [centre] centro m comercial 130
shopping list lista f das compras
shopping cart [trolley] carrinho m das compras
shopping, to go ir fazer compras
shore (sea/lake) costa/margem f
short curto 146
shorts calções mpl 144
show espectáculo m 97
show, to mostrar 18. 106, 133
shower chuveiro m 26, 30; ~ gel geleia f para o chuveiro [sabonete líquido m]
shrunk: they've ~ encolheram
shut fechado(-a) 14
shy envergonhado(-a)
sick: I'm going to be ~ vou vomitar
sickbay (ship) enfermaria f
side (of road) lado m 95
side order à parte 38
side street transversal f 95
sidewalk, on the no passeio
sights lugares mpl interessantes
sightseeing tour circuito m turístico 97
sightseeing, to go ir ver os lugares interessantes
sign sinal m
signpost placa f de sinalização

silk seda f

silver prata f 149; ~ plate casquinha f [folheado m a prata] 149; ~ware talheres mpl

similar, to be ser parecido com

since *(time)* desde

singer cantor m/cantora f 157

single individual 81; ~ room quarto m individual 21; to be ~ ser solteiro(-a) 120

sink lava-louças m [pia f]

sister irmã f 120

sit, to sentar(-se) 77, 126; ~ down, please sente-se, por favor

six-pack of beer embalagem f de seis cervejas 160

size número m/tamanho m 115, 146

skates patins mpl

skating rink rinque m de patinagem [patinação]

skid: we skidded derrapámos

skiing esquiar

skin-diving equipment equipamento m para pesca submarina

skirt saia f 144

skis esquis mpl

sleeping bag saco m de dormir 31

sleeping car couchette f [vagão-leitos mpl] 77

sleeping pill comprimido m para dormir

sleeve manga f

slice fatia f 159

slide film filme m para slides

slip *(undergarment)* combinação f

slippers chinelas [pantufas] fpl 145

slope *(ski)* rampa f

slow lento(-a) 14

slow down! desacelere!

slowly (speak) devagar 11, 17, 94, 128

small pequeno(-a) 14, 24, 40, 134

small change troco m

smell: there's a bad ~ cheiro m está aqui um mau cheiro

smoke, to fumar 126; I don't ~ não fumo

smoking (area) fumadores [fumantes] 36, 69

smoky: it's too ~ cheio de fumo [fumaça]/está cheio de fumo [fumaça]

snack bar snack bar m [lanchonete f], cafetaria f 73

snacks snacks

sneakers ténis mpl

snorkel snorkel m

snow neve f

snow, to nevar 122

snowed in, to be estar bloqueado pela neve

soaking solution *(contact lenses)* solução f para imersão

soap sabonete m 142

soap powder sabão m em pó

soccer futebol m 114

socket tomada f

sock peúga [meia curta] f 144

sofa sofá m

sofa-bed sofá-cama m

soft drink (soda) refresco m 110; bebida f não-alcoólica/gasosa 160

solarium solário m

sold out (a lotação) esgotada 108

sole *(shoes)* sola f

soluble aspirin aspirina f solúvel 141

someone alguém 16

something alguma coisa 16

sometimes às vezes 13

son filho m 120, 162

soon em breve 13

sore throat dor f de garganta 141

sore: it's ~ doer: dói

sorry! desculpe/perdão!

sort género m 134; a sort of ... uma espécie de ...

sour azedo(-a) 41

south sul m 95

South Africa África f do Sul

South African sul-africano(-a)

souvenir lembrança f 98, 156; ~ guide guia m turístico 156; ~ shop loja f de lembranças 131

spa estância termal/termas fpl [spa f]

space lugar/espaço 30

spade *(shovel)* pá f 157

spades *(cards)* espadas

Spain Espanha f

spare *(extra)* sobresselente

speak, to falar 11, 41, 67, 128; **do you ~ English?** fala inglês? 11

special rate tarifa f especial 86

special requirements pedidos mpl especiais 39

spectacles óculos mpl

speed limit limite m de velocidade

speed, to ir com excesso de velocidade 93

spell, to soletrar 11

spend, to gastar

spin-dryer *(clothes)* centrifugador m

sponge esponja f 148

spoon colher f 39, 41, 148

sport desporto [esporte] m 114

sports: ~ club clube m desportivo [esportivo]; **~ stadium** pavilhão m desportivo [esportivo] 96

sporting goods store loja f de artigos de desporto [esportivos] 131

spring primavera f 219

square quadrado 134

squash *(game)* squash m

stadium estádio m 96

stain nódoa [mancha] f

stainless steel aço m inoxidável

stairs escadas fpl

stale seco(-a)

stalls *(theater)* plateia f

stamp selo m 150, 154; **~ machine** máquina f de selos

stand in line, to estar na fila/bicha 112

standby ticket bilhete m de standby

start início m

start, to começar 88, 112

starter hors-d'oeuvre, aperitivo m

statement *(legal)* depoimento m 93; *(bank)* extracto m

station estação f 73, 78, 96

station wagon carrinha f [minivan m]

stationer papelaria f

statue estátua f

stay estadia f 32

stay, to ficar 23

stereo stereo m

sterilizing solution solução f esterilizante

stern *(ship)* popa f

still: I'm ~ waiting ainda estou à espera

stocking meia f 144

stolen, to be ser roubado(-a) 71

stop *(bus/tram)* paragem [parada] f 79, 80

stop, to parar 77, 78, 84, 98; **~ here** pare aqui 84

stopcock torneira f de passagem [de segurança]

stopover escala f

storekeeper dono(-a) da loja

store guide planta f da loja 132

straight ahead sempre em frente 95

strange estranho(-a) 101

straw *(drinking)* palha f para chupar [canudinho]

strawberry *(flavor)* morango 40

stream ribeiro m / corrente f 107

string cordel m [corda f]

striped *(patterned)* às riscas [listado(-a)]

stroller cadeira f de bebé [nenê]

strong *(potent)* forte

store loja f

student estudante m/f 74, 100

study, to estudar 121

stupid: that was ~! isso foi idiotice!

styling mousse mousse f para o cabelo

subway metro 80; **~ station** estação f de metro 80, 96; *(underpass)* passagem f subterrânea 96

suede camurça f

sugar açúcar m 38, 39

suggest, to sugerir 123

suit fato [terno] m 144

suitable próprio(-a) 140

sun block protector m solar 142

sun lounger cama f para banho de sol

sunbathe, to tomar banho de sol

sunburn queimadura f de sol 141

sundeck *(ship)* solário m

sunglasses óculos mpl de sol 144

sunshade *(umbrella)* um chapéu m de sol 117

suntan lotion creme m / loção f de bronzear

super *(gas/petrol)* super 87

superb soberbo(-a) 101

supermarket supermercado m 131, 158

supplement *(extra charge)* suplemento m / taxa f

suppository supositório m
sure: are you ~? tem a certeza?
surfboard uma prancha f de surf
surname apelido [sobrenome] m
sweatshirt sweatshirt m [blusa f de moleton] 144
sweet *(taste)* doce
sweets *(candy)* rebuçados mpl [balas fpl] 150
swim, to nadar 116
swimming natação f 114; **~ pool** piscina f 22, 26, 116; **~ trunks** calções mpl de banho 144
swimsuit fato [maiô] m de banho 144
switch interruptor m
switch on, to ligar
switch off, to desligar
swollen, to be estar inchado(-a)
synagogue sinagoga f
synthetic sintético

T **T-shirt** camiseta f 144, 156
table mesa f 36, 112; **~ cloth** toalha f de mesa; **~ tennis** ping-pong m
tablet comprimido m 140
tailback *(traffic)* fila f de trânsito
take away, to para levar 40
take photographs, to tirar fotografias 98, 100
take someone home, to acompanhar alguém a casa
take, to *(carry)* levar 71; *(medicine)* tomar 140; *(room)* ficar 24; *(time)* demorar 78; *(buy)* **I'll take it** levo 135
talcum powder pótalco [talco] m 142
tall alto(-a) 14
tampons tampões mpl higiénicos 142
tan bronzeado m
tap *(faucet)* torneira f 25
taxi táxi m 70, 71, 84;
~ driver chauffeur [motorista f] m de táxi; **~ stand [rank]** praça f [ponto m] de táxis 96
tea chá m 40; **~ bags** saquinhos mpl de chá 160
tea towel pano m da louça 156
teacher professor(a)
team equipa f [times fpl] 114

teaspoon colher f de chá 140, 148
teat *(for baby)* chupeta f
teddy bear urso m de peluche [de pelúcia] 57
telephone telefone m 22, 70, 92, 127;
~ bill conta f telefónica; **~ booth [box]** cabine f de telefone [orelhão m] 127;
~ calls telefonemas 32; **~ directory** lista f telefónica; **~ kiosk** quiosque m do telefone; **~ number** número m de telefone 127
telephone, to telefonar
television televisão f 25
tell, to dizer 18, 79; **tell me** diga-me
temperature temperatura f
tennis ténis m 114; **~ ball** bola f de ténis; **~ court** campo m [quadra f] de ténis 115
tent tenda f 30, 31; **~ pegs** cavilhas fpl 31; **~ pole** estaca f 31
terminus estação f
thank you obrigado(-a) 10; **thanks for your help** obrigado(-a) pela sua ajuda 94
that que; **~ one** esse, essa 16, 134; *(more distant)* aquele, aquela
that's all é tudo 133
theater teatro m 96, 99, 110
theft os roubos 71; roubo m 153
their(s) seus/suas, deles/delas 16
them eles/elas 16
theme park parque m temático
then *(time)* então/depois 13
there ali 17
there is ... há ... 17
thermometer termómetro m
thermos bottle [flask] garrafa f termos [térmica]
these estes, estas 134
they eles/elas
thick grosso(-a) 14
thief ladrão m, ladra f
thin fino(-a) 14
think, to pensar 135; **I think** creio 42; acho 77
thirsty com sede
this one este/esta 16, 134

those (close by) esses/essas 134; (more distant) aqueles/aquelas 134
thread linha f
throat lozenges pastilhas fpl para a garganta
through pelo/pela/através de
ticket bilhete m 68, 69, 74, 75, 77, 79, 80; ~ **machine** posto m de venda de bilhetes; ~ **office** bilheteira [bilheteria] f 73
tie gravata f
tight apertado(-a) 146
tights collant m 144
till receipt recibo m
time horas fpl 76, 78; **free ~** tempo m livre 98
tin foil papel m de alumínio
tin opener abre-latas [abridor de latas] m 148
tinted (glass/lens) fumado(-a) [escuro(-a)]
tipping as gorjetas fpl 42
tire [tyre] pneu m 83
tired, to be cansado, estar
tissues lenços mpl de papel 142
to (direction) para 12
toaster torradeira f
tobacco tabaco m
today hoje 124
together junto(-a) 42
toilet (item) sanita f [vaso m sanitário]
toilet paper papel m higiénico 25, 142
toll portagem f [pedágio m]
tomorrow amanhã 84, 124, 218
tongs tenazes fpl
tonic water água f tónica
tonight hoje à noite 110, 124; **for ~** para hoje à noite 108
tonsillitis amigdalite f
too (extreme) demasiado 15, 17, 93; (also) também; ~ **much** demasiado 15
toothache dor f de dentes
toothbrush escova f de dentes
toothpaste pasta f de dentes 142
top floor último andar m
tour passeio m/visita f/excursão f; ~ **guide** guia m; ~ **operator** agência f de viagens 26; ~ **representative** guia m turístico 27

tourist o(-a) turista; ~ **office** posto m de turismo [informações turísticas fpl] 97
tow rope corda f de reboque
tow, to rebocar
toward para/na direcção de 12
towel toalha f 2
toweling pano m turco
tower torre f 99
town cidade f 94; ~ **hall** câmara f municipal 99; ~ **map** mapa mpl de cidade 150
toy brinquedo m 157
toy and game store armazém m [loja f] de brinquedos 131
track trilho m
tracksuit fato m de treino [training]
traffic trânsito m; ~ **jam** engarrafamento m 94; ~ **circle** rotunda f
tragedy tragédia f
trail caminho m 106
trailer rulote f [trailer m] 30, 81
trailer park parque m de campismo [camping]
train comboio [trem] m 75, 76, 77, 80; ~ **station** estação f de caminho de ferro [estação f (ferroviária)] 73
train times horário m dos comboios [trens] 75
tram eléctrico [bonde] m 78, 79
transfer transferência f; (transport) transbordo m
transit, in em trânsito
translate, to traduzir 11
translation tradução f
translator tradutor m
trash (rubbish) lixo m 28; **trash can** lixeira f 30
travel agency agência f de viagens 131
travel sickness enjoo m 141
travel, to viajar
traveler's check cheque m de viagens 136, 138
tray tabuleiro m
tree árvore f
trip excursão f 97
trolley carrinho m 158
trouble: I'm having ~ with estou a ter [tendo] problemas com

trouser press máquina f de engomar [passar] as calças

trousers calças fpl 144

truck camião [caminhão] m

true: that's not ~ isso não é verdade

try on, to (clothing) provar 146

tube bisnaga f

tunnel túnel m

turn, to virar 95; **~ down** (volume, heat) baixar; **~ off** desligar 25; **~ on** ligar 25; **~ up** (volume, heat) aumentar

turn [turning] curva f

TV TV f 22; **~ room** sala f de televisão 26

tweezers pinça f

twin beds duas camas fpl 21

type tipo m 109; **what ~?** que tipo? 112

tyre pneu m 83

U

ugly feio(-a) 14, 101

United Kingdom Reino m Unido

ulcer úlcera f

umbrella (parasol) um chapéu m de sol 117; (rain) guardachuva m

uncle tio m 120

unconscious, to be perder os sentidos 92, 162

under (place) debaixo de

underdone mal cozido(-a) 41

underpants cuecas fpl 144

underpass passagem f inferior 96

understand, to compreender 11; **do you ~?** compreende?; **I don't ~** não compreendo 11, 67

uneven (not flat) acidentado 30

unfortunately infelizmente 19

uniform uniforme m

unit unidade f 155

United States Estados mpl Unidos 119

university universidade f 99

unleaded gas gasolina f sem chumbo

unlimited mileage sem limite de quilometragem

unlock, to abrir

unpleasant desagradável 14

unscrew, to desaparafusar

until até

upmarket de luxo

upper (berth) superior 74

upset stomach indisposição f gástrica 141

upstairs em cima

up to até 12

us nós; **for ~** para nós; **with ~** connosco

use, to usar, utilizar 139

use uso m 67

useful útil

V

vacancy quarto m vago 21

vacant vago(-a) 14

vacate, to deixar 32

vacation férias fpl 66, 123

vaccination vacinação f

valet service lavagem f e limpeza interior do carro

valid válido(-a) 75; **not ~** não é válido

validate, to (ticket) validar 79

valley vale m 107

valuable de valor

value valor m 155

vanilla (flavor) baunilha 40

VAT (sales tax) IVA 24; **~ receipt** factura f com IVA

vegan, to be ser vegan

vegetable store lugar m da hortaliça [quitanda f]

vegetables legumes, vegetais 38

vegetarian vegetariano(-a) 35, 39; **to be ~** ser vegetariano(-a)

vehicle veículo m; **~ registration document** os documentos do carro

velvet veludo m

vending machine máquina f de vender

Venezuela Venezuela f

ventilator ventilador m

very muito 17

vest (UK) camisola f interior [camiseta f]

veterinarian veterinário m

video vídeo m; **~ cassette** cassete f [m] de vídeo 157; **~ game** jogo m de vídeo [vídeo game]; **~ recorder** gravador [aparelho] m de vídeo

view vista f; **with a ~ of the sea** com vista para o mar

viewing point miradouro m 107

village aldeia f 107

vineyard (winery) vinha f 107

viniculture vinicultura f

visa visto m

visit visita f

visit, to visitar; **places to visit** sítios [lugares] para visitar

visitor center centro m de acolhimento

vitamin pills comprimidos mpl de vitaminas

voice voz f

volleyball voleibol m 114

voltage voltagem f

W **waist** cintura f

wait (for), to esperar 41, 76, 89, 140; **wait!** espere! 98

waiting room sala f de espera 73

wake, to (self) despertar; **~ someone** acordar alguém 27

wake-up call chamada f para despertar

Wales País m de Gales 119

walk home, to ir a pé para casa

walk: to go for a ~ ir dar um passeio

walking passear; **~ boots** botas fpl para caminhar 145

walking route itinerário m a pé 106

walking/hiking gear equipamento m desportivo 145

wall parede f

wallet carteira f (de documentos) 42, 153

want, to desejar 18

ward (hospital) enfermaria f

warm morno(-a) 14; (weather) quente 122

warm, to aquecer

warmer mais quente 24

wash, to lavar

washbasin lavatório m

washing, to do lavar roupa

washing: ~ instructions instruções fpl de lavagem m; **~ powder** detergente m em pó para a roupa 148; **~-up liquid** detergente m líquido para a louça

wasp vespa f

watch relógio m de pulso 153; **~ band [strap]** correia f do relógio

watch TV, to ver televisão

water água f 87; **~ bottle** botija f [garrafa f de água]; **water carrier** garrafão m [vasilha f] de água; **~fall** cascata [catarata] f 107; **~ heater** esquentador [aquecedor] m 28

waterproof à prova de água; **waterproof jacket** impermeável m 145

waterskiing esqui m aquático

waterskis esquis-aquáticos mpl 117

wave onda f

waxing depilação f a cera 147

way (direction) caminho m 83, 94; **I've lost my ~** stou perdido(-a) 94

we nós

weak fraco(-a); **I feel ~** sinto-me fraco(-a)

wear, to trazer vestido 152

weather tempo m 122; **~ forecast** previsão f do tempo 122

wedding casamento m; **~ ring** aliança f

week semana 23, 24, 97, 218

weekend fim-de-semana

weekend rate tarifa f de fim-de-semana 86

weekly (ticket) semanal 79

weight: my weight is ... eu peso ...

welcome to ... benvindo a ...

well-done (steak) bem-passado

Welsh galês m / galesa f

west oeste m 95

wetsuit roupa m de mergulho

what? que? 18; **what kind of ...?** que variedade de ...? 37, que espécie de ...? 106

what time? a que horas? 68, 76, 78, 81

wheelchair cadeira f de rodas

when? quando? 13

where? onde? 12, 99; **~ are you from?** donde é? 119; **~ else** em que outro lado 135

which? qual? 16; **~ stop?** qual é a estação? 80

while enquanto

whist (cards) uíste m

white branco(-a) 143; **~ wine** vinho m branco 40

who? quem? 16

whole: the ~ day todo o dia

whose? de quem? 16

why? porquê?
wide largo(-a) 14
wife mulher f 120, 162
wildlife animais m e plantas selvagens
window janela f 25, 77; *(store)* montra f 149
window seat lugar m à janela 69, 74
windshield [windscreen] pára-brisas 90
windsurfer prancha f à vela 117
windy, to be haver vento 122
wine vinho m 40; **~ list** carta f dos vinhos 37; **~box** pacote m de vinho 160
with com 17
withdraw, to *(money)* levantar [sacar] 139
without sem 17
wood *(forest)* mata f 107; *(material)* madeira f
wool lã f 145
work, to trabalhar 121; *(function)* funcionar 28, 83, 89; **it doesn't ~** não funciona 25
worry: I'm worried estou preocupado(-a)
worse pior 14; **it's gotten [got] ~** está pior
worst pior m
wrap up, to embrulhar
write down, to escrever 136
write: write soon! escrever: escreve depressa!
writing pad bloco m de papel
wrong errado(-a) 14
wrong number engano m 128

yacht iate m
yellow amarelo 143
yes sim 10
yogurt yogurte m
you você, senhor(a) 118; *(familiar)* tu / ti 16
young jovem 14
your *(singular)* seu / sua; *(plural)* vosso(-a), *(familiar)* teu / tua 16
yours teu / tua, vosso(-a) 16
youth hostel pousada [albergue] f da juventude 29

zebra crossing passadeira f [faixa de pedestres]
zero zero m
zip(per) fecho [zíper] m éclair
zone zona f
zoo jardim m zoológico 113; zoo m
zoology zoologia f

Dictionary
Portuguese–English

This Portuguese–English Dictionary covers all the areas where you may need to decode written Portuguese: hotels, public buildings, restaurants, stores, ticket offices, and on transportation. It will also help with understanding forms, maps, product labels, road signs, and operating instructions (for telephones, parking meters, etc.). If you can't locate the exact sign, you may find key words or terms listed separately.

A

à lista a la carte
à prova d'água waterproof
à tarde p.m.
abadia abbey
abajur lampshade
aberto open
aberto 24 horas 24-hour service
aberto a noite inteira open all night
aberto diàriamente open daily
abra aqui open here
abril April
acenda os faróis switch on headlights
acesso para deficientes físicos access for handicapped
acesso reservado a funcionários staff only
acesso só a residentes access for residents only
acesso único access only
acessórios de automóveis car accessories
achados e perdidos lost property
acidentes casualty
acostamento hard-shoulder
açougue butcher *(Braz.)*
acrílico acrylic
açúcar sugar
admissão admissions
adoçante natural natural sweetener
adro da igreja churchyard
aerobarco hovercraft/hydrofoil
aeródromo airfield
aeroporto airport
agência de câmbio currency exchange office [bureau de change]
agência de viagem/viagens travel agent

agitar antes de usar shake well before use
Agosto August
água benta holy water
água potável drinking water
aguardar vez aqui wait here
albergue de juventude youth hostel
aldeia village
aldeia turística holiday village
alfândega customs
algodão cotton
alojamento accommodations
alpinismo mountaineering
alta tensão high voltage
altura máxima headroom
aluga-se for rent
aluga-se apartamento apartment to rent
aluga-se quartos rooms to rent
alugam-se carros car rental
aluguel de bicicletas bicycle rental
amanhã tomorrow
ambulância ambulance
5 amp. 5 amp
andebol handball
anfiteatro operatório operating room
antiguidades antiques
ao ar livre open air
aperitivos snacks
apertar o cinto fasten your seatbelt
após as refeições after meals
apresentar identidade proof of identity required
aproximação de cruzamento crossroads ahead
aproximação de estrada com prioridade yield [give way]

aproximação de rotunda traffic circle [roundabout]
aproximação de túnel tunnel ahead
área construída built-up area
área para piqueniques picnic area
areia sand
areia movediça quicksand
armazém department store
arroz rice
artigos a declarar goods to declare
artigos de informática computer goods
artigos da free-shop duty-free goods
artigos desportivos sports goods
artigos fotográficos photographic goods
artigos para animais pet store [shop]
artigos para bebês children's clothes and goods
ascensor elevator
assinatura signature
atalho cutting/wayside
atendimento admissions
atendimento ao cliente customer service
atração turística tourist feature
atrasado delayed
atravesse agora cross now
atrelado trailer
auto-escola driving school
auto-estrada highway [motorway]
autocarro bus
automóvel car/automobile
avariado out of order
avarias breakdown services
avião plane
aviso warning

B **bagagem** baggage
baia bay
bailarino dancer
balcão de registo check-in counter
balcão de informações information desk
balcão dress circle *(theater)*
balcão segundo circle *(theater)*
balé ballet
balsa ferry *(Braz.)*
banco bank
bandeira flag *(special rate)*
banheiros bathrooms/restrooms [toilets]
banho bath/bathroom
barbeiro barber

barco boat
barco salva-vidas lifeboat
basebol baseball
basquetebol basketball
bebidas drinks
bebidas (não) incluidas drinks (not) included
beco cul-de-sac
bemvindo welcome
biblioteca library
bicicleta bicycle
bilhete de embarque embarkation card
bilhete de ida e volta round-trip [return] ticket
bilhete duplo round-trip [return] ticket *(subway)*
bilhete semanal weekly ticket
bilhete simples/unitário (metrô) one-way [single] ticket *(subway [metro])*
bilhete só de ida one way [single] ticket
bilheteira/bilheteria ticket office
bilhetes tickets
bolachas cookies [biscuits]
bolos e doces cakes and candies
bomba pump
bomba de gasolina filling station
bombeiros fire department [brigade]
bonde tram *(Braz.)*
botas de ski ski boots
boutique boutique
box(e) boxing
brasileiro (-a) Brazilian
brinquedos toys
bufete dining car

C **cabaré** cabaret
cabeleireiro/cabelereiro hairdresser
cabeleireiro de homens barber
cabina dupla double cabin
cabina simples single cabin
cachoeira waterfall *(Braz.)*
café da manhã breakfast *(Braz.)*
café coffee/coffee shop
cafezinho coffee *(Braz.)*
cais docks/quay
caixa expresso express checkout
caixa cashier
calçado shoes
calçado ortopédicos orthopedic shoes

cálcio calcium
calculadoras calculators
calorias calories
cama extra extra bed
câmara municipal town hall
câmbio currency exchange office/exchange rate
camião truck
caminho path
caminho de ferro railway
camioneta coach
camping campsite
campo de batalha battle site
campo de desportos playing field [sports ground]
cana de pesca fishing rod
canal canal
cancelado canceled
candeeiros lamps
canoagem canoeing
capela chapel
cardápio menu (Braz.)
carnaval carnival
carne meat
carro car
carta registada registered letter
carteira wallet
casa house
casa de banho bathroom
casa de câmbio currency exchange office [bureau de change]
cassetes cassettes
castelo castle
catedral cathedral
cavalo horse
caverna cave
caves cellars
cemitério cemetery
cêntimo cent
central in the center of the town
centro comercial shopping mall
centro da cidade downtown area
centro desportivo sports center
cereais cereals
cerveja beer
chá tea
chalé cottage
chamada gratuita toll-free
chamadas internacionais international calls
chamadas interurbanas regional calls
chamadas locais local calls

charcutaria delicatessen
chegadas arrivals
churrasco barbecue
chuveiro shower
ciclistas cyclists
cidade city
cidade antiga/histórica old town
cigarros cigarettes
cinema movie theater [cinema]
circo circus
circular à esquerda/direita keep to the left/right
cirurgia surgery
clínica de saúde health clinic
cobre copper
código de área area code
colete de salvação life jacket
colina hill
coloque as moedas necessárias/o cartão insert required coins/card
com banheiro with bathroom
com chumbo leaded
com cozinha with cooking facilities
com depósito returnable
com iva incluído includes sales tax [VAT]
com piscina with swimming pool
com (satélite) TV with (satellite) TV
com vista para o mar with sea view
combóio rápido express/intercity train
combóio suburbano local train
combustível fuel
comida típica local specialties
completo full (up)
comprimidos pills/tablets
computadores computers
comunhão communion
concerto de música clássica classical music concert
concerto pop pop concert
condicionador conditioner
confecção de homem menswear
confeitaria baker/pastry shop/confectioner's
congelado frozen
conserto de calçado shoe repairs
consertos repairs
conservar no frigorífico keep refrigerated
conservas preserves
conserve o bilhete please retain your ticket

consulte (o) seu médico antes de usar consult your doctor before use
consultório consulting room
consumir em ... dias best before ... days
contador de electricidade electric [electricity] meter
conteúdo contents
controle de passaportes passport check/control
convento convent
correio(s) post office
correio azul express mail
correio normal regular mail
correspondência change (to other subway lines)
corte aqui cut here
cosméticos cosmetics
costa coast
couro leather
credifone phone card
creme para depois do sol after-sun cream
crianças children
cruz vermelha red cross
cruzamento crossing/crossroads
cruzeiros cruises
cuidado caution
cuidado com a bolsa beware of pick-pockets
cuidado com o cão beware of the dog
cuidado com o degrau watch your step
cuidado, (aproximação de) escola caution, school
cuidados intensivos intensive care
cume peak
curva perigosa dangerous bend

D da responsabilidade do próprio at the owner's risk
dança dance
data date
data de nascimento date of birth
data de validade do cartão de crédito credit card expiration [expiry] date
de manhã a.m.
de preferência antes de ... best before ...
deck de automóveis car deck
deck de cabines cabin deck
deck inferior lower deck
deck superior upper deck

deixe o carro em primeira leave your car in first gear
dentista dentist
depilação a cera waxing
depósito refund
depósito de bagagem baggage check
descartável disposable
descontos reductions
desembarque arrivals
desembarque pelo lado direito/esquerdo do combóio exit by left/right side of the train
deserto desert
desligar/desligue o motor turn off your engine
desnatado skimmed (milk)
desporto sport
destino destination
desvio detour [diversion]
detergentes detergents
devagar slow
devolução refund
Dezembro December
dia da independência independence day
dia de Ano Novo New Year's Day
dia de Portugal Portugal Day
dia do trabalhador Labor Day
diária room rate
dias úteis weekdays
dicionários dictionaries/reference
dieta/dietético diet
dietéticos dietary/health (food)
dique dam
direcção management
dirija com cuidado drive carefully
discoteca music store
disque ... para obter linha dial ... for an outside line
disque ... para recepção/portaria dial ... for reception
dissolver em água dissolve in water
distância aproximada em km approximate distance in kilometers
doca docks
documentos de registo registration papers
doentes externos outpatients
domingo Sunday
Domingo de Páscoa Easter Sunday
Domingo de Ramos Palm Sunday

A-Z

A-Z

dormidas rooms available
doces desserts/candy
drogaria drugstore
duas estrelas two-star
duna dune

E € euro
ecológico ecologic
eléctrico streetcar

electrodomésticos/eletrodomesticos electrical appliances
elevador elevator
em construção under construction
em pó powdered
em serviço occupied
embaixada embassy
embalagem perdida non-returnable
embalagens packages
embarque departures/embarkation point
embarcadouro docks/quay
embarque imediato boarding now
ementa menu
ementa turística tourist menu
emergência emergency (services)
empacotado em ... packaged in ...
empurre/empurrar push
encerrado à hora do almoço closed at lunch time
encerrado para férias closed for vacation [holiday]
encerrado para obras closed for repairs
encosta perigosa dangerous slope
endereço address
endereço comercial business address
endereço residencial/do domicílio home address
enfermaria (hospital) section [ward]
enlatados canned goods
enseada bay
entrada entrance/way in
entrada gratuita/grátis/livre admission free
entrada pela porta da frente/traseira enter by the front/rear door
entrada proibida no entry
entrada proibida a estranhos trespassers will be prosecuted
entradas starters
entrega de bagagem baggage claim
entregas deliveries
envio de fax faxes sent

equipamento de mergulho diving equipment
equipamentos eletrónicos electronic goods
equitação horseback riding
ervanário health food store
escada rolante escalator
escadas stairs
escalar climbing
escarpa cliff/escarpment
escavações arqueológicas excavations
escola school
escolha o destino/zona select destination/zone *(instruction)*
escolha você mesmo pick and mix
escritório de achados e perdidos lost-and-found office
especialidade da casa specialty of the house
especialidades da região local specialties
espectáculo show/performance
espectadores spectators
espere pelo sinal wait for tone
esquadra da polícia police station
esqui aquático waterskiing
esquiagem skiing
esquis skis
esquis aquáticos water skis
esta noite this evening
estação station
estação de caminhos de ferro train station
estação de metro subway station
estação de serviço filling station
estação de ferroviária train station *(Braz.)*
estação rodoviária bus [coach] station
estacionamento parking lot [car park]
estacionamento de rulotes trailer [caravan] site
estacionamento para clientes customer parking
estacione aqui park here
estádio stadium
estância turística tourist resort
estanho can
estátua statue
estrada road
estrada em construção road under construction
estrada fechada/bloqueada road closed

estrangeiro foreign
estreia premiere
estreitamento de rua narrow road
estuário estuary
exceto feriados except for holidays
exceto transportes de carga except
  heavy vehicles
exceto aos domingos e feriados except
  Sundays and bank holidays
exclusivo para residentes residents only
exclusivo para pedestres pedestrians only
exclusivo para pessoal autorizado
  authorized vehicles only
exige-se a identificação proof of
  identity required
exposição fair/art exhibition
extintor (de incêndios) fire extinguisher

F fábrica factory
   fabricado em ... made in ...
   fábrica manual made by hand
fala-se inglês English spoken
farmácia drugstore
farol lighthouse
favor fechar a porta please shut the door
favor não tocar please do not touch
favor tocar a campainha please ring
  the bell
fazenda farm (Braz.)
fechado closed/day off
fechado até ... closed until ...
fechado para almoço closed for lunch
fechar/feche a porta close the door
feira fair/market
feira popular amusement park
feito à mão handmade
feito por medida made-to-measure
feito a pedido made-to-order
feriado nacional national holiday
ferroviário railroad (Braz.)
Fevereiro February
fila única stay in lane
fim das obras end of roadwork
fim de auto-estrada end of highway
  [motorway]
fim de saldos closing down sale
fim do desvio end of detour [diversion]
floresta forest
florista florist
fogo de artifício fireworks
fonte fountain/spring
fortaleza fortress
forte fort

fortes rajadas de
  vento gales
fotocópias photocopies
fotografia photographic
  store/photography
foz river mouth
fraldas diapers [nappies]
free shop duty-free
frente front
fresco fresh
fronteira border crossing
fruta fruit
fumadores smoking (area)
fumantes smoking (area) (Braz.)
futebol soccer [football]
futebol americano American football

G galeria balcony
   galeria de arte art gallery
   garagem garage
garantia guarantee
gare platforms
gasolina gas
genuíno genuine
gerente manager
ginásio fitness room
golfe golf
gotas drops
grátis/gratuito free
grelha de churrasco barbecue
grelhados grilled
gruta cave
guarda-sol sun umbrella
guias de viagem travel guides

H handebol handball
   helicóptero helicopter
   hipermercado hypermarket
hipismo horseback riding
hipódromo racetrack [racecourse]
hoje today
homens men
hóquei hockey
hóquei no gelo ice hockey
horário timetable
horário comercial hours [business]
  hours
horário de abertura opening hours
horário de inverno winter hours
horário de tiragem times of collection
horário de verão summer hours
horário de visitas visiting hours
24 horas por dia 24-hour service

A-Z

horas das refeições meal times
hospital hospital
hotel hotel
hotel-fazenda farmhouse hotel (*Braz.*)

I ida e volta round-trip [return]
igreja church

ilha island
imposto de venda sales tax [VAT]
incluído included
incluído no preço included in the price
indicado para vegetarianos suitable for vegetarians
indicativo code
infantário kindergarten
inflamável inflammable
informações information
informações a clientes customer information
informações turísticas tourist information
ingredientes ingredients
início de auto-estrada highway [motorway] entrance
inquebrável unbreakable
inserir o cartão insert card
instruções para uso instructions for use
integração 1 subway + 1 bus trip
integral wholewheat (*bread*)
interdito ao trânsito traffic-free zone
internacional international
introduza as moedas insert coins
introduza ficha insert token
inverno winter
iva (com/sem iva incluído) sales tax [VAT] (included/not included)

J Janeiro January
jardim garden
jardim botânico botanical garden
jardim zoológico zoo
joalharia jeweler
jogo match
Julho July
Junho June

L lã wool
lago lake/pond
lancha motorboat

lanches snacks
largo square
laticínios dairy products
lavagem de carros car wash
lavagem de roupa laundry facilities
lavandaria laundromat
lavandaria a seco dry-cleaner
lavar a seco dry-clean only
lavável à máquina machine washable
lembranças souvenirs
lençóis bed linen
limite da cidade city limits
limite de bagagem baggage allowance
limite de carga load limit
limpeza cleaning
língua language
línguas estrangeiras foreign languages
linha platform
linha de bonde streetcar [tramway] (*Braz.*)
linha férrea railroad [railway]
liquidação clearance [sale]
líquido liquid
Lisboa Lisbon
lista menu
lista telefónica directory
lista de preços price list
litoral coast
livraria bookstore
livre vacant/free
livrete car registration papers
local de embarque embarkation point
local de nascimento place of birth
loção para depois da barba after-shave lotion
loja de antiguidades antiques store
loja de artigos de desporto sporting goods store
loja de brinquedos toy store
loja de departamentos department store
loja de presentes gift store
lojas duty-free duty-free store
lotação esgotada sold out
lotaria/loteria lottery
louça china
lubrificação lubrication
lugar à janela window seat
lugar de orquestra orchestra seat
lugar na asa aisle seat
lugar nº seat number
luxo luxury

M
madeira wood
maestro conductor
magro fat-free/lean
Maio May
malas luggage/suitcases
manejar com cuidado handle with care
mantenha-se à direita/esquerda keep to the right/left
mantenha congelado keep frozen
mantenha a distância keep clear
mantenha fora do alcance das crianças keep out of reach of children
mapa da cidade city map
mapa dos arredores area map
máquina automática automatic machine
máquina fotográfica camera
mar sea
Março March
marionetes puppet show
marque ... para linha externa dial ... for an outside line
marque ... para recepção dial ... for reception
massas noodles, pasta and spaghetti
mata wood
mata-burro cattlegrid (Braz.)
material fotográfico photographic equipment
maternidade maternity
matrícula do automóvel license plate [registration] number
meia entrada half price ticket
meia pensão half board
menu menu
menu turístico tourist menu
mercado market
mercadorias goods
mercadorias isentas duty-free goods
mercearia grocer
mergulhar diving
mesas no andar superior seats upstairs
metropolitano/metro/metrô subway
mina mine
miradouro viewpoint
missa mass
missal prayer book
mobiliário furniture
moda feminina ladieswear
moda infantil childrenswear
moda masculina menswear
modo de usar instructions for use

moeda comprada a ... currency bought at ...
moeda estrangeira foreign currency
moeda vendida a ... currency sold at ...
moedas coins
moinho mill
moinho de vento windmill
molhada wet
montanha mountain
montanhismo mountaineering
monte mount/hill
monumento monument
monumento comemorativo (war) memorial
morro hill
mosteiro monastery
moto de montanha dirt (motor)bike
motorizada motorcycle
móveis furniture
mpb (música popular brasileira) mpb (popular Brazilian music)
mudança de óleo change of oil
mudar change
mudar em ... change at...
mulheres women
multa por viajar sem bilhete penalty for traveling without ticket
múltiplo 10 10 trips (subway [metro])
múltiplo 2 round-trip [return] (subway [metro])
muralha wall
muralha da cidade city wall
muro wall
museu museum
música music
música ao vivo live music
música clássica classical music
música folk folk music
música pop pop music

 N
nacional national
nacionalidade nationality
nada a declarar nothing to declare
não abrir a janela do not open the window
não abrir em andamento do not open while (the train is) moving
não bloqueie a entrada do not block entrance
não buzinar use of horn prohibited

A-Z

A-Z

não dá troco no change given
não debruce nas janelas do not lean out of windows
não deixar/deixe obje(c)tos de valor no (seu) carro do not leave valuables in your car
não desbota colorfast
não é permitida a entrada a crianças com menos de … no children under …
não entrar no decorrer do serviço/sessão no entry during services
não entre keep out
não estacionar em frente do not block entrance
não falar com o condutor do not talk to the driver
não fumadores non-smokers
não fumantes non-smokers (Braz.)
não fumar no smoking
não funciona out of order
não inclui/incluído exclusive
não inclui serviço no service charge included
não ingerir not for internal consumption
não jogue papel no vaso sanitário don't put paper in the toilet
não lavar à máquina handwash only
não passar a ferro do not iron
não perturbar/perturbe do not disturb
não pisar a relva keep off the grass
não se aceita cartões de crédito no credit cards
não se aceita cheques no checks [cheques]
não se aceita devoluções no refunds
não se aproxime keep clear
não se troca artigos goods cannot be exchanged
não serve para uso interno not for internal consumption
não tirar fotografias no photography
não tocar do not touch
não ultrapasse no passing [overtaking]
não usar flash no flash photos
Natal Christmas
navegação à vela sailing
navio ship
nome name
nome da esposa/do marido name of spouse (wife/husband)

nome da mãe mother's name
nome de família last name
nome de solteira maiden name
nome do pai father's name
nomes dos pais parents' names
Novembro November
novo new
número de segurança social social security number
número de telefone telephone number
número de voo flight number
número do cartão de crédito credit card number
número do passaporte passport number
número do registo do automóvel license plate [registration] number

O

obras construction [roadworks]
oculista optician
ocupado occupied/engaged
oferta especial special offer
oficina office
óleo oil
ônibus bus/coach (Braz.)
ônibus direto direct service (Braz.)
ônibus elétrico streetcar [tram] (Braz.)
ônibus noturno night service (Braz.)
operador(a) operator
orações prayers
ordem de pagamento money order
orquestra orchestra
orquestra sinfônica symphony orchestra
ourivesaria goldsmith
ouro gold
outono fall [autumn]
outras nacionalidades other nationalities
Outubro October

P

paço palace
padaria baker/bakery
pães bread rolls
pagamento payment
pagar ao balcão pay at counter
país da nacionalidade country of nationality
palácio palace
palácio da justiça law court
palco stage
pantomina pantomime
pão bread
papel higiénico toilet paper

papel reciclado recycled paper
papelaria stationery store
para cabelo normal for normal hair
para cabelo oleoso for oily hair
para cabelo seco for dry hair
para deficientes físicos for handicapped
para diabéticos for diabetics
para dois for two
para microondas microwaveable
para uso externo external use only
paragem/parada requisitada request
  stop
paragem/parada de autocarro/ônibus
  bus stop
parapente gliding
paraquedas parachuting
pare stop
parede wall/cliff
parque park
parque da cidade city park
parque de campismo campsite
parque de diversões amusement park
parque de estacionamento parking lot
  [car park]
parque florestal country park
parque indígena Indian reserve
parque nacional national park
parque para clientes customer parking
parque privativo private parking
partidas departures
partidas internacionais international
  departures
Páscoa Easter
passadeira pedestrian crossing
passageiros passengers
passagem de nível railroad [level]
  crossing
passagem de peões pedestrian
  crossing
passagem fechada/interdita pass
  closed (mountain)
passagem interrompida
  no throughway
passagens ticket office
passaporte passport
passe mensal monthly ticket
passeio walkway
passeio panorâmico scenic route
passeios a cavalo horseback riding
passeios com guia guided tours
passeios circulares round trips
pastelaria pastry/cake shop
pastilhas lozenges

patinagem no gelo ice
  skating
patins skates
património do estado
  public (building)
pavilhão de desportos
  sports center
pedestres pedestrians (Braz.)
pedestres aguardem o sinal verde
  pedestrians wait for the green light
peixe/peixaria fish store [fishmonger]
pensão bed & breakfast, guest house
pensão completa full board (American
  Plan [A.P.])
peões pedestrians
pequeno almoço breakfast
percurso alternativo alternative route
percurso alternativo para camiões
  alternative truck route
percurso da natureza nature trail
percurso de bicicleta cycle track
percurso panorâmico scenic route
perigo danger
perigo de avalanches danger of
  avalanches
perigoso dangerous
pesca fishing
pesca com autorização fishing by
  permit only
pesca proibida no fishing
pico peak
pílulas pills
ping-pong table tennis
pintado de fresco wet paint
piscina swimming pool
pista de corrida(s)
  racetrack (Braz.)
pista de ônibus bus lane (Braz.)
pista dupla dual roadway (Braz.)
pista escorregadia slippery road (Braz.)
pista fechada/bloqueada road blocked/
  closed (Braz.)
pista simples/mão dupla two-way
  traffic (Braz.)
placa de matrícula do carro car license
  plate [registration] number
planador gliding
planetário planetarium
plateia stalls
pneus tires [tyres]
poço well
pode cozinhar cooking facilities
pode ir ao micro-ondas microwavable

A-Z

polícia police/police station
polícia de trânsito traffic police
polícia federal immigration control/ federal police (*Braz.*)
polícia rodoviária highway/traffic police
poltrona no. seat no.
pomada ointment
pomar orchard
ponte bridge
ponte baixa low bridge
ponte estreita narrow bridge
ponte levadiça drawbridge
ponte romana Roman bridge
ponto de encontro meeting place [point]
ponto de luz power point
ponto de ônibus bus stop (*Braz.*)
ponto de táxi taxi stand [rank] (*Braz.*)
por favor please
porcelanas e cristais china and glass
porta door
porta-moedas purse
porta de embarque boarding gate
porta de incêndio fire door
portagem toll
portão gate
portas automáticas automatic doors
porteiro (da noite) night porter
porto port/harbor
posters posters
posto de ambulância ambulance station
posto de venda de selos stamps sold here
posto gas [petrol] station (*Braz.*)
pousada guest house
povoado village
praça square
praça de táxis taxi stand
praia beach
praia de nudismo nudist beach
prancha de surfe surfboard
prancha de windsurf windsurfing board
prata silver
prato do dia dish of the day
pre-pagamento (de combustível) please pay for gas [petrol] before filling car
preço por litro price per liter

preços com IVA incluído all prices include sales tax [VAT]
prefeitura town hall (*Braz.*)
preferencial yield [give way]
presentes gifts
primavera spring
primeira classe first class
Primeiro do Ano New Year's Day (*Braz.*)
primeiro nome first name
primeiros socorros first aid
prioridade priority
prioridade a deficientes, idosos e grávidas please give up this seat to the disabled, the elderly, and pregnant mothers
privado private
produtos de limpeza cleaning products
produtos dietéticos/naturais health foods
proibida a entrada no entry
proibida a entrada a pessoas estranhas staff only
... proibido(-a) ... forbidden
proibido acampar no camping
proibido ao trânsito closed to traffic
proibido buzinar use of horn prohibited
proibido estacionar no parking
proibido fazer fogueiras no fires
proibido fotografar no photography
proibido fumar no smoking
proibido jogar à bola no ball games
proibido nadar no swimming
proibido pescar no fishing
proibido tomar banho no bathing
proibido ultrapassar no passing [overtaking]
proibido usar telemoveis no mobile phones
pronto socorro-emergência accident and emergency
próximo comboio next train
puxe/puxar pull

Q **quantia exacta** exact fare
quarta-feira Wednesday
quartel de bombeiros fire station
quarto duplo double room
quartos para alugar rooms to rent
quatro estrelas four star
quebrar o vidro em caso de emergência break glass in case of emergency
queda de água waterfall
queda de pedras falling rocks
quilómetro/quilômetro kilometer

quinta farm
quinta de turismo rural family-owned
  farm providing accommodations
quinta-feira Thursday
quiosque de jornais newsagent

R raios-x x-ray
  rampa ramp
  rápidos rapids
receita federal customs control
recepção reception
recibo receipt
reciclado recycled
reduções reductions
reduza a velocidade slow down
reembolso refund
refeições meals
refrigerantes soft drinks
regente conductor (*music*)
reparações gerais general repairs (*car*)
represa dam
rés-do-chão first floor
reserva de bilhetes ticket reservations
  [advance bookings]
reserva natural nature reserve
reservado reserved
reservas reservations [advance
  bookings]
reservatório reservoir
residencial guest house
respeite este lugar de culto please
  respect this place of worship
restaurante restaurant
retire o bilhete take ticket
revelação em 2 horas two-hour film
  processing service
revistas magazines
rezas prayers
ribeira stream
rio river
rochedo cliff
rolo film (*camera*)
rotunda traffic circle [roundabout]
roupa interior underwear
rua street/road
rua fechada ao trânsito road closed
rua particular private road
rua principal main road
rua sem saída closed road/
  no-through road
rua com sentido único one-way street
ruínas ruins

S sábado Saturday
  sabonete soap
  saída exit
saída de camiões truck
  exit
saída de emergência
  emergency exit
saída de viaturas vehicles exit
sal salt
sala de operações operating room
sala de concertos concert hall
sala de conferências/convenções
  conference room
sala de espera lounge/waiting room
sala de jantar dining room
sala de jogos game room
saldo sale
salsicharia delicatessen
salva-vidas lifeguards
sapatos shoes
sé cathedral
secador de cabelo hair dryer
secção de bebé babywear
seda silk
segunda classe second class
segundo andar second floor
segunda-feira Monday
segundos seconds
segurança security
selos stamps
sem açúcar sugar-free
sem álcool alcohol-free
sem cafeína caffeine-free
sem chumbo unleaded
sem gordura fat-free
sem iva incluído excludes sales tax [VAT]
sem sal salt-free
semáforo traffic light
semi-desnatado semi-skimmed
senha ticket
senhoras ladies
serra mountain range
serviço service charge
serviço a clientes customer service
serviço de avarias breakdown service
serviço de quarto room service
serviço incluído/não incluído service
  included/not included
serviços de imigração immigration
  control
Setembro September
sexta-feira Friday

A-Z

Sexta-Feira Santa Good Friday
silêncio silence
sinaleira traffic light (*Braz.*)
sinalização provisória temporary traffic lights
só a dinheiro cash only
só autocarros buses only
só cargas e descargas loading and unloading only
só com licença permit-holders only
só dias da semana weekdays only
só domingos Sundays only
só entrada access only
só máquinas de barbear shavers only
só para esquiadores for skiers only
só para pedestres pedestrians only (*Braz.*)
só para residentes residents only
só para uso externo for external use only
só sexo feminino women only
só sexo masculino men only
só veículos autorizados unauthorized parking prohibited
sobremesas desserts
soirée evening performance
solário sun lounge
solo escorregadio slippery road surface
solteiro single (*room*)
sòmente aos domingos e feriados Sundays and bank holidays only
sopa soup
sos 115 emergency services (*Port.*)
sucos fruit juices
supermercado supermarket
suplemento supplement

T **talheres** utensils [cutlery]
talho butcher
tarifa fare/rate
tarifa de pedágio toll fare (*Braz.*)
tarifa mínima minimum charge
taxa de serviço service charge
taxi taxi
táxi aéreo air taxi
taxi comum shared taxi
taxímetro taxi meter
teatro theater
teatro de arena open-air theater
teatro infantil children's theater
teatro municipal opera house (*Braz.*)

teleférico cable car/chair lift
telefone telephone
telefone comercial business phone number
telefone de emergência emergency telephone
telefone público public telephone
telefone residencial home phone number
telefonista operator
telegramas telegrams
temperos seasoning/spices
ténis tennis
ténis de mesa table tennis
terapia intensiva intensive care
terça-feira Tuesday
termas spa
terminus/término terminal
tinta fresca wet paint
tipografia printing
tipos de acomodação available accommodations
toalhas linen
tocar a campainha please ring the bell
tocar para sair press the button to get off
toldo awning
tóxico toxic
tráfego lento slow traffic
trailer trailer
trajecto do autocarro bus route
trampolim diving board
trânsito impedido closed to traffic
travão brake
travão de emergência emergency brake
trem expresso express train (*Braz.*)
trem local local train (*Braz.*)
trevo intersection [crossroad] (*Braz.*)
trocar em ... change at ...
trolley-carro trolleycar [tram]
túmulo grave/tomb
túnel tunnel
turismo tourist information office

U **universidade** university
use fichas ddd use regional tokens
utensílios de cozinha kitchen equipment
utensílios domésticos household goods

vagão-cama sleeping car
vagão restaurante dining car
vagas vacancies
vago vacant
vale valley
vale postal money/postal order
válido até ... valid/use until ...
válido para ... zona(s) valid for ... zone(s)
varanda balcony
vegetais vegetables
veículos vehicles
veículos lentos slow vehicles
veículos longos long vehicles
veículos pesados heavy vehicles
veleiro sailboat
velocidade máxima maximum speed limit
venda de bilhetes ticket office
venda de selos stamps
venda sob prescrição médica sold only under medical prescription
vende-se cartões de telefone phone cards on sale here
venenoso poisonous
verão summer
verdureiro fruit and vegetable store (*Braz.*)
vésperas vespers
vestuário changing rooms/ fitting room
via de dois sentidos two-way traffic
via de sentido único one-way street
via em mau estado poor road surface
via rápida highway [motorway]
via turística scenic route
vidro glass
vidro claro clear glass
vidro de cor colored glass
vidro reciclado recycled glass
vila (small) town
vilarejo village
vinhas vineyard
vinho do porto port (*wine*)
vinhos wines
visitas guiadas guided tours
voleibol volleyball
voo número... flight number
voos domésticos domestic flights
voos internacionais international flights

 zona aduaneira customs zone
zona comercial business district
zona de pedestres/calçadão pedestrian zone [precinct]
zona de piquenique picnic site
zona histórica historic area
zona residencial residential zone

Numbers

GRAMMAR

Note that in Brazil, the numbers 16, 17 and 19 are spelled slightly differently: **dezasseis, dezessete, dezenove.**
Note that Portuguese uses a comma for a decimal point and a period [full stop] or space to indicate 000s, e.g. 4,95; 4.575.000 or 4 575 000.

0	**zero** _zehroo_		16	**dezasseis** _dzer-saysh_	
1	**um(a)** _oom(er)_		17	**dezassete** _dzer-set_	
2	**dois (duas)** _doysh (_doosh_)_		18	**dezoito** _dzoytoo_	
3	**três** _traysh_		19	**dezanove** _dzer-nov_	
4	**quatro** _kwatroo_		20	**vinte** _veent_	
5	**cinco** _seenkoo_		21	**vinte e um(a)** _veent ee oom(er)_	
6	**seis** _saysh_		22	**vinte e dois (duas)** _veent ee doysh (_doosh_)_	
7	**sete** _set_		23	**vinte e três** _veent ee traysh_	
8	**oito** _oytoo_		24	**vinte e quatro** _veent ee kwatroo_	
9	**nove** _nov_		25	**vinte e cinco** _veent ee seenkoo_	
10	**dez** _desh_		26	**vinte e seis** _veent ee saysh_	
11	**onze** _onz_		27	**vinte e sete** _veent ee set_	
12	**doze** _doaz_		28	**vinte e oito** _veent ee oytoo_	
13	**treze** _trayz_		29	**vinte e nove** _veent ee nov_	
14	**catorze** _ker-toarz_				
15	**quinze** _keenz_				

30	**trinta** _treenter_	fifth	**o/a**	
31	**trinta e um(a)**		**quinto/-a**	
	treenter ee oom(er)		_oo/er_	
			keentoo/-er	
32	**trinta e dois (duas)**			
	treenter ee doysh (dooush)	once	**uma vez**	
			oomer vaysh	
40	**quarenta** _kwer-raynter_			
50	**cinquenta** _seenkwaynter_	twice	**duas vezes**	
			dooush vayzish	
60	**sessenta** _ser-saynter_			
70	**setenta** _ser-taynter_	three times	**três vezes** _traysh vayzish_	
80	**oitenta** _oytaynter_	a half	**meio(-a)** _mayoo(-er)_	
90	**noventa** _noovaynter_	half an hour	**meia hora**	
100	**cem** _saym_		_mayer orer_	
101	**cento e um(a)**	half a tank	**meio depósito [tanque]**	
	sayntoo ee oom(er)		_mayoo der-pozzytoo_	
			[tanki]	
102	**cento e dois (duas)**			
	sayntoo ee doysh (dooush)	half-eaten	**meio comido(-a)**	
			mayoo koomeedoo(-er)	
200	**duzentos(-as)**			
	doozayntoosh (-ush)	a quarter	**um quarto** _oom kwartoo_	
500	**quinhentos(-as)**	a third	**um terço** _oom tairsoo_	
	keenyayntoosh(-ush)	a pair of ...	**um par de ...**	
			oom par der	
1 000	**mil** _meel_			
10 000	**dez mil** _desh meel_	a dozen ...	**uma dúzia de ...**	
			oomer doozyer der	
35 750	**trinta e cinco mil**			
	setecentos e cinquenta	1999	**mil novecentos e noventa**	
	treenter ee seenkoo meel		**e nove** _meel_	
	setsayntoosh ee		_novsayntoosh ee_	
	seenkwaynter		_noovaynter ee nov_	
		the 1990s	**a década de mil**	
1 000 000	**um milhão**		**novecentos e noventa**	
	oom meelyawm		_er dekader der meel_	
			novsayntoosh ee	
first	**o/a primeiro/-a**		_noovaynter_	
	oo/er primayroo/-er			
		the year	**o ano dois mil**	
second	**o/a segundo/-a**	2000	_oo anoo doysh meel_	
	oo/er ser-goondoo/-er			
		the	**o milénio**	
third	**o/a terceiro/-a**	Millennium	_oo meelaynyoo_	
	oo/er tersayroo/-er			
		2001	**dois mil e um(a)** _doysh_	
fourth	**o/a quarto/-a**		_meel ee oom(er)_	
	oo/er kwartoo/-er			

Days Dias

Monday	**segunda-feira** *ser-goonder fayrer*
Tuesday	**terça-feira** *tairser fayrer*
Wednesday	**quarta-feira** *kwarter fayrer*
Thursday	**quinta-feira** *keenter fayrer*
Friday	**sexta-feira** *sayshter fayrer*
Saturday	**sábado** *saber-doo*
Sunday	**domingo** *doomeengoo*

Months Meses

January	**Janeiro** *zher-nayroo*
February	**Fevereiro** *fer-ver-rayroo*
March	**Março** *marsoo*
April	**Abril** *er-brill*
May	**Maio** *mighoo*
June	**Junho** *zhoonyoo*
July	**Julho** *zhoolyoo*
August	**Agosto** *er-goashtoo*
September	**Setembro** *staymbroo*
October	**Outubro** *ohtoobroo*
November	**Novembro** *noovaymbroo*
December	**Dezembro** *derzaymbroo*

Dates Datas

It's July 10.	**Estamos a 10 de Julho.** *ishtamoosh er desh der zhoolyoo*
It's Tuesday, March 1.	**Hoje é terça-feira, 1 de Março.** *oazh eh tairser fayrer oom der marsoo*
yesterday	**ontem** *ontaym*
today/tomorrow	**hoje/amanhã** *oazher/amer-nyah*
this ...	**deste(-a)** *daysht (deshter)*
last ...	**do(-a) passado(-a)** *doo(-er) per-sadoo(-er)*
next ...	**próximo(-a) ...** *prossymoo(-er)*
every ...	**todos(-as) os(as) ...** *toadoosh(-ush) os(ush)*
week/month/year	**a semana/o mês/o ano** *er ser-maner/oo maysh/oo anoo*
on [at] the weekend	**no fim de semana** *noo feem der ser-maner*

Seasons Estações

spring	**a primavera** er preemer-_vehrer_
summer	**o verão** oo ver-_rawm_
fall [autumn]	**o outono** oo oh_toa_noo
winter	**o inverno** oo een_vehr_noo
in spring	**na primavera** ner preemer-_vehrer_
during the summer	**durante o verão** doo_rawnt_ oo ver-_rawm_

Greetings Cumprimentos

Happy birthday!	**Parabéns!/Feliz aniversário** per-rer-_baynsh_/fer-_leesh_ anniver_sahr_yoo
Merry Christmas!	**Feliz Natal!** fer-_leesh_ ner-_tal_
Happy New Year!	**Feliz Ano Novo!** fer-_leesh_ _a_noo _noa_voo
Happy Easter!	**Feliz Páscoa!** fer-_leesh_ _pash_kooer
Best wishes!	**Felicidades!** fer-lysy_da_dish
Congratulations!	**Felicitações!** fer-lysyter-_soynsh_
Good luck! / All the best!	**Boa sorte!** _boa_er sort
Have a good trip!	**Boa viagem!** _boa_er vya_zhaym_
Give my regards to …	**Os meus cumprimentos a …** oosh _me_oosh koomprymayntoosh er

Public holidays Feriados

Major national holidays in Portugal (*Port.*) and Brazil (*Braz.*), excluding movable feasts:

		Port.	Braz.
January 1	New Year's Day	Port.	Braz.
January 6	Epiphany		Braz.
April 11	Tiradentes Day		Braz.
April 25	Freedom Day	Port.	
May 1	May Day	Port.	Braz.
June 10	Camões Day	Port.	
August 15	Assumption Day	Port.	
September 7	Independence Day		Braz.
October 1	Our Lady of Aparecida Day		Braz.
October 5	Republic Day	Port.	
November 1	All Saints' Day	Port.	Braz.
November 15	Proclamation Day		Braz.
December 1	Restoration Day	Port.	
December 8	Immaculate Conception Day	Port.	
December 25	Christmas Day	Port.	Braz.

Time As horas

uma hora

uma hora e cinco

uma hora e dez

uma hora e um quarto

uma hora e vinte

uma hora e vinte e cinco

uma hora e meia

vinte e cinco para as duas

vinte para as duas

um quarto para as duas

dez para as duas

cinco para as duas

Excuse me. Can you please tell me the time?	**Desculpe. Pode dizer-me as horas, por favor?** *dish<u>koolp</u>. pod dee<u>zair</u>-mer ush <u>o</u>rush poor fer-<u>voar</u>*
It's five past one.	**É uma e cinco.** *eh <u>oo</u>mer ee <u>seen</u>koo*
It's ten past two.	**São duas e dez.** *sawm <u>doo</u>ush ee desh*
a quarter past three	**três e um quarto [e quinze minutos]** *traysh ee oom <u>kwar</u>too [ee keenz mee<u>noo</u>toosh]*
twenty past four	**quatro e vinte** *<u>kwa</u>troo ee veent*
twenty-five past five	**cinco e vinte e cinco** *<u>seen</u>koo ee <u>veent</u> ee <u>seen</u>koo*
half past six	**seis e meia** *<u>sayz</u> ee <u>may</u>er*
twenty-five to seven	**vinte e cinco para as sete** *<u>veent</u> ee <u>seen</u>koo <u>per</u>-rer ush set*
twenty to eight	**vinte para as oito** *veent <u>per</u>-rer uz <u>oy</u>too*
a quarter to nine	**um quarto para as nove** *oom <u>kwar</u>too <u>per</u>-rer ush nov*
ten to ten	**dez para as dez** *desh <u>per</u>-rer ush desh*
five to eleven	**cinco para as onze** *<u>seen</u>koo <u>per</u>-rer uz onz*
twelve o'clock	**doze horas** *doaz <u>o</u>rush*
noon/midnight	**meio-dia/meia-noite** *<u>may</u>oo <u>dee</u>er/<u>may</u>er noyt*

at dawn	**de madrugada** *der mer-droogader*
in the morning	**de manhã** *der mer-nyah*
during the day	**durante o dia** *doorawnt oo deeer*
before lunch	**antes do almoço** *awntish doo almoasoo*
after lunch	**depois do almoço** *der-poysh doo almoasoo*
in the afternoon	**de tarde** *der tard*
in the evening / at night	**à noite** *ah noyt*
I'll be ready in five minutes.	**Estou pronto(-a) em cinco minutos.** *ishtoh prontoo(-er) aym seenkoo minootoosh*
He'll be back in a quarter of an hour.	**Ele está de volta daqui a um quarto de hora [a quinze].** *ayl ishtah der volter der-kee er oom kwartoo dorer [ah keenz]*
She arrived half an hour ago.	**Ela chegou há meia hora.** *eler sher-goh ah mayer orer*
The train leaves at …	**O comboio [trem] parte às …** *oo kawmboyoo [trayn] part ash*
13:04	**treze horas e quatro minutos** *trayz orush ee kwatroo minootoosh*
0:40	**zero horas e quarenta minutos** *zehroo orush ee kwaraynter minootoosh*
10 minutes late / early	**dez minutos atrasado/mais cedo** *desh minootoosh er-trer-zadoo/mighsh saydoo*
5 seconds fast / slow	**cinco segundos adiantado/atrasado** *seenkoo ser-goondoosh er-dyawntadoo/ er-trer-zadoo*
from 9:00 to 5:00	**das nove às cinco horas** *dush nov ash seenkoo orush*
between 8:00 and 2:00	**entre as oito e as duas horas** *ayntrer uz oytoo ee ush dooerz orush*
I'll be leaving by …	**Parto daqui antes da(s) …** *partoo der-kee awntish der (dush)*
Will you be back before …?	**Está de volta antes da(s) …?** *ishtah der volter awntish der (dush)*
We'll be here until …	**Ficamos aqui até à(s) …** *feekamooz er-kee er-teh ah (ash)*

Valença

Viano do Castelo

Braga

Bragança

Porto

Vila Real

Aveiro

Viseu

Guarda

**Atlantic
Ocean**

Coimbra

Portugal

Leiria

Castelo

Santarém

Portalegre

LISBON (Lisboa)

Évora

Spain

Setubal

Beja

Lagos

Faro